L.P. VIDYARTHI

CONTRIBUTION TO THE DEVELOPMENT OF ANTHROPOLOGY

PROF. L. P. VIDYARTHI
(February 28, 1931 - December 1, 1985)

L. P. VIDYARTHI

Contribution to the Development of Anthropology

Edited by

M. K. GAUTAM A. K. SINGH

CONCEPT PUBLISHING COMPANY, NEW DELHI

First Published 1986

Published by
Naurang Rai
Concept Publishing Company
H-13, Bali Nagar
NEW DELHI-110015 (India)

Printed in India by
Lohia Composing Agency
at Sunil Printers
CB-1067, 75/1, Ajay Palace
Ring Road, Naraina,
NEW DELHI-110028

Dedicated to the inspiring thoughts of many gurus (teachers), friends, well-wishers and students, which moulded Vidyarthi as a most considerate and devoted Social Scientist

Publisher's Note

This volume was intended to honour Professor L.P. Vidyarthi for his contribution to the Development of Anthropology. While work on its production was in progress, the cruel hands of death snatched the doyen of Indian Anthropologists from us.

We are presenting this book in the form it was originally prepared. It may be treated as a memorial to the learned scholar's life and work.

THE PUBLISHER

Foreword

It is a pleasure to participate in a book honouring Prof. L.P. Vidyarthi's important contributions to Third World Anthropology. I was Chairman of the Department of Anthropology of the University of Chicago when, in 1958, Lalita Vidyarthi was awarded the degree of Doctor of Philosophy, I remember that it happened to be our 100th Ph.D. degree granted, since the first one in 1897, and I was struck by the fact that Vidyarthi's was the very first to a candidate from the Third World. Since then he has had many "firsts", among which I personally observed his ascendancy to the Presidency of the first International Congress of Anthropological and Ethnological Sciences to be held in a Third World country, making him also the 10th President of the International Union. Our path have thus crossed many times in our professional lives. For example, on my very first visit to India in January of 1959 when my flight from Moscow to Delhi was delayed for two days and nights, upsetting a busy schedule, it was Prof. Vidyarthi who welcomed me at the airport and relieved my anxieties. But perhaps I am most grateful for his having translated into Third World terms and used the ideas about "action anthropology" which my students had developed in work among North American Indians. It is, thus, not only a personal pleasure but an honour to participate in this recognition of Prof. Vidyarthi's prominent contributions to anthropology in general and to Third World scholarship in particular.

Chicago
1984

SOL TAX
UNIVERSITY OF CHICAGO

Contents

WHAT MEDIA SAYS

List of Contributors

N. K. BOSE
Former Commissioner for Scheduled Castes and Scheduled Tribes and former Director,
Anthropological Survey of India

CHARLES FRANTZ
Professor, Department of Anthropology
State University of New York
Buffalo, New York, USA.

M.K. GAUTAM
Institute Kern
Leiden University,
Leiden, The Netherlands

D. N. MAJUMDAR
Professor and Head, Department of Anthropology
Lucknow University, Lucknow, India

MORRIS E. OPLER
Professor (Retired),
Cornell University, Ithaka, USA

SHELLEY PORTEOUS
Department of Anthropology,
University of Western Ontario
London, Canada

L. M. PRASAD
Department of Anthropology
Ranchi University, Ranchi, India

BAIDYA NATH SARASWATI
Visiting Professor, Department of Anthropology
North-Eastern Hill University
Nongthymmai, Shillong (Meghalaya)

S. N. SEN
Vice-Chancellor, University of Calcutta, India

AJIT SINGH
Lecturer in Anthropology
Ram Lakhan Singh Yadav College
Ranchi University, Ranchi, India

S. C. SINHA
Director, Institute of Social and Economic Change
Calcutta

JULIAN H. STEWARD
Professor of Anthropology
University of Illinois, USA

MARIO D. ZAMORA
Professor of Anthropology
College of William and Mary
Williamsburg, Virginia, USA

List of Photographs

BETWEEN PAGES 80-81

8. Prof. Vidyarthi at a party after receiving the Distinguished Service Award at Chicago, in 1983. Prof. Sol Tax (extreme right) and Mrs. Sol Tax are also in the picture.
9. In a fighting mood! Prof. Vidyarthi, with his fellow investigator (of Chicago University) at the fair of Red Indians in 1957.
10. Prof. Vidyarthi congratulating Mr. Ushiyama after he received the Award at the Japanese Press Club in Tokyo in 1984.
11. Prof. Vidyarthi addressing a tribal gathering on October 2, 1984, at the birthplace of Jatra Bhagat, father of Thana Bhagat, in the village Chingri near Bishunpur in Ranchi district. Sitting (on his right) are Mr. R. M. Bhagat, Mrs. K. Oraon, Dr. Biswanath Prasad, Vice-Chancellor, Ranchi University, and Mr. Bandi Oraon, a State Minister.

BETWEEN PAGES 96-97

12. Prof. Vidyarthi responding to the felicitation address after the announcement of his being chosen for the Distinguished Service Award. Also seen in the picture (facing the camera) are Dr. A. K. Dhan, Vice-Chancellor, Ranchi University, and Dr. A. K. Singh.
13. Prof. Vidyarthi with the Ainu leaders and a local Japanese Professor near Sappro in Hokkado (Japan).
14. Prof. Vidyarthi distributing gifts to the tribals on the Andaman Islands in 1978. Also in the picture is Mr. S. N. Krishnarthi the then Commissioner of the Andaman and Nicobar Islands.
15. Working with the 'Maler' tribe in Rajmahals in 1958. The researcher is seen in the village with the informants and the villagers.

❀ श्री गणेशाय नमः ❀

अथ गयाश्राद्धपद्धतिः

व

गयाश्राद्ध की विधि

यात्री को उचित है कि गयाश्राद्ध गयावाल (पण्डा) के आज्ञानुसार करै ये तीर्थ गुरु हैं। गयावाल ब्राह्मणों को तृप्त करने से पितर और देवता दोनों ही सन्तुष्ट हो जाते हैं। To Satisfy the ancestors + Gods

ब्रह्मप्रकल्पितान् विप्रान् हव्यकव्यादिनार्च्चयेत्।
तैस्तुष्टस्तोषिताः सर्व्वे पितृभिस्सह देवताः ॥१॥

गयाश्राद्ध करने वाले यात्री के नियम—

कामं क्रोधं तथालोभं त्यक्त्वा कार्य्यादिका क्रियाः
ब्रह्मचर्य्यैकभोजी च भूशायी सत्यवाक्शुचिः।
सर्व्वभूतहिते रक्तः स तीर्थफलमश्नुते ॥२॥

काम क्रोध लोभ मोह आदिक त्याग करके ब्रह्मचर्य होकर एक समय भोजन करता हुआ पृथ्वी में शयन करै और सत्य बोलता रहै निरन्तर पवित्र रहै सर्व प्राणियों के हित की इच्छा करते हुए पिण्डदान करै तो गयाश्राद्ध का फल मिलता है। अत्र नीचे लिखे मन्त्र से मस्तक पर जल छिड़के।

ॐ अपवित्रः पवित्रो वा सर्वावस्थांगतोपि वा।
यः स्मरेत् पुण्डरीकाक्षं सबाह्याभ्यन्तरः शुचिः ॥३॥

हाथ में जल लेकर हाथ जोड़े हुए निम्नलिखित श्लोक पढ़े।

देव देव जगन्नाथ, शङ्ख चक्र गदाधर।
देहि विष्णो ममानुज्ञां तुतीर्थसेवनाइनम् ॥

मेरा नाम श्री राम लाल कंगा एवं मेरे श्रद्धेय पिता का नाम श्री मुरलीधर लाल जी कंगा (४२ वर्ष) है। मेरा जन्म ता० १४ नवम्बर १९ [illegible] ई० को [illegible] तिथि-१ अगहन (मार्गशीर्ष) १९८[illegible] सं० को अपने पैतृक निवास स्थान (मु० कृष्ण [illegible]) पर हुआ। मेरा [illegible] गया [illegible] जिले [illegible]

मैं अपने पिता का प्रथम सन्तान था [illegible] में [illegible] अभी नहीं थी। किन्तु मेरा दुर्भाग्य जिसने केवल तीन मास के बाद ही मेरे परिवार के [illegible] बदल डाला। मेरी स्नेहमयी माता जी के [illegible] स्वर्गवास [illegible] आकस्मिक मृत्यु मेरे जीवन की सबसे विषादपूर्ण तिथि है। यद्यपि उस समय मैं केवल तीन मास का था एवं उस दुर्घटना का किंचित भी आभास मुझे नहीं है, परन्तु [illegible] की ममता [illegible] का [illegible] जीवन के हर क्षणों में पाता रहता हूँ।

उपरोक्त घटना मेरे पालन-पोषण में [illegible] बाधक रहा। किन्तु यह बाधा स्व० दादाजी (श्री मुत महेशलाल जी कंगा) एवं दादीजी एवं श्रद्धेय पिता के [illegible] सम्मिलित सहयोग के [illegible] [illegible] जाता रहा। मेरे लिये [illegible] रखा गया। इस भाँति किसी प्रकार शैशव काल में अनेक सम्बन्धियों एवं भाइयों के गोद में पलता रहा।

प्राय: ८ वर्ष तक

प्राय: तीन वर्ष के उपरान्त मेरा मुंडन संस्कार हुआ। इस संस्कार के उपरान्त भी मैं सदैव [illegible] रहा। अस्वस्थता का मूल कारण मेरे समझ से अनेक माताओं का सम्पर्क था [illegible] यद्यपि मैं उनका अनुग्रह क्यों न मानूँ किन्तु यह [illegible] है कि इस काल मेरे रक्त में विकार उत्पन्न हो गया और अनेक प्रकार के रोगों से मैं सदैव ग्रसित रहा। [illegible] भी मेरे परिवार के लिए एक दर्द ही रहा एवं मेरे चिकित्सा में अनेक [illegible] होते रहे। ८ वर्ष के उपरान्त मैं कुछ स्वस्थ हुआ तब मेरा उपनयन संस्कार सम्पन्न हुआ। इसी समय मुझे शिक्षा-दीक्षा की ओर प्रवृत्त [illegible] गया एवं प्राथमिक स्कूल में मुझे भर्ती करा दिया गया। [illegible] एक शिक्षक नित्य पढ़ाने आया [illegible] स्व० दादाजी [illegible] का [illegible] अंग्रेजी में [illegible] एवं [illegible] अपने संरक्षण में [illegible] स्व० दादीजी का [illegible] यदि वह न होते मैं आज जिन्दा न होता। मुझे किसी प्रकार का अभाव [illegible] [illegible] स्कूल पढ़ने जाना। [illegible] पर स्नान-भोजन [illegible] फिर दादाजी के [illegible] विषयों का शिक्षा ग्रहण करना उस समय मेरे दिनचर्या का मुख्य विषय था। [illegible] अपने चचेरे चाचा के [illegible] में उनके लड़कों के साथ खेलने चला जाता। [illegible] फुटबाल खेला जाता। घर आकर स्नान [illegible] एवं शिक्षक के [illegible] घंटा [illegible] सोने चला जाता। सम्बन्धियों का उस समय के व्यवहार में प्रथम पिताजी [illegible] होने के [illegible] आज भी याद है। उस [illegible] दिलाना मेरे दादाजी का दादीजी से ही सम्भव होता था। [illegible] उसी समय मेरे पिताजी की पुनर्विवाह [illegible] अनेक [illegible] सम्बन्धियों [illegible] मेरे परिवार के सभी सदस्यों की भी इच्छा थी किन्तु मेरे पिता ही सदैव इन्कार करते रहे। स्पष्ट उन्होंने कहा कि सन्तान के होते हुए मुझे अब विवाह की कोई आवश्यकता नहीं है। यह घटना [illegible] उस समय के लिये [illegible] होते हुए भी मेरे [illegible] लिए [illegible] एवं [illegible] खाना, पढ़ना, खेलना, सोना इत्यादि स्वयं ही नियन्त्रित होता रहा। [illegible] दिनचर्या मुझ में आज भी प्राय: उसी भाँति विद्यमान है [illegible] बचपन की यह [illegible] [illegible]

Introduction

It is a real pleasure to introduce Dr. L.P. Vidyarthi, who is not only a devoted social scientist but also a most valuable friend to many people. Apart from his professional qualities, we know him as an open-minded, meek, smiling and relaxed person. Vidyarthi always offers a sympathetic ear to anyone who comes to him, for suggestions or for any type of advice. In this way he plays his role in the service of academic community as a social anthropologist, ready to pick up any new piece of social information or to contribute new ideas and theories to the development of the science of anthropology. Personally speaking, Vidyarthi is a true, traditional Indian who thinks that the development of Indian anthropology must emerge from the Indian climate. Mere transplantation of Western concepts, without taking into consideration Indian references, will be disastrous to the cause of development. One must think from the points of view of the country's culture and traditions, and only then we can really solve the problems of our country. His most pioneering service to the science of anthropology has been in developing the concept of Third World Anthropology, different from the existing legacy of Western and colonial paradigms. Veering away from the so-called old traditions of British, European and American thoughts he provides a new foundation with a perceptible development towards a synthetic approach with an interdisciplinary flavour specially geared to the developing nations. According to him, in order to understand the problems and development phases of India it is essential to study Applied and Action Anthropology. As early as mid 50s he established an Action Research Unit in the Department of Anthropology at Ranchi University and carried out research in the Chotanagpur region. It would not be wrong to say that today Indian anthropology is proud of him as the founding father of Action and Applied Anthropology in South Asia. Though ideas of applied anthropology and the need for related researches were inspired by the late D.N. Majumdar, the real "take-off" was by Vidyarthi who, as a student of Majumdar, applied his ideas in empirical situations.

In 1952, during the Vienna Congress of the International Union of Anthropological and Ethnological Sciences (IUAES), the idea to study "integrated man" had already been formulated as an *urgent need*, but the real empirical work started in late 50s. The Philadelphia Congress of IUAES received some papers which took a new course and deviated from the traditional approach of the British school of anthropology. The consequent 7th, 8th and 9th International Congresses of IUAES made it amply clear that applied and action anthropology was the only means to study the problems of Third World society (Vidyarthi, 1979). Discussions on such issues whether pursuing Western academic patronage in the study of society is relevant or the indigenous notions should be discovered became a decisive factor in shaping the contours of new developing nations. Such issues were often debated in regional meetings and conferences of the social scientists. In the Indian case, as early as 1936, "Reform" is possible only "from within"; Gandhi's real meaning of *Swarājya* (self-reliance) was considered to be the only way to solve the problems of India. In any case dependence on Western thoughts can never help and promote the development of Third World countries, because indigenous phenomena and their various shades do not and cannot fit in Western theories (Nakane, 1972; Alatas, 1974). Having watched the progress of the colonial administration in developing countries, Sol Tax in the 50s, in order to realize the development and the progress of the new nations, coined the term "action anthropology". Vidyarthi, being the product of the Chicago school, took these ideas of Sol Tax and gave them a "new taste and flavour" by adding the wing of "Indianness" to the descipline of Applied and Action Anthropology. In his Presidential Address during the Science Congress, of the anthropological section, at Varanasi (1969), Vidyarthi stressed the urgency to understand, study and evaluate change, and continuity, among the tribes of India and deviated from the existing researches on "caste-dominated rural society" (Srinivas, 1966). By his renewed emphasis on tribal studies Vidyarthi did not completely ignore the study of the "Great Tradition". One should not forget that his earlier research was on the religious complex of the Gayawals of Gaya (Vidyarthi, 1961). Looking at the vastness of South Asia he pleads that its "unified cultural diversity" can be protected only when a comprehensive action research oriented strategy in anthropology is devised and used. The alarming situation of the Andaman Islands and various other tribal groups in India (as well as other parts of the world) had already caused a setback to the anthropologists (Vidyarthi, 1968; Gautam, 1969). According to Vidyarthi, in order to ensure the success of the Indian Five Year Plans, anthropology must stress the applied and action aspect. It should be called "Development anthropology" as Zubrow (1981) has suggested where a *Praxis* (thoughts plus action) is required to recognize the multiple paths of development and with new paradigms (Frantz, 1981). Whether it is micro- or macro-level research, the anthropologist must have some feeling and involvement for his community of study. He can never be a value-free non-involved scientist. The welfare of the community should be part of his conducted research. Only then the results of the action and applied aspect can be fully realized

(Gautam, 1978 ; Gautam & Pott, 1983). And only then, the ideas of the Five Year Plans can induce change for development and welfare in an Indian context, which can be "selected" and not "imposed" upon (Vidyarthi, 1968). In such a situation one may be able to understand the "processes" and the evolving "new forms". Concepts, such as sanskritization, santalization, tribe-caste continuum, detribalization, revitalization, etc. then can be properly seen with reference to their local, regional and national climates (Gautam, 1977). The impact of various forces, such as communication channels, industrialization, ruralization, urbanization, education, money economy, bureaucracy, formation of political parties, etc. have to be seen in relation to inter-ethnic relations and interactional processes. Then only matrix factors and references can be understood. Action and Applied Anthropology's five categories as proposed by Vidyarthi can be of the utmost use not only to the administration, but also to the private and public sectors in development processes of any Third World country (Vidyarthi, 1978). It will provide a willingness to work on a joint team of anthropologists and administrators (Gautam, 1973). Since many European-American anthropological thoughts are inapplicable to understand Indian society and "Indianness", it is necessary to revise our methodology and look at our own thoughts. The ideologies of Deuris, Freud and Marx cannot and do not fit in the Indian canvas. Adaptation of foreign models can take place only after a very critical examination of its suitability, applicability and usefulness. Indian anthropologists must look at the thoughts of Indian thinkers such as Tilak, Tagore, Gandhi, J.P. and many others. Only then would we be able to understand the percolation of the ideal of our heritage as the continuous force of our society. This was a turning point of focus on India's vast problems from an Indian point of view through Indian anthropology (Vidyarthi, 1978 : Presidential Address at Varanasi). In this way, the search for Indian unity through Indian paradigms and thoughts for change and development were established and gave momentum to urban researches (Vidyarthi, 1969), industrial complexes (Vidyarthi, 1970), social forestry, nutrition and problems of scheduled castes, etc. Vidyarthi's contribution to the development of Indian anthropology is rich and can easily be understood because of its practicability through empiricism. What perhaps one needs is another attempt to condense these facts into more constructive theories. Let us hope that in coming years Vidyarthi will give more serious thought to creating some new anthropological theories, tools and models specially geared to the South Asian situation, which perhaps could also be used in comparative studies.

This volume covers the contribution of known anthropologists such as Zamora, Frantz, Saraswati, Porteous, Singh and Prasad ; reviews on Vidyarthi's major works ; excerpts from media, etc. Evaluating the contribution of Vidyarthi to the growth of science of anthropology

Dr. Zamora highly appreciates his warm and cordial relations which have been an asset in maintaining human relations and understanding the various social factors. Perhaps this quality of "winning friends' confidence" has made Vidyarthi a most successful field anthropologist.

Dr. Frantz, looks at Vidyarthi in totality and discusses his "holistic" approach in studying societies. He traces certain important influences on Vidyarthi's personality at Chicago which were responsible for moulding him as a practical anthropologist. His two mentors Redfield and Singer contributed equally in developing his earlier work on the sacred complex and helped him discover his concept of "Indianness". The third paper of Dr. B.N. Saraswati discusses the depth of the sacred complex in a transanthropological perspective which inspired him to conduct his prolonged work on the sacred complex of Kashi. The sacred and secular continuum as well as polarity has served to analyse the totality of the complex. Saraswati discusses the analysis of traditional and classical vision. The paper of Shelley Porteous discusses Vidyarthi as a "forming personality of an anthropologist" from childhood to the present stage and focusses on various aspects which inspired him to develop the force of Indian anthropology.

Dr. Ajit Singh goes even further and treats some new aspects of Vidyarthi's contribution, such as sacred complex, nature-man-spirit complex, urban-industrial complex, applied and action anthropology, village studies, scheduled castes, folklore research, leadership and even contributing new concepts in anthropological theories. The last paper of L.M. Prasad deals with the political aspects of Vidyarthi's contribution in history, politics and administration. As a political scientist he evaluates Vidyarthi's contribution as an overall contribution in the field of social science.

To conclude, the present work is meant to provide an overall picture of the contribution of Dr. L.P. Vidyarthi who has contributed a new aspect to the study of anthropology in general and specifically to the study of "Indianness".

I am thankful to Prof. Sol Tax who has done me a big favour and honour by accepting my proposal to write a Foreword about the contribution of Vidyarthi, his illustrious student.

Finally my thanks go to my colleague and friend, Dr. Ajit Singh, for his tremendous work involved in compiling the information and completing the references to the work of Vidyarthi.

Leiden, The Netherlands
November, 1984

DR. M.K. GAUTAM
Institute Kern
Leiden, University

References

Frantz, Charles, (ed.) 1981 : "Introduction" *in Ideas and Trends in World Anthropology*, New Delhi, Concept Publishing Company.

Gautam, M.K., 1969 : "The Ethnographical Museum : An anthropological bridge between research and education" *in Ethnographical Museum Yearbook*, Oslo.

Gautam, M.K., 1973 : "Reciprocity of Information", *in Man*, Vol. 8 : 4.

Gautam, M.K., 1977 : *In Search of an Identity : A Case of the Santal of Northern India*, Leiden.

Gautam, M.K., 1977 : "Are we doing justice to the tribal studies in India ?" *in* Rupert Moser and M.K. Gautam (eds.), *Aspects of Tribal Life in South Asia I : Strategy and Survival*, Berne : University Press.

Gautam, M.K. & P.H. Pott, 1983 : *Anthropology and the Functions of Ethnographical Museums in Third World Countries : A Case Study of a Multi-ethnic Society in South Asia*, Leiden.

Nakane, 1972 : *Human Relations in Japan*, Tokyo : Ministry of Foreign Affairs.

Srinivas, M.N., 1966 : *Caste in India and other Essays*.

Vidyarathi, L.P., 1961 : *Sacred Complex in Hindu Gaya*, New York : Asia Publishing House.

Vidyarthi, L.P., 1968 ; "Presidential Address to the Anthropology and Archaeology Section", *Journal of Social Research*, under the title "Culture Change in the Tribes of Modern India".

Vidyarthi, L.P., 1968 : "Unity and diversities in the cultural elements of Andaman and Nicobar Islands and other Essays" *in* special number of the *Journal of Social Research*.

Vidyarthi, L.P., 1968 (ed) : *Applied Anthropology in India*, Allahabad : Kitab Mahal (2nd Edition).

Vidyarthi, L.P., 1969 : *Cultural Configuration of Ranchi, Survey of an Emerging Industrial City of Tribal India*, Planning Commission Publications, Distribution Council of Social and Cultural Research, Deptt. of Anthropology, Ranchi University.

Vidyarthi, L.P., 1970 : *Socio-cultural Implications of Industrialisation in India : A Case Study of Tribal Bihar*, Council of Social and Cultural Research, Bihar, Dept. of Anthropology, Ranchi University.

Vidyarthi, L.P., 1978 : Presidential address to the IXth ICAES, published in Charles Frantz (ed.), *Ideas and Trends in World Anthropology*, Concept Publishing Company.

Vidyarthi, L.P., 1979 : *Rise of World Anthropology : As Reflected through the International Congresses (1934-58)*, New Delhi : Concept Publishing Company.

Vidyarthi, L.P., 1979 : *The Changing Dietary Patterns and Habits* (co-author), New Delhi : Concept Publishing Company.

Zubrow, 1981 : "International Trends in Theoretical Archaeology" *in* Charles Frantz (*ed.*), *Ideas and Trends in World Anthropology*, New Delhi : Concept Publishing Company.

ARTICLES

1

A TRIBUTE TO AN INDIAN ANTHROPOLOGIST

Mario D. Zamora

Dr. Mohan Gautam, Chairman of the Commission on Museums and Cultural Heritage of the International Union of Anthropological and Ethnological Sciences (IUAES), is to be commended for initiating a project to honour Dr. Lalita Prasad Vidyarthi, University Professor and Head, Department of Anthropology, Ranchi University, Ranchi, Bihar, India.

I wish to join Professor Vidyarthi's friends, admirers and colleagues from India and other countries in felicitating him on this historic occasion. It has been my privilege to have had the friendship and professional collaboration of Dr. L.P. Vidyarthi for the past several years. I first met him during the 1973 International Congress of Anthropological and Ethnological Sciences (ICAES) in Chicago, when he was named to succeed Professor Sol Tax as President of the IUAES. I was introduced briefly to him by his student, Dr. B.N. Sahay. Dr. Vidyarthi asked me to help organize a symposium on shifting cultivation at the 1978 ICAES in India, a plan which was ultimately realized when I co-chaired the symposium ably organized by Prof. L.K. Mahapatra, University Professor and Head, Department of Anthropology, Utkal University, Orissa, India.

When my colleagues at the College of William and Mary, Drs. Nathan Altshuler and Vinson H. Sutlive and I established an international journal entitled *Studies in Third World Societies* in 1974-75, I was assigned to choose the members of our international editorial advisory board. Prof. Vidyarthi was one of those who accepted to serve on our board. At the 1978 ICAES, I renewed my acquaintance with Prof. Vidyarthi. He invited me to join a select group of scholars from many parts of the world to a memorable evening of dinner and fellowship after hectic days of conferences. There, I met some of the top leaders of the ICAES and also the publishers of the Concept Publishing Co. of India. Since then, my correspondence with Dr. Vidyarthi has been regular. He invited me to become a founder-member of the International Centre for Asian Studies and as a member of the editorial board of the *International Journal of Asian*

Studies. In 1983, he was chosen to receive the Distinguished Service Award of the Association for Anthropological Diplomacy under my presidency. He was cited for his significant contributions to international anthropology, especially in his role as President of both the IUAES and the ICAES in 1978.

Having described my professional relationships with the honouree, I now summarize briefly his academic background and then assess his contributions to Indian and international anthropology. (The details can be found in his vita, in this text.) In the last part of this brief paper, I will present some of the ideas I heard from him personally which have implications for India and the world.

Dr. Vidyarthi was a consistent honours graduate in his student days, both at the graduate and post-graduate levels. He obtained his predoctoral training from schools in his home State of Bihar and Uttar Pradesh. On a Fulbright/Smith-Mundt grant, he studied at the University of Chicago where he was conferred the Ph.D. degree in anthropology in 1958; among his professors were Sol Tax, Milton Singer and Fred Eggan, three intellectual pillars of anthropology in the United States.

Although I have not had the opportunity to read all of Dr. Vidyarthi's numerous books and articles I, however, have an idea about his major concerns in anthropology. Among such fundamental concerns are the study of sacred complexes and pilgrimage sites, his focus on tribes and their socio-economic welfare and advancement, industrialization and urbanization, the history of Indian anthropology, and the history of the IUAES and the ICAES.

In my view, Dr. Vidyarthi's significant contributions to Indian and Third World anthropology are his systematic efforts to advance the cause of anthropology through his organizational and managerial skills. His serious and persistent activities to mobilize personnel and resources are commendable. His vita reveals vividly his involvement in many international, national, and local organizations designed to enhance scholarship in our discipline. These efforts culminated in his appointment as President of both the IUAES (1973-78) and the ICAES (1978) which was held in India. He has been the leader of the Indian Anthropological Association, the founding father of the International Centre for Asian Studies, and the founding editor of the *International Journal of Asian Studies*, located at Ranchi University. He has been editor for a long time of the social research journal of Ranchi University. He has played an active role as Chairman of the Commission on Development of the IUAES. One of the great achievements of this Commission was the holding of the successful symposium on underprivileged communities (SUNCOM) in New Delhi. There are now plans to hold regional symposia along the same pattern as the Indian SUNCOM. He was also an active organizer/chair of several sessions at the ICAES in Vancouver in 1983.

In his capacities as President of the IUAES and the ICAES, Dr. Vidyarthi brought honour and glory to India and Indian anthropology. His successful management, in cooperation with Indian colleagues, of the Xth ICAES in India attested to his dynamic leadership. As one of those fortunate to attend the Xth ICAES, I was very much impressed with the congress preparations and its overall thrust and direction. The themes chosen were useful and timely, the discussions were substantive and lively, and the social activities revealed the best side of Indian hospitality. It was one of the most memorable and enjoyable conferences I have ever attended in my many years of membership in professional meetings in the U.S.A. and abroad.

Dr. Vidyarthi's bold initiatives, energy, enthusiasm, and determination in the anthropological profession are worthy of emulation. His resourcefulness and helpfulness to others, especially to younger colleagues and his students, merit our gratitude and commendation. Moreover, Dr. Vidyarthi has a larger vision and a noble mission. One afternoon, while having refreshments at the convention site of the American Anthropological Association in Chicago last year, I had a good opportunity to exchange ideas with him about Indian anthropology and anthropologists. He shared with me his knowledge about the background, status and direction of Indian anthropology. In all those candid talks, I never heard him even once speak ill of any of his Indian colleagues. He was always concerned with the larger issues. My respect for him as a colleague, friend and fellow human being has increased through time.

In addition to the above qualities, Dr. Vidyarthi is a man full of gratitude and thoughtfulness. During the banquet/programme in honour of the awardees of the Association for Anthropological Diplomacy, he paid glowing tributes to Prof. Sol Tax and his other former teachers at the University of Chicago. In appreciation of Dr. Milton Singer's contributions to his intellectual growth and development, he and Prof. Michael Ames of the University of British Columbia are coordinating the publication of a *festschrift.* At the world congress of anthropology in Vancouver, Dr. Vidyarthi surprised my family with a lovely gift, a shawl from India; coming from a man whose mind was preoccupied with many things at that time, my wife and I were very impressed with his thoughtfulness and sentiments.

Finally, I would like to summarize briefly some of the main ideas he generated in his remarks before the banquet/programme in Chicago and in his discussion of the papers presented at the symposium on the anthropology of war and peace. Dr. Vidyarthi urges a truly holistic and interdisciplinary approach to the study of the human being He believes that anthropology, to be a genuinely holistic science, should at the same time be relevant. According to him, anthropologists should take advantage of their wisdom and expertise about the human being and the human condition to help solve many of the issues and problems confronting humankind : war and peace, poverty and injustice, pollution and deforestation, population expansion, crime and delinquency, among others. Anthropologists should address themselves to the study of the causes and consequences of conflict both at the tribal and the global levels. He believes that despite differences in culture, history and state of technology, many nations, especially the super-powers, can still learn from the practical teachings of heroes such as Mahatma Gandhi of India who preached truth and non-violence. Anthropologists, according to Dr. Vidyarthi, should go beyond the study of little tribes and villages; they should investigate more intensively the behaviour and values of nations in order to understand fully the issues and solutions to global conflicts and social pathologies.

As a final note, it is with pride and joy that I felicitate Dr. Vidyarthi on the occasion of a publication dedicated to his life and career as an accomplished anthropologist devoted to the cause of enhancing anthropology internationally, through teaching, research, publication and public service.

2

ECOLOGICAL AND INTELLECTUAL WINDS OF CHANGE

A Young Scholar in the Windy City of Chicago

Charles Frantz

Lalita Prasad Vidyarthi was the first student from India, and the hundredth altogether, to receive a doctorate in anthropology from the University of Chicago, the initial ones having been granted in 1897. He is thus a singular phenomenon in the history of Chicago and Indian, if not world, anthropology. As his experiences may perhaps best be understood contextually, in the Chicago tradition of anthropology, attention will be given to salient features of his life before, during, and after being exposed to the scintillating ecological, social, and cultural attributes of the Windy City.

I will not seek for any ultimate causes to explain Vidyarthi's distinguished career. Rather, I am inclined to follow the traditions of natural science/history in seeking to understand his development primarily in terms of social relationships, within their spatial/ecological and temporary settings, allowing also for bio-genetic factors which I cannot specify or explicate (cf. Redfield 1955). Methodologically, therefore, I may be less holistic than Vidyarthi, who believes that most events happen not as the result of human choices, but rather are due to the actions or influences of some supernatural power or divine guidance. In sum, my approach parallels the kind of anthropological attention frequently given to some secondary marriage systems, i.e. looking not only at liminal *rites de passage* but also at the anticipatory levirate or sororate and the ensuring post-nuptial behaviour. Both form and substance will receive attention in this discourse, which uncontrollably may or may not be consonant with other contributors to this volume. Much of the material I draw upon derives from a taped conversation (Vidyarthi 1983), personal experiences and correspondence since 1967, and various published sources cited in the Bibliography.

When Vidyarthi arrived in the United States during the summer of 1956, he was an anticipatory Chicagoan social-cultural anthropologist. His first academic marriage had been with geography, but while studying at Lucknow that bond dissolved and the ideas in anthropology courted him strongly. These soon led him into a second marriage, one of considerable longevity and commitment, even though remembrances of ideas encountered during the first marriage were never completely submerged or ignored. A happy first marriage, it seems, simply was less promising and enriching than the second.

Vidyarthi was born to a family having middle caste status in a small, multi-caste village near Patna, one in which the children of many castes played together. At that time, individuals identified more with a village than with a caste, and Vidyarthi came to feel discomfort about the distancing or restrictions on inter caste behaviour while he was still quite young. As his father resided elsewhere, in Gaya, he thus remained with his mother and sisters through primary schooling, during which he frequently was disinclined to "listen to females". His middle and secondary schooling took place in Gaya, where he lived with his father. During this period he accompanied his father, a great devotee, to numerous city temples, not so much as a participant as an observer. In this way, Vidyarthi experienced considerable exposure to varieties of Hinduism (which may suggestively be compared to cross-cultural experiences), and this was responsible for his "discovery"—although not yet a conceptualization--of the "Sacred Complex" of Gaya. Significantly, at that time he also became friends with several individuals who, because of caste rules, were excluded from participating in temple rituals. As the youngest of four sons, Vidyarthi was also influenced greatly by his second eldest brother, an intellectually alert and politically liberal man who worked as a secretary for the district tax collection. It was this brother who later urged Vidyarthi to continue higher studies at Patna.

Vidyarthi successfully won a secondary school scholarship of five rupees (equivalent to fifty U.S. cents, at present) per annum, an amount sufficient to pay the tuition fees. During this time, he became pro-Gandhian, as the joint product of newspaper reading, participation in a debating society which he organized, and especially certain teachers.

Enrolling in the Arts College rather than the Science College at Patna, he began to be exposed increasingly to non-Indian cultures through his concentrated studies in history and geography. His teachers took him to visit different cities, mines, and so on. He also became more active in the movement toward national independence and warmly supported the socialist movement which, among other things, was seeking destructure of the caste system. He also developed a flair for writing for newspapers and radio, by which means he earned half of his income. His Special Paper (comparable to a thesis) for the baccalaureate degree, in human or economic geography, was the result of studying the city of Gaya. He found much of the professional literature—including that of Ellen C. Semple and Ellsworth Huntington—to have overly deterministic explanatory schemata, hence it was only later that he developed the idea of the "Man-Nature Complex". His geography professor suggested the possibility of Vidyarthi's starting anthropological instruction in a newly-established college in Ranchi, and said that the Government was interested in supporting an outstanding candidate to do advanced study in that discipline. Vidyarthi successfully obtained a fellowship to embark into this new field and, after a year's interregnum, he entered Lucknow University upon the advice of its Vice-Chancellor.

Vidyarthi's first year at Lucknow was spent in specializing in geography, but during that time he took his first course in anthropology. This was offered by the Sociology Department and taught by Dhirendra Nath Majumdar. He did some brief fieldwork among the Santals, the first tribe he had contacted, but he wrote his Special Paper on the dying priestly communities, *Gayawal*, in Gaya. In 1953, he sent this paper to Robert Redfield, at the University of Chicago, and received an encouraging reply inviting him (and offering to pay expenses) to meet Milton Singer during an upcoming visit to Calcutta. This meeting proved to be fruitful, leading eventually to Vidyarthi's enrollment in Chicago and the development of the idea of the "Sacred Complex" to characterize the city of Gaya. Meanwhile, at the age of 22 and before his Master's thesis had been published, Vidyarthi began teaching at Ranchi College, a unit of Bihar University, which offered post-graduate instruction in only three subjects : history, Hindi and anthropology. Library resources then were extremely scarce, and most of the students were local recruits. Three years later, he flew to Chicago to begin his doctoral programme, being funded with Fulbright-Hays and Smith-Mundt grants and with programmatic funds that Redfield had obtained from the Ford Foundation.

During the previous quarter of a century, the privately endowed University of Chicago had become pre-eminent in social science among U.S. universities, and a number of significant innovations had been introduced at both the undergraduate and post-graduate levels. In the 1940-50s, a number of interdisciplinary committees and programmes, such as those on Social Thought, Race Relations, Communication, South Asian Studies and Human Development, had been established. The quality of the Anthropology Department's programme and its staff also were generally acknowledged to be among the best in the nation. One of the Department's major changes before Vidyarthi arrived was to shift emphasis from areal ethnology to topical and problem-centred courses (Stocking 1979 : 45), as well as seeking at a fairly abstract level to integrate the approaches and data of archaeology, the "new" physical (biological) anthropology, culture history, and social anthropology. Ties were strong with the Oriental Institute and such departments as sociology, geography, philosophy, economics, history, zoology, and psychology (cf. Vidyarthi 1979).

Various professors in the department were among the most prominent in national and international anthropological societies. Robert Redfield and Fred Eggan had been presidents of the discipline's major organization, the American Anthropological Association, in 1944 and 1953, and Sol Tax was to assume that office in 1959. Eggan also had been Secretary of the A.A.A. from 1941 to 1943. Fay-Cooper Cole, the person most responsible for the department's remarkable growth (Cole 1932, Stocking 1979), and Alexander Spoehr also served on the Executive Board of the Association, 1955-58, as did Sherwood L. Washburn from 1957 to 1960. In the early years after Vidyarthi returned to Ranchi, Norman A. McQuown, Robert J. Braidwood, Donald Collier, and F. Clark Howell were also elected to the Executive Board. Tax, furthermore, had been the Editor of the major disciplinary journal, *American Anthropologist*, from 1953 to 1955, and Eggan had served as editor of the Association's *Memoirs*. Tax also was active in helping the Wenner-Gren Foundation to launch the international journal, *Current Anthropology*, in 1960, and he served as editor during its first 15 years. During the latter part of this active period, 1968-73, Tax in addition held the office of President of the International Union of Anthropological and Ethnological Sciences. Beyond anthropology *per se*, most of Vidyarthi's Chicago mentors were also prominent in both private and governmental organizations concerned with the subdisciplines of anthropology, as well as the social sciences, humanities and sciences in general.

As with most post-graduate students in the department, Vidyarthi attended courses, lectures and seminars given by Redfield, Tax, Washburn, McQuown, Singer, Eggan, Braidwood, Howell, Julian Pitt-Rivers and Lawrence Krader; these individuals collectively constituted almost the whole departmental faculty. He also attended courses in statistics (which he confesses to having mastered with only modest success), geography and Sanskrit, as well as interdisciplinary seminars that involved South Asianists, economists, and other specialists. Although Vidyarthi had studied and received a diploma in the German language at Lucknow, he was permitted at Chicago to pass Sanskrit to fulfil the foreign language requirement. Among fellow graduate students who befriended and assisted him with his doctoral dissertation and courses were McKim Marriott, Leonard Borman, Manning Nash and myself. Beyond the formal classroom, he was also befriended by Redfield, Singer and Tax, his major mentors. Vidyarthi recalls vividly the first party for graduate students, held shortly after his arrival at Tax's residence, where Redfield introduced him to many co-minglers as a "practising anthropologist" rather than as a "student".

Intellectually, Vidyarthi was most influenced by Redfield, Singer and Tax, an attraction to and empathy with the first two having preceded and contributed to his choosing Chicago. The young scholar was particularly impressed with Redfield's inspirational didactic styles during lectures and seminars, for these contrasted strongly with the "British" type of university instruction that he had experienced in Patna and Lucknow. Redfield had both studied and practised law before going into anthropology, and he possessed a sensitive, inquiring and provocative mind not constrained by disciplinary boundaries (Leslie 1976, Singer 1976, Tarn 1981, and Cole and Eggan 1959). From 1934 to 1946, he had played the crucial formative role of Dean of the Social Science Division at the University. Although Martindale (1960 : 92) describes him as "undoubtedly the single most able exponent of the classic phase of positivistic organicism" in U.S. sociology/anthropology at that time, Redfield also was the first U.S. anthropologist to conduct field studies among peasants (Silverman 1981 : 256) and then, much as did Alfred L. Kroeber, moved on to a general concern with the nature of nation-states and civilizations. By the time Vidyarthi arrived in Chicago, Redfield had become more historical and interdisciplinary in his interests and writings (Singer 1976 : 188-191), especially seeking to understand the "minds", "spirits", and "world views" of civilizations (Leslie 1976 : 150). Redfield's newer interests and activities were greatly facilitated by the Ford Foundation funds he obtained in 1951 to finance over a decade a new "Programme in Intercultural Studies", which included several interdisciplinary seminars, conferences and publications (Stocking 1979 : 35).

Singer moved into anthropology from philosophy during the decade prior to Vidyarthi's arrival, mainly because of the growing intellectual mutuality and association he had with Redfield (Singer 1976 : 198). Singer's interest in the relationships of personality to culture and civilization greatly stimulated Vidyarthi, and were to be reflected later when at Ranchi he introduced a course on culture and personality. Singer also provided "delicate intellectual surgery" on Vidyarthi's course papers and dissertation.

Tax was the third professor most responsible for contributing to transformations in Vidyarthi's mind. In 1956, his "action anthropology" programme among the Mesquakie (Fox) Amerinds living in the State of Iowa was in full swing, as were his interests in undertaking and contributing to the betterment of the existential situations of indigenous populations in Guatemala, Mexico and the U.S.A. In a manner different from Redfield, Tax was similarly stimulating, provocative and critically-minded, although more controversial, emotive, and practical-minded (cf. Hinshaw 1979). His influence on Vidyarthi was also to be reflected in courses, seminars and publications that followed his return to India. In addition, there is much evidence to suggest that Tax was a crucial role model for

Vidyarthi in the latter's subsequent administrative and organizational activities, both within India and throughout the world.

A fourth professor at Chicago who had significant, although lesser, influence on Vidyarthi was the anthropological linguist, McQuown. Upon returning to Bihar, Vidyarthi offered a course in Linguistic Anthropology, the first to be given in any Indian university.

As the result of his commitment to both formal courses and doing heavy additional reading, Vidyarthi had little time to interact socially with fellow students or to experience life elsewhere in the city and nation. He completed all the necessary requirements for the doctorate in 18 months, a remarkably short period compared to the norm among his peers. As a non-smoker and teetotaller, Vidyarthi was not particularly interested in student parties or drinking in bars, and was disinclined to play games and sports, do ballroom dancing, watching moving pictures and television, or attend concerts, dramatic productions, art shows, and poetry readings. On the other hand, he actively attended lectures on social and political issues, and kept abreast of world events through reading newspapers and magazines.

Vidyarthi had some contact with a few instructors in the various theological colleges associated with the University of Chicago, as well as with a "tribal" from Bihar who was enrolled in one of them. Vidyarthi also had the experience of working for the Chaplain of Rockefeller Chapel, located on the university campus. Although paid for this labour, which mainly involved the filing of papers and articles, Vidyarthi also benefited from having many opportunities both to converse with the Chaplain and to read materials in his files. During Thanksgiving and Christmas holidays, Vidyarthi participated in U.S. family celebrations, and he also occasionally visited Christian missionary families who had lived in India. During the whole of his time in the Windy City, he lived in the large multi-storied International House, at the edge of campus, which had been built with private philanthropic funds to provide residence and social activities primarily for foreign students. Meals could be taken there, but Vidyarthi developed only a limited taste for American bread and other foods; hence, he generally cooked spiced dishes, rice, pulses, and other foods quite economically in his own room. Often, however, he went out to dine at "The Tropical Hut" restaurant a few blocks away, where he would consume much chicken and vegetable salad.

Outside Chicago, Vidyarthi had few experiences with U.S. Americans. These included a trip to Milwaukee, Wisconsin, to visit another anthropologist, James Silverberg, and several days as the house-guest of Julian H. Steward near Urbana, Illinois. The latter was instrumental in Vidyarthi's formulation of the "Nature-Man-Spirit Complex," and provoked a re-stimulation of his pre-anthropological interest (i.e. during his first intellectual marriage) in ecological/geographical factors related to societal and cultural systems. In 1957, Vidyarthi read a paper at the Annual Meeting of the American Anthropological Association. When he had first arrived in the U.S.A., he had joined other foreign recipients of study, travel and research awards in a month's orientation programme that was held at Bard College, in Annandale-on-Hudson, New York. He also was able to attend the week-long International Congress of Anthropolgoical and Ethnological Sciences, held in Philadelphia. There, he became acquainted with several Russian and other non-American anthropologists, and these ties proved useful as he increasingly moved from being a regional to a national and international figure in anthropology and the social sciences. Finally, during the summer of 1957 he took brief leave from his courses and dissertation-writing to participate in a conference for foreign students outside the city of Chicago.

During his stay in the U.S.A., Vidyarthi mainly dressed in Indian clothing. His demeanor, even when he was under heavy academic pressure, was always serious, gentle, helpful, kind and happy. Although he sometimes missed the meaning of various gestures, verbal nuances, and customs of his fellow students, he never allowed this to bring forth sarcasm, withdrawal, or negative criticism. His formal-appearing attire, carefully prepared pattern of speaking English, diligent studiousness, and succesful control of emotions led some fellow students to think of him variously as *guru*, *gayawal*, *brahmin*, *yogi* and *mandarin*. Throughout his residency in Chicago, he was almost unanimously liked and respected by his peers and colleagues.

Vidyarthi's experiences with the intellectual winds of change in the new ecological milieu of Chicago had both immediate and lasting impacts on his subsequent career. His range of research, university courses and ideas embrace those of *several* of his U.S. mentors. His corpus of ideas has expanded not only to include those of, or similar to, Redfield, Singer and Tax, but also such others as Julian H. Steward and Victor Turner, who were not members of the Chicago faculty (although Turner was later to be). Vidyarthi's breadth of publications substantively covers problems tackled by *several* Chicago professors, and in addition he wrote textbooks designed for students in India. I feel quite confident in asserting that the quantity of his publications, which seems to average about one book and several articles each year, exceeds that of *all* individuals who were doing post-graduate work with him in 1956-58 ; in fact, it is quite possible that *no* product of the anthropology department at the University of Chicago has published so extensively in the course of the last quarter-century. Finally, in terms of his administrative and organizational activities, there are few who have been equally ambitious or successful, not only in building a new post-graduate department but also in holding offices within his or her university, state, nation, and the world.

The Chicago exposure transformed some of Vidyarthi's mind, but it also helped him to fulfil or realize some ideas and interests that had developed during his first marriage to geography, as well as during the period of his anticipated second marriage to anthropology. The 18 months in the Windy City stimulated him to clarify and enrich some of his earlier formative paradigms. Perhaps the most significant new additions came from Tax, who was committed to action and applied anthropology, and who also was extraordinarily vigorous in transnational organizational activities. Also, Vidyarthi benefited from accretions deriving from Singer's efforts to integrate aspects of the psychological and social sciences with philosophy and history; and from McQuown's special approach to the relations between language, thought and action.

In conclusion, it seems to me that Vidyarthi's intellectual (and cultural) core remains strong and intact, and that some characteristics of his first marriage to geography have been profitably revised and enhanced. He is still concerned, perhaps more now than ever before, with rediscovering or retaining and developing the peculiar "Indianness" of anthropology in and for India, and by extension for anthropological paradigms everywhere. Finally, it may be worth noting that during the 1950s both Redfield and Singer were undergoing changes in their minds toward less Euro-centric and perhaps more Indo-centric, or at least more trans-cultural and trans-civilizational, world views in their own endeavours to broaden and strengthen anthropology. The complementary transformation, in sum, of Vidyarthi, Redfield and Singer has left a common legacy that continues to generate creative thought and action by anthropologists in many parts of the world.

References

Cole, Fay-Cooper, 1932 : The Department of Anthropology. *University Records.* University of Chicago, 8 : 207-210.

Cole, Fay-Cooper, and Eggan, Fred, 1959 : Robert Redfield, 1897-1958 : *American Anthropologist*, 61 : 652-662.

Hinshaw, Robert (ed.) 1979 : *Currents in Anthropology* : *Essays in Honour of Sol Tax.* The Hague : Mouton.

Leslie, Charles, 1976 : The Hedgehog and the Fox in Robert Redfield's Work and Career. In Murray, John V. (ed.), *American Anthropology* : *The Early Years*, pp. 146-166. St. Paul, Minn. : West Publishing Co.

Martindale, Don, 1960 : *The Nature and Types of Sociological Theory.* Boston : Houghton Mifflin.

Redfield, Robert, 1955 : *The Little Community : Viewpoints for the Study of a Human Whole*, Chicago : University of Chicago Press.

Silverman, Sydel (ed.), 1981 : *Totems and Teachers* : *Perspectives on the History of Anthropology.* New York : Columbia University Press.

Singer, Milton, 1976 : Robert Redfield's Development of a Social Anthropology of Civilization. In Murra, John V. (ed.), *American Anthropology : The Early Years*, pp. 187-260. St. Paul, Minn. : West Publishing Co.

Stocking, George W., Jr. 1979 : *Anthropology at Chicago*. Chicago : Joseph Regenstein Library, University of Chicago.

Tarn, Nathaniel, 1981 : Robert Redfield. In Silverman, Sydel (ed.), *Totems and Teachers : Perspectives on the History of Anthropology*, pp. 255-284. New York : Columbia University Press.

Vidyarthi, Lalita P., 1979 : *Trends in World Anthropology*. Delhi : Concept Publishing Co.

Vidyarthi, Lalita P., 1983 : Interview with Charles Fantz. Buffalo, New York, 16th November. Tape recording.

3

THE SACRED COMPLEX

A Transanthropological Perspective

Baidyanath Saraswati

INTRODUCTION

To honour my teacher, Professor L.P. Vidyarthi, I could have chosen for this volume no better theme than the anthropology of sacred. For, that is a subject in which both the human and divine dimensions are integrated, and of which Professor Vidyarthi is not merely a specialist but a believer—a man in good faith. Also because whatever smattering of the anthropology of sacred I have acquired I owe to him. My dedication to him stands truly in line with the pupils of the ancient world who had sought new experiences in the intellectual consciousness of their mentors. Theirs was a personal offering, an expression, of the highest form of love.

Here I wish to lay the groundwork for a new interpretation of Vidyarthi's original and initial concept of the Sacred Complex. In so doing, his ancther stimulating concept, the "Nature-Man-Spirit Complex", will also be taken into account, for these two concepts are intrinsically related.

In his monumental work, *The Sacred Complex of Hindu Gaya* (1961), Vidyarthi introduces the concept of "Sacred Complex" formed of three interrelated phenomena : (1) Sacred geography, (2) Sacred performances, and (3) Sacred specialists. He describes the sacred geography of Hindu Gaya in terms of sacred centre, sacred cluster and sacred segments. A sacred centre represents a single spot where a sacred performance takes place. Such a sacred centre may be variously located. It may be isolated. Then a sacred centre may be in a cluster of many other sacred centres in its adjacent neighbourhood. To denote such a combination of sacred centres around a dominant sacred centre, the term sacred cluster has been used. On another local and organizational level two or more clusters forming a continuous segment may be termed the sacred segment. The sacred performances are linked with the sacred centres. These may be analysed into floral offerings, meditational exercises, oblations, libations, artritic performances, and religious donations. The various types of sacred specialists are connected, on the one hand, with the sacred centres and performances there and, on the other, with the sacrificers (*Yajmans*)—the pilgrims. Among the sacred specialists are mentioned temple priests, florists, drummers, barbers, Pandas, Gumastas, and such other functionaries professionally associated with sacred performances.

Vidyarthi applies this model of Hindu Sacred Complex to tribal cultures in his another seminal work, *Maler : A Study in Nature-Man-Spirit Complex* (1963). He demonstrates how ecology influences the economic life and culture of the Maler of the Raj Mahal hills in Bihar who practise the slash-and-burn cultivation. Man in Maler tribal society has been discussed in the context of social institutions, and the Maler's belief in spirits in terms of their sacred centres, sacred performances and sacred specialists. Integrating all these aspects of tribal culture, Vidyarthi makes out a conceptual model to which he calls "Nature-Man-Spirit Complex".

It may be stated at this point that nowhere has Vidyarthi defined the term "Sacred", yet there is no ambiguity in his treatment of the subject. The term "sacred" has been used precisely in the Durkheimian sense of distinction, as the opposite of the "profane", i.e. the opposite of the "secular". In point of functional and cultural importance the city of Gaya has been demarcated into two zones : the sacred and the secular. The sacred-secular distinction recurs throughout the book : sacred zone, secular zone ; sacred place, secular place ; sacred service, secular service ; sacred specialists, secular agencies ; sacred performances, secular jobs ; sacred intelligentsia, secular scholars. All these allusions show that the sacred-secular dichotomy has been maintained with unfaltering clarity.

Vidyarthi's model has been applied to various centres of Hindu pilgrimage in India and Nepal, as also in tribal contexts. Most of his followers and students have asserted that the concept of the sacred complex with its attending terminology has a much wider applicability and that it reflects one of the important dimensions of Indian civilization.

SACRED-SECULAR CONTINUUM

Following the lead so ably provided by Vidyarthi, I began to feel, in early 70s, that his concept of the sacred complex deserves a more extended treatment than what it has so far received. Studying the sacred traditions of Kashi I found, in 1972, that all the Hindu pilgrims visiting this sacred city do not participate equally in its sacred complex. Earlier, in 1970, I had suggested that in accordance with the modes of transmission of knowledge, Indian cultural traditions can be classified into Oral Cultural Tradition (OCT), Textual Cultural Tradition (TCT) and Transcendental Cultural Tradition (TranCT). It was observed that at the behavioural level the pilgrims of the three main traditions, namely, the potter pilgrims of the OCT, the Brahman pilgrims of the TCT, and the Dandi Sannyasee pilgrims of the TranCT, do not treat the Sacred Complex of Kashi in the same manner. Also at the ideational level, these traditions have three different notions of the sacred—the malevolent sacred, identified by the OCT, the benevolent sacred, identified by the TCT, and then a third dimension of the sacred, repudiating of both the malevolent and the benevolent, as envisioned by the TranCT. This threefold notions of the sacred, I have stated, reflects a continuum in Indian thought structure, and together forms a real set of Hindu Sacred complex.

In 1974, I published a small note on the concept of Man saying that, unlike Christianity, in Brahmanical sacredotal tradition Man is not a despised being, nor is man subservient to God. The examples of the Vedic *Rishis* and the Brahmanic ritual craft show that by means of *Tapas* Man has been "creating" sacred and by means of ritual he has been reversing the course of the sacred—the will of the Gods. To strike a difference between the glorious Man of the Veda and the Biblical Man burdened with a guilt complex, my purpose was to explain why the Western mind is so receptive to the duality of the religious phenomena in terms of the sacred-secular opposition. I made this point more clear and explicit in a later work, in 1975, demonstrating that the sacred and the secular are dialectically rather than dichotomously related.

My basic assumption is that the sacred-secular continuum is not merely an ideational principle—a philosophical speculation—but an empirical reality that can be observed at critical moments in life as also in the social organization of sacred traditions. In a sacred place like Kashi, for instance, in the organization of its space, in the performance of rituals, and in the profession of ritual specialists, it is almost impossible to make a clear-cut distinction between the sacred and the secular. In the drudgery of social life one may find certain diacritical marks artificially dividing people into high and low, pure and impure, sacred and profane, but as one mounts higher and higher in the spiritual disciplining of life (*sadhana*), these differences begin to evaporate. The purity-pollution boundaries have been repeatedly transgressed by saints and mystics, and the sacred laws have been prescribed in Hindu classical traditions in order to rise above the petty differences in social life. This is regarded as the spiritual necessity of every Hindu who wishes to be truly liberated. When a Brahman, the tallest and the purest in the society, comes to Kashi for the cremation of his deceased kinsman he asks for the sacred fire from the so-called untouchable, and Doms, who are its custodians. Without this sacred fire the deceased cannot attain *Mokṣhạ*—the supreme sacred.

From such examples how can one dichotomize "sacred" and "secular" or "sacred" and "profane" in the Durkheimian sense ? Indeed, the sacred and the secular are the two sides of the same coin—the difference lies in the perception of the observer, depending from what angle he looks at it. Nothing solely sacred, or nothing solely profane exists in the supreme experience of life, in the ultimate analysis of things.

TRADITIONAL VISION OF THE SACRED

It now appears to me that the exisiting methods in anthropology are inapt in explaining the sacred complex of any society. The realities of the sacred cannot be understood by a simple observation method, or by questioning the non-specialists in the matter. This is true especially of the Indian classical society, because Indian mind does not seem objectifiable. It considers the other equally truthful, as propounded in the theory of *Anekantavada*. The Truth in Indian sacred tradition is beyond objective-subjective knowledge. It comes through revelation or what is better known as *Rtambharaprajna*, which is neither a simple process of believing nor a complex method of learning. Revelation, by definition, is a mystical experience that cannot be fully explained or interpreted but can be shared only partially in the form of sarced myth, in the spiritual consciousness of a person or a culture. Hence any inquiry relating to the sacred complex has to be necessarily transempirical. It demands an orientation into what I call transanthropological perspective—a perspective developed through the processes of both de-anthropologization and re-anthropologization (Saraswati 1982b).

There are various ways of sharing the vision of the sacred. These may be grouped under two broad anthropological categories : (1) the archaic, and (2) the classical. This section is intended to make them explicit.

The archaic vision of the sacred

Myth orients the archaic people in reality, in the knowledge of authentic existence of life and death. The source of myth is invisible, but it flows out of the supreme principle that governs human life and culture. Hence in myth man discovers his roots, his origins, his relationships with the Cosmos and the Gods. The archaic people find a close communication between Man, Cosmos and the Supernatural—the three spheres or elements which, in their opinion, constitute a single reality. To illustrate it with concrete examples, we may take up the tribes of North-East India.

Elwin (1968) has recorded five types of creation myths of the NEFA tribes :

(1) The world arose from a primaeval ocean, or was formed upon its surface (Gallong and Sherdukpen).
(2) The world as a macrocosm, transformed from some great personage or even a tree (Apa Tani, Bori, and Hill Miri).
(3) The world was created directly by heavenly beings (Bugun and Sherdukpen).
(4) The world was born from the cosmic egg (Khampti).
(5) The earth and sky have descended from a Universal Mother (Singpho).

There are myths describing the union and separation of heaven and earth. Earth and sky are wife and husband. When they first loved each other every kind of tree and grass and living creature came into being.

Traditions about the creation of Man are unclear. There does not seem to have any real distinction between man, animal and spirit: A woman gives birth to twins, of whom one is human and the other a tiger; animals talk, and also behave, like man; of two brothers, one is the father of mankind, and the other the father of the spirit. Following are the main traditions about the origin of man:

(1) Man was born of the union o earth and sky (Dhammai and Singpho).
(2) Men came direct down from the heaven (Nocte).
(3) Men and women are made by divine beings as an artist would model clay (Bugun and the Kaman Mismi).
(4) Human beings emerge out of the ground, or from a gourd, or even the tusk of an elephant (Bugun, Singpho, Taraon Mishmi).
(5) The original race of man was destroyed by fire and flood, and the world was repopulated, either from a surviving human couple, or by the direct creation of a new race (Idu Mishmi).

The picture of the other world has to be necessarily more detailed and clear, as it is believed to be Man's ultimately permanent residence. The tribes of North-East India believe in the continued existence after death of what might be called the soul. There is a Land of the Dead—in some cases several such Lands—which is reached by a difficult path and often guarded by some spirit of the other world who examines the souls' credentials before he admits them. The soul can leave the body even during lifetime to visit the shadowy country. The Tagin, for instance, believe that part of men's personally called *Yalo* should normally go and make arrangements for his permanent residence there while he is still alive. It is on the basis of such visits and the experience of the Shamans during trance that the NEFA tribesmen have built up the picture of the

Land of the Dead. Fürer Haimendorf (1953) has thus recorded the Apa Tani's eschatological beliefs :

> The Apa Tanis believe that the souls, *Yalo*, of all those who die a natural death go to *Neli*, the place of the dead, which looks like an Apa Tani village with long rows of houses . . . . As an Apa Tani lived on this earth so will he live in *Neli* : a rich man will find the cattle he has sacrificed during his lifetime . . . . Every woman returns to her first husband, but those who died unmarried may there marry and beget children. Life in *Neli* is similar to life on the earth : people cultivate and work, and ultimately they die once more and go to another Land of the Dead.

Such beliefs support the theory that in the archaic vision, Man, Cosmos and the Supernatural are not separate realities but are related and closely communicable, to the extent that the Land of the Dead is the archetype of the Land of the Living.

The primordial oneness of man, nature and the supernatural is reflected not only in the belief system—in the myths—but also in the archaic way of life. I have discussed this point elsewhere (Saraswati, 1978).

Briefly

The archaic cultures recognize man as part of society which in turn is an integral part of Nature and the Cosmos. The wellbeing of man is contingent upon his harmonious relationship with Nature,[1] which means harmony with society. To bring a disorder in society amounts to the disordering of Nature, which means disordering oneself, destroying oneself. In the interest of his own existence man must, therefore, continually seek for balance. The balance can be maintained if the members of society think[2] alike and act alike. Hence in the archaic societies all human activities are corporate actions. This can be seen in their institutions of collective ownership of land and forest, vested in territorial group, collective living, as in the institution of youth dormitory, collective performance of rituals, clan members forming a ritual unit, village group performance, for collective good. In fact, there is nothing personal in the archaic society. In primitive jurisprudence the clan is the only legal person, the only body and entity. The unit is not the individual but the kin, the individual is but part of the kin.[3] Even in the finer aspects of life there is no personal venture. All archaic or folk poetry are collective and anonymous. They are of equal merit. There is nothing like good poetry or bad poetry. Here everyone is a poet, everyone is a singer, everyone is a dancer. The collective identity of the archaic people is so strong that some tribes will identify themselves as "man" and others as "Not-man". For instance,

Singpho means man, Konyak (or *Keniak*) means man, Mizo (or *Mi*) means man. The universe of man is thus limited to one's own tribe, constituted of clans which have their origin in the natural objects, and all natural objects are connected with the supernatural beings. Thus, there exists in the archaic vision a genetic affinity between the three spheres of realities : Man, Nature and the Supernatural.

The classical vision of the sacred

As in the case of the archaic so also in classical cultures, myth is the ultimate reference point of Truth. Hence, both share in common a similar vision of the basic unity between Man, Cosmos and Gods. The similarities exist not merely in the description of myths but also at the level of belief lived in (as indicated in Table 1).

TABLE 1

Elements of archaic and classical myths believed and lived in (+presence; —absence)

Sl. No.	Elements	Archaic	Classical
1.	The myth of primaeval ocean from which all things have emerged	+	+
2.	The macrocosmic myth of the world	+	+
3.	The myth of direct creation by heavenly beings	+	+
4.	The myth of world born from the cosmic egg	+	+
5.	The myth of earth and sky descended from a Universal Mother	+	—
6.	The myth of man born of the union of Earth and Sky	+	—
7.	The myth of man descending from the heaven	+	—
8.	The myth of man made by divine being	+	+
9.	The myth of man emerging out of the ground	+	—
10.	The myth of primaeval flood which destroyed the original race of man, and the world was repopulated	+	+
11.	The myth of the incest of the primordial couple, to perpetuate the human race	+	+
12.	Social groups such as clan, tribe/caste sharing a common mythic origin	+	+
13.	Men sharing equally the strands of nature (*guns*, in Brahmanic culture)	+	—
14.	Human activities to be shared equally by all	+	—
15.	Collective ownership of land	+	—
16.	Collective living	+	—
17.	Collective performance of rituals for collective good	+	+
18.	Collective identity	+	+
19.	Social laws are sacred laws	+	+
20.	Social laws to maintain harmonious relationship with nature	+	+
21.	Unfaltering belief in sacred reality	+	+

In the Brahmanic classical culture, for instance, the cosmic, the human and the divine are the three subsets of the Ultimate Reality Brahmana The Vedic *Rishis* had the direct vision of this reality which they described in the form of His *Vibhuti*, that is, his *sakar* (manifest) attributes of excellence in every field and He as the cause of creation. The essence of this truth has been expressed in various ways, and more importantly in the myth of Prajapati (Rigveda, Book X) : In the beginning there was nothing, not even nothingness. That which was hidden by the void wanted to be, and there it was Prajapati. Prajapati desired a second and so he set out on sacrifice (*Yajna*). He divided himself into as many parts as were necessary to complete the creation. From this primordial sacrifice, from the limbs of Prajapati, were born strophes and melodies, horses and every animal, the four human castes (Varnas), the sky, the atmosphere, the ocean, the earth, the moon, the sun, Indra and Agni (the gods), the wind, and so all the rest. Even evil was created by Him. Having thus created the World by total self-immolation, Prajapati asked Agni : "Remake me". With the *agnihotra* the Gods came to His aid, carried his Limbs back to Him, and remade Him.

This myth of primordial sacrifice makes man aware of the Supreme Principle underlying both the ontological and existential realities. According to Panikkar (1983 : 71), "radical solitude is the primary symbol of the unity and transcendence of the Indescribable, its perfection as well as its simplicity, its original, primordial character".[4] The dismembering of Prajapati shows the primordial oneness of all who were thus created out of His limbs. The remaking of Prajapati stands for the principle of immortality, the principle of "return to life by sacrifice". The ritualistic explanation of the sacrifice is that it is by the sacrifice that the Gods have existence and immortality ; Man, being the integral part of Prajapati, is divinized ; and that as an organ of Prajapati, Man performs all His functions, follows Him in the sacrifice, and re-enters Him.

In the Brahmanic culture, Man is essentially a ritual being. Following the supreme Principle of sacrifice he moves on the earth in the Prajapati way. The best illustration of this is exemplified in a *Tirtha* (a sacred place of Hindu pilgrimage). I have discussed at length elsewhere (Saraswati 1982) how in such sacred places, as Kashi, Man has constructed the replica of the paradigmatic universe where he imitates the paradigmatic work of the Gods, and performs the symbolic merger with the creator. Here the relevant part of my interpretation is reproduced, without pursuing details.

Kashi is the replica of the paradigmatic universe. As the name suggests, Kashi, the luminous city, represents the primaeval egg which had a golden colour (*Hiranyagarbha*), and where in the Prajapati Brahma, the progenitor of all creatures and regions himself was born. Here the eight directions as well as the Lords of the planets, the sun, and the moon had their origin. Kashi is situated on the Shiva's *trisula* (trident) at the centre of space and time, the meeting place of heaven and beyond. The cosmological structure of the *Panchakrosatmka* Kashi-Kshetra[5] represents the five subtile and transforming *Tanmatras* of which this universe was created. The *Panchakrosi* of Kashi-Kshetra stands for the five primordial fundamental materiality (*Panch-kosa*) : *Annamaya Kosa, Pranamaya Kosa, Manomaya Kosa, Vijnanmaya Kosa*, and *Anandamaya Kosa.* Its three segments[6] signify *Triloka*, the "three worlds", totality of the universe, consisting of three realms : earth, atmosphere and heaven. In Kashi, *Pralaya* is overcome and all beings rest for ever. Kashi is the Brahman itself, of which this turning world is but an expression. It is thus an earthly representation of a transcendental model. Kashi pilgrimage also reactualizes the cosmic principle, and imitates the paradigmatic work of the Gods. By circumambulating Kashi-Kshetra the pilgrims reactualize the cycle of birth and death, and experience the cosmic rhythm. Men pilgrimage to Kashi because the Gods have pilgrimaged to this sacred city. In *Masa-yatra* (monthly cycle of pilgrimage), the pilgrims follow the divine and the semi-divine beings in their scheme of pilgrimage. Performances of various types of sacrifices (*yajna*) in Kashi are meritorious ; and the highest merit is attached to cremation in Kashi for that is the reactualization of the primaeval sacrifice of Prajapati. Such performances as visitation of the shrines, touching the deities, rolling on the sacred ground, bathing in the sacred wells and river, ritual sweeping of the streets of Kashi, death, cremation, and immersion of the relics of the dead are all symbolic acts of uniting and dissolving. The *Panchakrosi yatra* originates from Muktimandap and brings to an end there. This symbolizes the return to the primordial. Staying in Kashi, for varying durations,[7] also amounts to the same symbolic return to the point of origin. The central thrust in the sacred complex of Kashi is thus clear.

CONCLUSIONS

Taking the thought structure of the archaic and the classical cultures of India, we find that the meaning which the people themselves attach to their religious phenomena stands different, often in opposition, to that of the anthropologists. Thus, for instance, the anthropological theory of essential duality of the religious phenomena in terms of the sacred-profane opposition does not hold good in the auto-interpretation of Indian cultural traditions.

At one point in the Indian thought structure, the sacred and the secular form a continuum, which implies a peculiar attitude of mind toward the manifest world. Generally, a subjective distinction is made between things for the business of life. But as one mounts higher in the spiritual life, this distinction gets obliterated. Man is ordinarily conditioned by attachment to life, by his desire of *artha* and *kama* which binds him to the "secular", a terrestrial transitory halting place in the passage, which is only as real as one takes it to be. But the moment one is freed from his bondage he moves on to an authentic existence to the sacred reality. Men struggling for freedom are placed at different points of progress. One characteristic of traditional cultures is that while people do differentiate, in actual life situation, between things "sacred" and "secular", at no point is the differentiation made to the extent that the ultimate unity of reality is broken. Thus, in the self-awareness of a traditional culture there always exists a continuum between the sacred and the secular.

All living cultures remain in perpetual pursuit of experiencing and interpreting. Traditional cultures are conditioned by their self-experience ; hence, both description and interpretation of the experienced object vary from one culture to another. But they all are in agreement, that the supreme experience cannot be fully described or interpreted ; and that it can only be shared partially in the for m of myth, in the spiritual consciousness of a person or a culture.

There are two modes of sharing the vision of the sacred : (1) the archaic, and (2) the classical. Their difference stands as follows : In the archaic cultures, myths are uncritically taken as bare facts, as real ; in the classical cultures, myths are examined by a philosophically critical and mystical mind. The archaic perception is radically terrestrial ; the classical perception is markedly transcendental. The archaic people draw up their vision of the sacred in "collective consciousness" ; the classical culture builds up on "individual consciousness". However, these cultural distinctions fade away, as the supreme experience is achieved.

The assumption, that the archaic people take myths uncritically and that their perception is radically terrestrial, deserve some explanation.

This is not to say that the archaic mind is "empty cabinet", deficient or incapable of experiencing the transcendence. This only means that theirs is a different way of understanding the religious phenomena. As stated, both in the archaic and in the classical belief system the basic material is myth. It is but natural for the archaic Oral Cultural Tradition to preserve the primitive innocence of their myths. The classical Textual Cultural Tradition, on the contrary, codifies the myths, destroys its innocence, and builds up a complex philosophical system, comprehensible only to the specialist. This transition from simple to complex is due primarily for the reason that in archaic cultures all experiences are collective (and hence greater homogeneity), and in classical cultures individual experiences are valued (and hence inevitably heterogeneous and complex). But in either case the purpose of myth is the same—to achieve the supreme experience. Also, as stated, both the cultures have reached the same conclusion—the oneness of Men, Cosmos and Gods. Thus, archaic and classical are two human modes of understanding, irreducible one to the other, but equally inseparable in their ultimate understanding of Reality.

If this be so, then the anthropological theory concerning primitive religion as animistic, a system of "low savage faith", out of which has evolved historical religion, cannot be acceptable. Sujata Miri (1981), a philosopher, has critically examined its validity and has arrived at the conclusion that such a theory is totally untenable. Taking Khasi religion as her referent point, she decries animism and brings Khasi religious beliefs to a philosophical domain.

> Knowledge of man consists fundamentally in the insight into the truth that man must lead his life within a framework of rules and duties. It is important, . . . that the Khasi world for religion is derived from *Nia* which means reason. Religious knowledge is thus also the knowledge that man's life has a rational foundation which derives ultimately from *U Blei* (the Khasi term for God) (p. 10). The Khasi religion is quite explicit in its assertion that there can be a sphere of human life on which religion does not have a crucial bearing (p. 15).
>
> In Khasi culture there are enough examples to show how divine sanctions are sought to enforce their social and political order. I am far from suggesting that one can give an exhaustive account of Khasi or any religion in functionalist terms alone. . . . While religious activities undeniably have a functional role—whether social, psychological or political—their meaning transcends the boundary of any such role. And it is characteristic of religious meaning that it necessarily binds together in one whole, of course in an inevitably oblique and complex manner, man, nature and the transcendent world. My plea is that instead of looking at Khasi religion (or any tribal religion) as a collection of more or less disconnected activities with more or less disparate areas for human life, we should consider it as a system of meanings with its centre in the concept of *U Blei* (p. 21).

One might say that Miri's *etic* view of Khasi religion is much too philosophized and far from the *emic* view of that religion. In defence of her interpretation, it may be mentioned that Miri's explanation stems from Mawrie's (1981) *emic* interpretation of Khasi religion. Mawrie, a Khasi reverted from Christianity to his indigenous faith, has ventured to take the auto-understanding of Khasi tradition into theological domain. One may still ask : To what extent is Miri's or even Mawrie's interpretation valid ? Perhaps, one can never be sure of interpreting religious phenomena correctly to its original context. Nevertheless, there could be more than one interpretation – all valid—provided the interpretations are made within the same framework of religious faith and no one obsolutizes truth. Certainly, then, both Miri's philosophy and Mawrie's theology are valid, to the extent that they are meaningful for Khasi religion.

Thus, we arrive at three major conclusions :

(1) That in the self-awareness of a traditional culture there always exists a continuum between the sacred and the secular.
(2) That in the supreme experience of religious phenomena, all traditional cultures recognize the primordial oneness of Man, Cosmos and Gods.
(3) That the archaic and the classical cultures are inseparable in their ultimate understanding of Reality.

These conclusions, based on transempirical understanding of religious phenomena, may not fully contain Vidyarthi's concept of the "Sacred complex" ; but they do justify and support his enterprise of (a) applying one single model of "sacred complex" to both the classical and archaic cultures, and (b) implying, empirically, the unity of nature, man and supernatural in archaic life and culture.

Notes

1. In the Zuni worldview, for instance, there is a harmonious identification of God, nature and man in one enduring recurrent system. Here the "duty of man is the performance of those collective rituals that maintain a perpetual and unchanging harmonious oneness of God, man and nature. The attitude is one of doing one's part in a persistent system." Robert Redfield, *The primitive world and its transformations* (New York, 1953), p. 99.
2. Redfield (Ibid, p. 69) has pointed out that among the Andamanese what one man thinks is not too different from what four of them think.
3. These are the words of Mr. Sidney Hartland. Cf. Bronislaw Malinouski, *Crime and Custom in Savage Society* (London, 1947), p. 48.
4. For the analysis of the Prajapati myth, see Panikkar (1983). The present analysis of the myth is gratefully owed to Panikkar's influence on my thought.
5. In the Pauranic description, the sacred territory of Kashi (Kashi-Kshetra) is of the extent of *Pancha Krosa* (16 km) in radius. The pilgrims circumambulate clockwise on this holy circuit.
6. The Kashi-Kshetra is divided into three segments (*khanda*), called Vishveshvara-khanda, Kedar-Khanda and Onkara-khanda, each having a presiding god. The holy circumambulation of each of the segments is called *antargrihi-parikrama*.
7. Because Kashi is *muktipuri*, the salvation bestowing city par excellence, every Hindu desires to come here and remain for ever. To reside in Kashi for nine months, not crossing its sacred boundary even once during the period of vow, is called *garbhavasa*. It is like living in mother's womb (*garbha*) for nine months. Staying in Kashi for one month during Kartika (October-November) is endowed with inexhaustible merits. The vow to dwell in the sacred territory of Kashi till death is called *kshetra-sannyasa*. A person who has taken this vow must never

cross the boundaries of Kashi, even for religious purpose. His salvation is already secured.

Thus pilgrims come to stay in Kashi for varying durations. Tradition demands that a pilgrim must stay in a place of pilgrimage at least for three nights.

References

Elwin, Verrier, 1968 : Myths of the North-East Frontier of India. Shillong.

Fürer-Haimendorf, C. von, 1953 : The after-life in Indian belief. *Journal of the Royal Anthropological Institute*, LXXIII.

Mawrie, H.O., 1981 : *The Khasi milieu.* New Delhi.

Miri, Sujata, 1981 : An introduction to the study of tribal religions *in* H.O. Mawrie, *The Khasi Milieu.* New Delhi; Concept.

Panikkar, R., 1983 : *Myth, Faith and Hermeneutics.* Bangalore.

Saraswati, Baidyanath, 1970 : *Contributions to the Understanding of Indian Civilization.* Dharwar.

Saraswati, Baidyanath, 1972 : Sacred Complexes in Indian Cultural Traditions, *in* Binod Chand Agarwal (ed.), *Anthropological Approaches to the Study of Complex Society.* New Delhi.

Saraswati, Baidyanath, 1974 : Structure of the Sacred Ritual Terracotta : A Reply to B.K. Roy Burman's Letter, *Man in India* 45(1).

Saraswati, Baidyanath, 1975 : *Kashi : Myth and Reality of a Classical Cultural Tradition.* Simla.

Saraswati, Baidyanath, 1978 : An Anthropologist Looks at Poetry, *Man in India* 58 (3).

Saraswati, Baidyanath, 1982a : Kashi pilgrimage : The end of an end less journey. Prepared for Barbara Nimri Azis's book on *Pilgrimage.*

Saraswati, Baidyanath, 1982b : *Ritual Language : A Transanthropological Perspective.* Varanasi.

Vidyarthi, L.P., 1961 : *The Sacred Complex of Hindu Gaya.* Bombay.

Vidyarthi, L.P., 1963 : *Maler : A Study in Nature-Man-Spirit Complex*, Calcutta.

4

EXPERIENCING VIDYARTHI

Shelly Porteous

VIDYARTHI'S BEGINNINGS

"This extra-ordinary internationally acclaimed anthropologist of the Third World spent his childhood very ordinarily" (Sahay, 1981 : 1). Born on the 28th of February, 1931, Lalita Prasad Vidyarthi spent his early years in the rural and caste-structured village of Bariarpur, Police Station Barh, District Patna in the State of Bihar. After he had completed his initial schooling, Vidyarthi's family moved to Gaya in 1940. There his father was employed as a "Mokhtar" (Assistant Lawyer) in the Mukhsudpur Estate. In Gaya, Vidyarthi attended a middle school named Mahabir School. He graduated with honours and distinction in mathematics and English, obtaining a "Middle School Leaving Certificate Examination". Vidyarthi considers this to be a turning point in his life as a student. He matriculated in 1946, achieving top merit in his school and a very high position in the State standings. Hence Vidyarthi was readily accepted at both Patna College (Arts) and Patna Science College of Patna University.

Vidyarthi's brothers were instrumental in encouraging him to further his studies. Vidyarthi was, for a time, torn whether to enter the arts or science faculty. He decided that a science training, such as medicine or engineering, would be too expensive for his family. Furthermore, his interests in "liberal education" (Sahay, 1981 : 1) made the arts a logical choice. Vidyarthi chose to study geography, of which "Human Geography" interested him the most. The young Vidyarthi helped to pay for his undergraduate course by writing for local weeklies.

In 1950 Vidyarthi received a first class degree in Geography (M.A.). It was shortly after that he heard of a scholarship of Rs. 75 to be given to a student entering anthropology. Vidyarthi applied for the scholarship and was once again faced with a dilemma when he was selected to study anthropology. He was unsure whether to remain in geography or to explore a new terrain. It was at this point that he met Sri Acharya

Narendra Deo, the then Vice-Chancellor of Lucknow University. Acharya Narendra Deo persuaded Vidyarthi to study anthropology and helped him get admission to Lucknow University. Hence, Vidyarthi left Patna for Lucknow, despite his doubts as to the future of anthropology in India. At that time, anthropology was offered only in Calcutta, Delhi and Lucknow.

"In the beginning, in Lucknow, he put up with the Vice-Chancellor, Sri Acharya Narendra Deo. However, he later shifted to the hostel" (Sahay, 1981 : 2). At Lucknow, Vidyarthi was to meet many comrades due to his old Socialist party connections.

> It was difficult for young Vidyarthi to keep himself away from active student politics and devote his full time and energy to pick up the elements of science of man. Nevertheless, the more he studied the more he became interested in knowing about man and his culture and society. From the beginning he was exposed to what may be termed as classic social sciences, anthropology, sociology and social psychology.
>
> (Sahay, 1981 : 2).

After a year at Lucknow University, Vidyarthi married on May 18, 1952, as he had promised his deceased father that he would do so after completing his post-graduate degree. "His wife, Lakshmi Vidyarthi, with her under-graduate degree has proved to be a very successful housewife with two daughters and two sons" (Sahay, 1981 : 2). The eldest daughter, Renu Kumari, has her M.A. in psychology and is presently teaching at the Women's College of Ranchi University. She is married to a geologist and has two young sons (Miku, 3 years ; Riku, 2 years). The second daughter, Kumkum Mohan, has a bachelor's degree in medicine and is married to a physician. The first son, Deepak Vidyarthi (20 years), is studying pharmacy at the Birla Institute of Technology and the second son, Pankaj Vidyarthi (19 years), is taking undergraduate anthropology at Ranchi University.

A "native" anthropologist

My initial reading of Vidyarthi proved highly satisfying. I was exalted to have found exactly what I was seeking : a "native" anthropologist of the "Third World" who was striving to endow anthropology with an indigenous mode of thinking. He is pleased with the esteem anthropology has gained in the eyes of Indian university and government officials over the past two decades. But Vidyarthi professes,

> The journey of Indian anthropology still continues. It has gone ahead under the influence of and in collaboration with British and then

1. A successful expedition : Prof. L.P. Vidyarthi (extreme left) with the Jorwa so-called hostile tribe) of the Middle Andamans in February, 1984.

2. Prof. Vidyarthi with the late Prime Minister, Mrs. Indira Gandhi, and Prof. M. Ames, at a luncheon meeting on the occasion of the 71st Indian Science Congress held at B.I.T., Mesra, on January 3, 1984.

3. Prof. Vidyarthi delivering the presidential address at the annual meeting of the Indian Anthropological Association (December 31 to January 2, 1984). Seated (on his left) are Prof. M. Ames, University of British Columbia, Dr. A. K. Danda, Director, Anthropological Survey of India, and (on his right) Dr. A.K. Dhan, then Vice-Chancellor, Ranchi University and Dr. Sunil Misra, Director, Audience, Research, All India Radio.

> American anthropologists. Of course these non-Indians will continue to wield powerful influence in expanding the scope of anthropology in India in the future. Science knows no barriers and the science of man in India has still much to learn in the field of theory and method from other scientifically advanced countries of the world. But this does not mean that social anthropology in India should overlook what may be termed its "Indianness". Perhaps to some extent social anthropology has not done so, because it has not progressed under the spell of unthinking imitation. Because of this salient feature Professor Kroeber has said that India has listened to England, America, and to herself. The result, we may say, has been a synthetic approach.
>
> (Vidyarthi, 1977 : 76).

The synthetic approach is one moulded by India's own unique heritage. Vidyarthi believes that social scientists in India must explore the ancient scriptures, such as the Vedas, the Upanishads, the Smritis, the Puranas, and the Great Epics, if they are to acquire a sensitive insight into the social realities of India. The scriptures reflect great wisdom in regard to such as man-nature relationships, man-man relationships, and man-spirit relationships. The basic elements of Indian lifestyle are inherent in the traditional practice of fourfold Ashramas, fourfold Purusharthas, the sixteen Sanskaras, etc., which still today hold a powerful position in the life of an average Indian. Vidyarthi calls for Indian social scientists to have an appreciation of traditional religion and not to be swayed by those Western scholars who proclaim only the negative influence of religion on development.

Vidyarthi also declares that social scientists must not ignore such vital Indian social thinkers as Sri Aurobindo, Rabindranath Tagore, Raja Ram Mohan Roy, Vinoba Bhave, Vivekananda and Mahatma Gandhi, to name but a few. They speak in terms of "spiritual humanism, universal love and non-violence" (Vidyarthi, 1979 : 134). Vidyarthi stresses the need to explore Gandhian philosophy. For, as suggested by J. Narayan, there remains untouched a much larger "submerged part of the ice-berg" (Vidyarthi, 1979 : 133). Vidyarthi feels that Gandhi's humanistic tribal writings are of immediate importance. He says of the tribal people, "It is for the Indian anthropologists to take them seriously and not to be carried away by the voluminous writings of the Western scholars who termed them to be 'animist', 'savages', and very different from the Hindus" (Vidyarthi, 1979 : 133). An understanding of India's ancient scriptures and own native sons is of utmost necessity in reaching the fullest understanding of what the "Indianness" of social anthropology in India can possibly mean.

Vidyarthi appeared to me as a scholar who held definite opinions as to the future role of anthropology in India. Vidyarthi advances numerous proposals as to how Indian scholars should approach their work. Vidyarthi believes that Indian anthropologists should emerge in fundamental as well as applied research, despite Edward Shils' claim that fundamental research is beyond the scope of Third World scholars. Vidyarthi encourages Indian anthropologists to tackle the problems of urbanization, industrialization and tribal development. He wishes to see Indian anthropologists re-evaluate the colonial history and hence derive a new and vital understanding of the place of social sciences in developing countries. Vidyarthi's own major fields of research are the tribal culture of India, the Andaman and Nicobar Islands, urban-industrial, political, and action anthropology, Indian civilization, the history of Indian culture, folklore, and village studies. He truly hopes that world anthropology "will allow the anthropologists of the developing countries to play its due role" (Vidyarthi, 1979 : 136).

ASPECTS OF VIDYARTHI'S MAJOR FIELDS OF RESEARCH IN TRIBAL CULTURE OF INDIA : TRIBAL DEVELOPMENT

After a quarter-century of independence for India and upon the verge of the Fifth Five Year Plan for tribal development, Vidyarthi had felt it was the anthropologist's task to evaluate and suggest new tactics for the modernization of tribals. His first hope was that all those involved in tribal development would bear in mind the approach to the problem taken by Jawaharlal Nehru, the first Prime Minister of India. Nehru's worthy position was to develop "the tribals along the lines of their own genius", and he expressed his disapproval of the attitude of labelling "some people primitive and to think of ourself highly civilized" (Vidyarthi, 1974 : 46).

It was in the late forties that Indian anthropologists began to take an active interest in tribal problems. They made it their role to act as advisers in tribal development. They did not wish to simply proclaim the devastating effects of culture contact on tribal people, as had the British colonial anthropologists. After India's independence in 1949, anthropologists began producing papers and presenting speeches advocating the importance of applied anthropology. A theory of "planned acculturation" (Vidyarthi, 1974 : 7) was proposed in an effort to combat the economic hardships of tribal groups.

> The Constitution for the Republic of India provides, The state shall promote with special care the educational and economic interests of the weaker sections of the people and in particular of the scheduled castes and the scheduled tribes and shall protect them from social injustice and all forms of exploitation.
>
> (Vidyarthi, 1974 : 46).

An administrative structure consisting of national leaders, social workers, tribal leaders and applied anthropologists was established in order to protect tribal interests. Religious agencies were also active in this sphere. The Government of India introduced a number of development programmes in the fields of economics, education, health and sanitation, communication and housing, and socio-culture and politics, but it was realized that development schemes should not be so numerous and overpowering as to bewilder the tribal groups.

The economic measures taken by the Government were in the areas of "agriculture and allied sectors, forests, tribal development blocks, co-operative indebtedness, industries, minerals and power" (Vidyarthi, 1974 : 55) In the realm of education much has been done to improve the tribal situation. Primary schools were built within a couple of miles of the home of every child. Overseas and Post-Matric Scholarships were established. Also, efforts were made to provide technical, industrial and foreign training ; education for girls, etc. But Vidyarthi declared, "It is sad that after a quarter of a century of independence some of the tribals are still at the lowest level of cultural development" (Vidyarthi, 1974 : 59). The opening of health centres with qualified doctors has improved the medical field. But certainly, much more work is needed in this field and the same is true of communication and housing. Tribal leadership has been successful in publicizing tribal issues, but Vidyarthi feels with "enlightened tribal leadership the solution of the problem of backwardness will be accelerated" (Vidyarthi, 1974 : 62).

Despite the efforts made by the Government on behalf of tribal interests, Vidyarthi feels that very little has actually improved. He criticizes Goverdment plans on a number of points, e.g. inadequate funding, an administrative personnel lacking in knowledge of tribal culture and certainly not devoted to tribal welfare, etc. Vidyarthi believes a re-evaluation of "regions" and "backwardness" (Vidyarthi, 1974 : 64) is necessary. Hence, special attention could be directed to those tribes classified as extremely "backward". Collaboration between anthropologists and other experts could result in viable development schemes. Vidyarthi firmly believes that "social anthropologists should play the role of a social doctor who not only diagnoses the disease, writes the prescription, but also follows up the treatment" (Vidyarthi, 1974 : 66).

Vidyarthi is calling for measures to be taken in order to stop the process of land alienation and indebtedness and put a halt to tribal exploitation by forest and excise officials. Industrialization and urbanization have inflicted devastating maladies upon the tribal people and, in many cases, have destroyed the traditional way of life. With proper planning Vidyarthi believes that the tribes can be spared the ill effects of industrialization and, yet, can be integrated successfully into the thriving modern world without loss of human dignity. It is the education of tribal men and women which will be the ultimate harbinger of social and economic change, i.e. promote modernization and eliminate poverty. Furthermore, the education of all people should work to make equality and integration between tribal and non-tribal people a reality.

TRIBAL CULTURE OF INDIA : TRIBAL EDUCATION

Dr. Vidyarthi is very much concerned that there should be a well-planned system of tribal education. He feels education for tribals is necessary in today's world, but need not be implemented at the cost of the loss of their traditional values. If planners were to absorb some of the traditional characteristics of tribal education into their system, it would perhaps put a halt to educated youth who scorn their elders and traditional milieu.

Vidyarthi propounds the need for educational planners to take into consideration the economic conditions of the tribes. School sessions should be arranged during months when families find it possible to spare their children from work in the fields. He also believes that schooling for tribals should not be exclusively that of the three R's. Agricultural, craft and other training is necessary so that students may earn while attending school. The teaching of a tribe's foremost craft should be central to the educational curriculum. Economic considerations are the first step to a successful education programme.

Vidyarthi has furtber advice for tribal education. Children, Vidyarthi says, should be taught in their mothertongue at least up to the lower primary stage, with the regional language gaining predominance thereafter. Non-tribals with a knowledge of tribal languages should receive proper training if they are to be appointed as teachers. Vidyarthi hopes that some knowledge of social anthropology and racial psychology will help to dispel the superior attitude and prejudices held by the non-tribals in their association with tribals. Vidyarthi would like to see traditional songs, riddles, folktales, and dances used as a method of imparting formal education, as such activities are the most familiar form of learning for tribal children. Textbooks should be prepared by a cultural board so as to incorporate the tribal mythology, traditions, heroes, etc., of each particular area. Only in the middle stage should texts begin to introduce traits needed for acculturation. Hence it is that education for tribal areas should be approached from a very different stance than that of other areas. (Vidyarthi, 1955-56 : 39-45).

TRIBAL CULTURE OF INDIA : TRIBAL ETHNOGRAPHY

The Maler are a major tribe of Bihar and according to Vidyarthi "one of the few primitive tribes of great anthropological interest in India" (Vidyarthi, 1963 : 1). It was in 1951 that Vidyarthi learned of the "excessive primitiveness" of the isolated Maler tribe. As so little research material had been compiled on the Maler tribe, he decided to make them the object of his "scientific investigation" (Vidyarthi, 1963 : 3).

Vidyarthi approached his task with what he felt to be proper anthropological tools. Of primary significance were observation and interview methods. In addition, census, surveys, and questionnaires were used to gather such information as geneologies and life histories. With the aid of his students, Vidyarthi was able to visit almost the entire Maler area. Of utmost importance in facilitating a successful study was the fact that the research group was able to spend days and nights in the villages. Hence, Vidyarthi declares they became as "one among the villagers" and

> In spite of their ignorance and initial suspicion, most of them could develop deep confidence in me and helped me in achieving my mission in all their possible ways. While I acknowledge their appreciation, I also assure them that I have not betrayed their confidence and have used their statements with all pious and scientific intentions to understand the laws of society and culture.
>
> (Vidyarthi, 1963 : 5, x-xi).

In his book, *The Maler : A Study in Nature-Man-Spirit Complex of a Hill Tribe*, Vidyarthi sought to unveil what Malinowski would call the "spirit" or the "soul" (Vidyarthi, 1963 : 7) of the culture. Hence, it was necessary to combine ethnographic detail with theoretical projection. Vidyarthi, termed his approach on "cultural ecology" and "functionalism" (Vidyarthi, 1963 : 9). Vidyarthi's theoretical understanding of the importance of the "Nature-Man" inter-relationship for the study of "primitive" (Vidyarthi, 1963 : 176) culture was derived from Evans-Pritchard (1940), Redfield (1955), and Thomas (1956). But, Vidyarthi discovered that an examination of the realm of the "spirits" was necessary in order to complete the Redfieldian "intuited whole" (Vidyarthi, 1963 : 176, 175).

Vidyarthi explains how the ecological basis of forests and "Khallu" cultivation (hill or slash-and-burn cultivation) shapes the socio-religio-economic life of the Maler. He studies man in relation to man. Namely, he views man as a social being ; member of the village, the tribe, and the region of contacts ; he presents man in a role as part of the dominant family organization (nuclear family and lineage) around which are centred the major economic, social, religious and reproductive activities, and finally, he focuses upon man as a biological and self-perpetuating creature in terms of hunger for sex, need for food, and the innate process of socialization. Lastly, Vidyarthi presents, the four types of Maler spirits, ("Gossaiyan"—benevolent spirits, "Jiwe urkkya"—Ancestors' spirits, "Alchi"—evil spirits, and "Chergani"—spiritual power of a witch or witchcraft) in a framework of sacred geography, sacred performances, and sacred specialists. The three constitute the religious or sacred complex of the Maler village. Nature, man and spirit of necessity interact. Elsewise, there would be total oblivion for the Maler people. The social and religious beliefs and practices of the Maler operate functionally, in order to combat the constant threats of starvation, sickness and death. Hence, "Nature-Man-Spirit" form the complex of Maler life. Vidyarthi has displayed what Redfield would term the "little tradition of the Maler, as it does not reflect the "great tradition" (Vidyarthi, 1963 : i) of India.

APPLIED AND ACTION ANTHROPOLOGY IN INDIA

Vidyarthi was a member of a conference held in July 1968, which was organized to discuss the need for urgent research in social anthropology in India. Vidyarthi felt the conference came to a vital conclusion, that is, the need to combine successfully theoretical investigations with an examination of immediate practical problems of national development. The issues stressed by the conference as requiring urgent attention were the following : the need to study a number of people in India who were in threat of vanishing ; the need to record the lifestyles of the "primitives" before the Government's vast plan of economic development altered traditional patterns, and the necessity of investigating and understanding tribal integration into an industrialized and urbanized India.

Vidyarthi notes a number of specific phenomenon, which he feels to be of great importance for immediate study and recording He speaks of the caste and tribal communities, which came into contact through ancient fairs and festivals, but whose interactions prove to be fast diminishing. He explains that many tribes, due to a fear of loss of identity, have sought to recover and in some cases exaggerate their unique cultural identity. Vidyarthi is further interested in the new cultures and new classes, which are emerging to replace the old. He wishes to see a full examination of the messianic movements and rebellions. He also calls for a theoretical investigation of the areas in India where patriliny has been replacing matriliny.

The conference itself adopted three final resolutions. The first was to promote a broader data base for scholars, e.g. an exchange of annual academic reports should take place between the departments of anthropology, sociology and allied disciplines ; M.A. and Ph.D. dissertations should be compiled and abstracts of Ph.D. dissertations published ; out-of-date and rare volumes should be made available ; the value of pamphlet literature for understanding popular culture should be stressed, etc. The second resolution was to emphasize the need for university and other institutional support in carrying out urgent anthropological research, e.g. field research should be instituted as an integral part of the anthropology and sociology departmental curriculum ; scholarships by the University Grants Committee should be made available to deserving students entering anthropology and sociology, as these disciplines deserve a new place of importance in a country which is engaged in development and social change ; anthropological and sociological information should be made part of high school studies, etc. The final resolution of the conference was a pledge to urge collaboration among scholars and institutions in promoting an efficient and urgent social anthropology, e.g. stress the need for increased communication between government research institutions and the university departments, and facilitate the exchange of scholars between institutions in India and with neighbouring countries (Vidyarthi, 1969 : 377-379).

Vidyarthi explains that applied anthropology in India actually originated when a few British anthropologists, such as Rivers (1906), Radcliffe-Brown (1922) and Hutton (1931) offered suggestions for the proper colonial administration of tribals. In 1931, Hutton stated his concerns regarding the devastating effects of culture contact on tribal peoples. According to Hutton, "the solution of the problems would be to create self-governing tribal areas with free powers of self-determination in regard to surrounding or adjacent units" (Vidyarthi, 1976 : 81-82). The Indian anthropologist, S.C. Roy, was also active in unveiling the effects of contact on tribal groups. D.N. Majumdar and A. Aiyappan were to approach the problem of culture contact through applied anthropological research. They both operated under the influence of British functionalism. Majumdar (1937) discovered that the Ho of Kolhan had undergone gradual degeneration due to culture contact. He describes the Ho as "a degenerate race of men with a weak constitution and a lower expectation of life" (Vidyarthi, 1976 : 82).

Verrier Elwin's (1939) remedy for tribal problems was one of "isolationism". He suggested a National Park be established for the Baiga and Gonds where outside contact would be minimal and hence they could live their lives with "utmost possible happiness and freedom" (Vidyarthi, 1976 : 83). Vidyarthi suggests that Elwin's proposal was sorely misunderstood. Vidyarthi states that it was Elwin's concern and respect for tribal peoples that caused him to take the stance of "isolationism". For instance, in his book, *Loss of the Nerve* (1941), Elwin states.

> But for the aboriginal in the Central Provinces, except in certain obvious cases, liquor is not a source of degradation or disease, the real evil of liquor to the aboriginal is that it brings him into contact with and often makes him dependent on a degraded type of alien.
>
> (Vidyarthi, 1976 : 83).

Furthermore, Vidyarthi proclaims that, "in recognition of the appreciation for the tribal culture he (Elwin) married two tribal women, one after the other" (Vidyarthi, 1976 : 83). G.S. Ghurye on the other hand was to refute Elwin's position, in favour of assimilation. Ghurye (1943, 1959) proclaims, "some of the tribes are so far Hinduised that they have got assimilated as different castes in the caste system". Furthermore, he does not believe that, "Hinduisation of the tribal is accompanied by the evil desire of the kinds postulated by O'Malley and by Elwin" (Vidyarthi, 1976 : 84).

The current position held by administrators and social scientists alike towards tribal groups is one where, "instead of the principles of imposition and paternalism, ideas of persuasion and self-determination are recommended" (Vidyarthi, 1976 : 85-86). Vidyarthi names such social scientists as Dube, Dey, Tyler, Luschinsky, Orenstein, Oscar Lewis, Srinivas, Fraser, and Sinha as forging a strong theoretical and methodological applied anthropology in India.

Applied social scientists in India are concerning themselves with numerous aspects of tribal development. They feel it is of utter necessity to consider the cultural orientations of the tribal peoples before implementing plants of social change. Effective tribal education is believed to be of utmost importance. Vidyarthi states, "Roles of the educational institutions as channels of mobility and transition, and also as buffers and bridges, between the great traditions and the little traditions, are fields of investigation of particular relevance for India" (Vidyarthi, 1976 : 88-89).

In the field of health, concern has returned to uncovering the social, cultural and behavioural factors which are significant in determination of many diseases. Social scientists are now working in conjunction with medical specialists to improve health standards, by starting with a "cultural definition of illness" (Vidyarthi, 1976 : 89). Vidyarthi himself was involved in just such a project. The anthropologists of Ranchi University were assisted by local doctors in an Action Research Programme concerned with the health of a number of tribal villages. Family planning is another area where cultural characteristics must be understood before introducing any plans. Of course, applied physical anthropology can play a significant part in health schemes for society.

The list of tribal concerns by applied social scientists in India is indeed a long one. A recent challenge for anthropologists is in agricultural development. Anthropologists are attempting to make viable agricultural innovations in accordance with the local ethos. Anthropological studies of industrial and urban centres have proven to be of great value to town planners and will hopefully continue to hold a place in town planning administration. The National Commission on Labour, chaired by Dr. Vidyarthi, was a study team which investigated the labour problems confronting tribals. Vidyarthi's report (1969) suggests the need for a consistent labour policy. Social scientists are also concerned that modern technology should not destroy the traditional character of a craft. The study of criminal tribes is considered an endeavour of importance by applied anthropologists. Applied anthropologists find leadership studies to be of extreme value in providing a firm vantage point by which to deal with development. Full-length study of leadership in Indian villages was initiated by the American, Oscar Lewis (1954), and his Indian collaborator, H.S. Dhillon (1955). Vidyarthi (1967) edited a volume entitled *Leadership in India* in which various aspects of tribal and rural leadership are explored. In his book, *Dynamics of Leadership*, B.N. Sahay (1969) studies aspects of leadership among the Maler and the Santal. He presents three types of leaders in their roles as social changers. The study of military organization is also of great interest to applied anthropologists, but they are restricted in this area due to security reasons.

Vidyarthi concludes, "Indian anthropologists have faced the challenge to act as social doctors in diagnosing social ills, in prescribing appropriate remedies and smoothing the course of transformation from traditional to transitional stage, and then to the 're-organizational' phase of our society" (Vidyarthi, 1976 : 102-103). Many factors, however, inhibit the work of the applied anthropologists. Indeed, there is much disagreement both in the governmental sphere and among anthropologists themselves as to the role of social anthropologists. Should anthropologists be analysts and/or advisers or co-operators? The question remains ill-answered and hence anthropological positions are widely varied. Some anthropologists act as consultants, others are co-administrators and still others are placed in temporary control of a development project.

A final category of applied social anthropologists is one in which social anthropologists can engage in Sol Tax's action anthropology. Action anthropology is one in which the anthropologist can combine both action and research. Vidyarthi describes Tax's action anthropology as follows :

> First of all there is the value of truth. In the tradition of anthropologists, he (Tax) believes in finding out the verifiable facts before action is prescribed. Secondly the action anthropologists strongly feel the value of freedom. Freedom in these contexts usually means freedom for the individual to choose his own way of life. The third value on the operational level is a kind of law of parsimony, according to which questions of value are not settled by the action anthropologists. This is a decision for the people. This provides only alternatives and offers them the right to self-determination instead of imposing values from outside.
>
> (Vidyarthi, 1976 : 103-104).

Vidyarthi regrets that applied social science is still not viewed favourably among many bureaucrats and academicians in India. He believes a harmful and false dichotomy has been constructed between pure or fundamental research and applied research. He strongly believes that the time for social scientists to take a firm stance in support of applied and action research is well overdue. Vidyarthi does not want social scientists to simply remain recorders of descriptive facts or theoreticians.

INDIAN CIVILIZATION : HINDU GAYA

Vidyarthi's work, *The Sacred Complex in Hindu Gaya,* is one of his greatest contributions to the field of anthropology. Gaya is a sacred city of Hindu pilgrimage. He describes Gaya in terms of "a sacred geography", a set of "sacred performances", and a group of "sacred specialists". These three concepts comprise the "sacred complex" (Vidyarthi, 1961 : 111), which is essentially a "great tradition" in character. The great tradition of the sacred complex is one which reflects Hinduism and works to unite the diverse people of India.

The study is based on the concepts propounded by Professor Robert Redfield and Professor Milton Singer. It presents an integrated approach to the study of Indian civilization, whereby high caste Hindus and tribal ethnic groups are simultaneously compared in the context of ancestor worship. As Vidyarthi states in the introduction of his book, *The Sacred Complex in Hindu Gaya*, anthropology had in the past been "wedded" to the study of "primitive" (Vidyarthi, 1961 : xxiii) communities.

Redfield proposes that a civilization consists of both "great and little traditions". For example, outside influences on a village would be those of the "great tradition" and influences from within the village are ones of the "little tradition". Redfield originated the term "cultural specialists" to designate organized groups of people who function as mediators between the great and little traditions. Singer's concept of "cultural media" (Vidyarthi, 1961 : xxiv) is the various methods by which the cultural specialists attempt to communicate to the masses and maintain continuity between the two traditions.

Vidyarthi's study of Hindu Gaya demonstrates that the sacred complex establishes and maintains continuity and compromise between the great and little traditions of Hindu civilization. Vidyarthi describes the sacred specialists as remaining distinct from the great and little traditions, but able to transmit elements of the great tradition to the little tradition. Vidyarthi describes how the sacred complex is being transformed due to the influence of Western civilization. He notes that it remains to be seen in the future whether the sacred complex can continue to maintain cultural continuity and compromise with the absorption of modern influences into its traditional flow.

INDIAN CIVILIZATION : CASTES

In agreement with Srinivas, Vidyarthi states that the caste system forms the structural basis of Hinduism. Furthermore, the impact of caste customs is far ranging and can be seen to have greatly affected the social organization of the non-Hindu communities in India. It was not until the 1940's and the 1950's that the need for serious caste studies in relation to village studies was realized. Caste studies in rural India were first made by Srinivas (1952), Marriott (1955), Dube (1955), Lewis (1958), Majumdar (1958), Prasad (1959), Bailey (1958, 1960), and Ansaril (1960).

Majumdar (1958) reports of a situation where the Thakurs (Rajput) are striving to maintain their high status control over the Nai. When given ownership rights to the land they cultivated, the Nai consciously began to seek equal privileges to those of the Thakurs. They referred to themselves as Nai-Thakur : a clear statement of their desire to be equal in status to the Thakurs.

Vidyarthi feels the time for city caste studies is well overdue. After all, the caste system is not restricted to rural settings. Traditional cities have a rural base and villagers migrating to large urban centres carry with them the caste tradition. Considerable friction has been seen to arise between the upper and lower castes of cities, due to the increasing impact of Westernization, urbanization and industrialization. Vidyarthi feels a social structural approach is necessary in the study of this recent phenomenon of tension between castes.

In his study of the tribal town of Ranchi, Vidyarthi discovered, through the use of survey, that the majority of those in favour of the retention of the caste hierarchy occupied the highest position. On the other hand, a large number of lower caste members disapproved of the caste system. Vidyarthi states,

> . . . the informants (28.8%) who approved of the caste system did so mainly on religious considerations. They believed the caste system to be god-ordained, a divine institution to be accepted without question. The other considerations for approving the caste system were : caste is a traditional institution (16%) ; it facilitates division of labour (4.4%) ; it does good to the society (24.3%) ; and brings unity among the different caste groups (18%). . . . Regarding the disapproval of the caste system a majority of the informants disapproved of it as it was dangerous to the nation (34.7%). Some (11.7%) disapproved of it as it was harmful to society, while some (29.1%) did not favour it as it was a bad institution. Other minor reasons for its disapproval were that public opinion was against it (8 3%) and that it created social disorder (6.9%).
>
> (Vidyarthi, 1963 : 236-238).

Vidyarthi feels the response of the lower caste members is facilitated by city life. City life allows for greater freedom from the rigid hierarchical social structure of rural society. For instance, people are allowed to range from their traditional occupations. This sense of freedom has caused them to reject the caste system. Vidyarthi states that "the caste tensions between the upper and lower castes seem to be implicit as they are reflected from their differential response" (Vidyarthi, 1963 : 239).

Vidyarthi notes an increasing horizontal solidarity of both city and village castes along regional and political lines. This would seem to be a further indication of growing tensions between castes. Vidyarthi believes that despite all criticisms, the caste system provided "peace and contentment" (Vidyarthi, 1963 : 230) in India for centuries. In conclusion, Vidyarthi proclaims,

> During the last few decades under the influence of westernism, we have pledged to do away with the caste system. In making the decision, perhaps, we have been wise, as we are dreamers of a new era, but in its actual realization in the society, we have not made much headway . . . caste is becoming further entrenched in the Indian social structure owing to our new experiments in democracy and power alliances. Owing to this new political function of caste a careful thinker is led to believe that the longevity of the caste system has been prolonged (Srinivas, 1957) (Vidyarthi, 1963 : 239).

ANTHROPOLOGY IN INDIAN UNIVERSITIES : RESEARCH METHODOLOGY

> There is today widespread recognition that the future of human civilization depends to a high degree upon man's capacity to understand the forces and factors which control his own social behaviour. Such an understanding, we all agree, depends on the development of the science of society. Science has many connotations, but one of its most important contributions to human understanding and welfare lies in its methodology. . . Since anthropology is basically a field science, research methodology constitutes an essential part of this subject.
>
> (Vidyarthi, 1974 : 173-174).

Vidyarthi feels that research methodology consists of an inter-relationship between theory and practical experience ; an inter-relationship which requires that theory taught in the class-room be applied in the field, if one is to derive a full understanding from the study. Research methodology involves the learning of everything from formulation of project proposals and techniques of data collecting to the processing, analysis and presentation of data. Many of the Indian universities require that students of anthropology conduct field work, in order to put into practice the techniques they have learned in research methodology courses. Post-graduate students are required to conduct field work lasting from three to eight weeks. The field work of undergraduate students is usually a period between ten days and three weeks.

Vidyarthi would like to see the teaching of research methodology become compulsory and uniform in Indian universities. Vidyarthi believes that thorough training in research methodology is necessary as anthropology is a field science. The anthropological approach to social science consists of participant observation, micro-study and part-whole analysis. Those anthropologists who studied small and folk communities were responsible for the development of participant observation as there were no records to be consulted. Participant observation is characterized by "(a) staying with the community, (b) acquiring the working knowledge of its language, (c) to play roles, (d) to establish rapport and (e) to participate actively in the life-ways of the community" (Vidyarthi, 1974 : 177). The anthropologist's micro-study of human relations is in contrast to the macro-study carried out by sociologists. From the micro-study, macro-level generalizations can be derived and the part can be related to the larger whole, i.e. a village community can be related to the workings of a total civilization.

Vidyarthi advocates a multi-disciplinary approach to the anthropological study of man, i.e. the adoption of psychological and statistical methods. He would also like to see the development of indigenous field methods. He is happy to report that Indian anthropologists of late have proved themselves not to be restricted in scope. For instance, urban studies are of recent origin for anthropologists. He states that apart from using the methods familiar to other social scientists of urban studies, it is necessary "to explain the relevance of our own new techniques and strategies to this new field of anthropological study" (Vidyarthi, 1974 : 179).

VIDYARTHI'S HISTORY OF SOCIAL ANTHROPOLOGY IN INDIA

Vidyarthi gives credit to D.N. Majumdar as the first to attempt to classify the development of social anthropology in India according to the prevalent trends of historical periods. Using the terms of T.K. Penniman (1935), Majumdar (1950) categorizes anthropological researches in India into three phases, being Formulatory (1774-1911), Constructive (1912-1937) and Critical (1938-present). The establishment of the Asiatic Society of Bengal, which was devoted to the scientific study of "nature and man" (Vidyarthi, 1977 : 67) in India, marked the beginning of the Formulatory period. Majumdar's second phase was initiated by the publication of the first full-length monograph on the Mundas by S.C. Roy (1912).

Majumdar felt the critical period began in 1938 with the meeting of the Indian and British anthropologists on the occasion of the Silver Jubilee of the Indian Science Congress in Lahore. Past, present and future developments in Indian anthropological research were discussed.

Vidyarthi characterizes the three-phase development of social anthropology in India a great deal differently from Majumdar. Furthermore, he acknowledges that anthropology in India has developed at different rates in different areas and, hence, it cannot be said that one phase completely replaces the other. It was at this point that I began to critically re-evaluate Vidyarthi's researches in terms of his own categorizations.

VIDYARTHI'S FORMATIVE PERIOD

Vidyarthi is in agreement with Majumdar that the founding of the Asiatic Society of Bengal by Sir William Jones was the beginning of anthropological investigation in India. Typical of the Formative period (1774-1919) was the compilation of historical, geographical and ethnographic data on tribes and castes by British administrators, missionaries and travellers. District gazetteers, handbooks, encyclopedic inventories, monographs and books were produced aimed at ensuring effective colonial administration. Much was published in *The Journal of the Asiatic Society of Bengal* (1784), *Indian Antiquary* (1872), *The Jaurnal of the Bihar and Orissa Research Society* (1915), and *Man in India* (1921). Early British anthropologists with published monographs on their work among the tribes of India, Ceylon and the Andaman Islands were Rivers (1906), Seligmann and Seligmann (1911), Radcliffe-Brown (1922) and Hutton (1931). S.C. Roy was the first Indian national to write extensive monographs on the tribes of India, the first being the work on the Munda tribe (1912). It was J.H. Hutton who, in his presidential address to the Indian Anthropological Institute in Calcutta on January 5, 1938, named Roy "the father of Indian ethnology" (Vidyarthi, 1977 : 69). Roy received "intellectual inspiration" (Vidyarthi, 1977 : 69) from British anthropologists and financial assistance from the British governor of Bihar, Sir Edward Tait. The publication of R.P. Chandra's book on the Indo-Aryan race in 1916 was to attract great interest in the cultural history of India.

VIDYARTHI'S CONSTRUCTIVE PERIOD

The Constructive period (1920-1947) saw the inclusion of social anthropology in the departmental curriculum of the universities in Bombay (sociology in 1919 with P. Geddes as head) and Calcutta (anthropology in 1921 with R. Chandra as head). S.C. Roy established the first Indian journal of anthropology, *Man in India*, in 1921. Anthropologists such as Ghurye, K.P. Chattopadhyay, Srinivas, Majumdar and Karve took up studies of kinship and social organization. Scientific anthropological research was initiated by "conducting field expeditions, by writing books and articles, and by training researchers for anthropological study of tribal and rural cultures" (Vidyarthi, 1977 : 70). The Constructive period was punctuated in 1938 with the joint session of the Indian Science Congress Association and the British Association. Majumdar, Srinivas and N.K. Bose began to critically analyze their material and, hence, were responsible for introducing a theoretical sophistication to Indian anthropological research. The work of Verrier Elwin and Von Fürer-Haimendorf added further recognition to Indian anthropology. "Indian anthropology, which had been born and brought up under the dominant influence of British anthropology, matured during its Constructive phase also under a British influence" (Vidyarthi, 1977 : 70-71). Both British and Indian anthropologists were engaged in tribal studies. Not unlike the anthropology at Cambridge, Oxford and London, Indian anthropology was foremost a study of kinship and social organization.

FORMING AND CONSTRUCTING VIDYARTHI

"Originally, the influence of Malinowski percolated in him (Vidyarthi) through late Dr. D.N. Majumdar, who happened to be a student of Malinowski" (Sahay, 1981 : 5). Professor Dhirendra Nath Majumdar (1903-1960) was one of Vidyarthi's teachers. Majumdar received his M.A. degree in Anthropology from the University of Calcutta in 1924. He received his Ph.D. degree in 1935 from Cambridge University, where he studied social anthropology with Professor T.C. Hadson and physical anthropology with Professor G.M. Morant. Majumdar also attended Malinowski's seminar at the London School of Economics and was greatly impressed and influenced by his functional theory of culture. S.C. Roy, who had considerable contact with such British anthropologists as Frazer, Rivers and Marret, was a teacher to Majumdar. Radhakamal Mukherjee and D.P. Mukherjee, both of the University of Lucknow, were also influenced by British thought and both were Vidyarthi's teachers. Vidyarthi claims that the influences of Malinowski, which had indirectly reached him, were not long lived. For, Vidyarthi rejected Malinowski's anti-historical stance. Nonetheless, in a number of respects Vidyarthi can be seen to have taken a British approach to anthropology.

The British school of anthropology made a definite division in the world between "us and others" ; civilized and primitive. This is evident by the types of societies British social anthropologists chose to study, as in comparison to those of British sociologists. The social anthropologist studied native societies, "other cultures" ; that is "primitive", preliterate, or tribal societies and the sociologist would study British society or societies of the British kind. Anthropology and sociology were introduced to India from outside, particularly from Britain and, hence, Indian scholars were to adopt British orientations. Anthropologists in India were to study tribal groups and sociologists in India were to study the advanced sectors of Indian civilization. W.H.R. Rivers was appointed the first head of the Department of Anthropology at Calcutta (but died before he could take his position) and Patrick Geddes launched the Department of Sociology at Calcutta. These two men displayed vividly the dichotomy between the disciplines.

Andr Béteille explains that despite the imposed formal academic structure in India, social anthropologists and sociologists have continually interchanged roles. And, it is precisely those scholars who have ignored the categorization of society into primitive and advanced sections, who have contributed most to the understanding of Indian society. N.K. Bose was just such a scholar. He was an Indian anthropologist who re-emphasized the extreme and potentially harmful distinctions between tribal and non-tribal people. He believed in the use of a single scientific method to study all sectors of society, from "primitive" to "advanced". Bose's fieldwork differed from that of British and American anthropologists. He engaged in an "extensive as opposed to an intensive fieldwork" (Béteille, 1974 : 16) and thus was able to cover a range of investigation from the Juang tribe of Orissa to a survey of Calcutta city. Bose furthermore believed that "in order to understand fully any segment of Indian society its relation to the whole design of this society must be seen" (Bteille, 1974 : 16).

The generation of Indian scholars succeeding Bose continued to integrate the fields of anthropology and sociology. For, as Béteille states,

> The distinction between sociology and social anthropology (or cultural anthropology, or ethnology) thrives on a dichotomous view of the world. Whites and natives, civilized and primitive, us and they : this, historically, has been the basis of the distinction made in the West between the two. But given the way in which Indian society is constituted, it provides very little basis for generating—or sustaining—this kind of dichotomous distinction.
>
> (Béteille, 1974 : 17).

Béteille explains that in India, the distinction between tribal and non-tribal society is very unique, as there is much similarity between the two peoples in terms of modes of livelihood and economic organization, etc. Furthermore, there are great continuities between urban and rural life in India, as "city and village have co-existed in India for more than two millennia" (Béteille, 1974 : 18). It is thus only natural that those scholars who started by studying rural India, at some point, direct their endeavours to urban India.

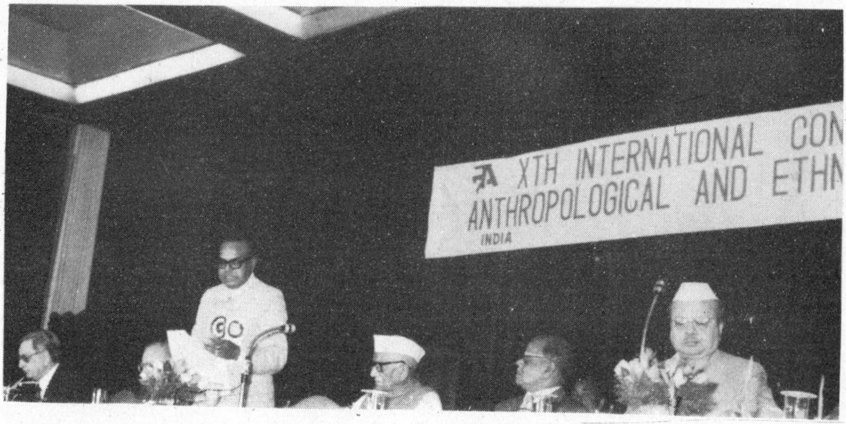

4. Prof. Vidyarthi delivering the presidential address at the Xth International Congress of Anthropological and Ethnological Sciences at Delhi on December 10, 1978. Sitting on his left is the then Prime Minister of India, Mr. Morarji Desai.

5. Prof. Vidyarthi with Mr. Morarji Desai, the then Prime Minister of India, Dr. Chander, the then Education Minister, and Prof. Krader, Secretary General of IUAES, 1972.

6. Addressing a convocation meeting of Ranchi University. Prof. Vidyarthi was Dean, Faculty of Social Sciences, Ranchi University.

7. At the reception given by the Indian Ambassador in Japan, Mr. Badr-ud-Din Tyabji, to the Indian deligation to the IXth Pacific Science Congress in Tokyo in 1966. From left : Dr. S. Tomonaya, Nobel Prize winner and President of the Congress, Mrs. Tyabji, Ambassador Tyabji and Prof. Vidyarthi.

It must be said that Vidyarthi, not unlike numerous Indian scholars, purports to support an inter-disciplinary approach to the social sciences. However, I feel there is an underlying attitude in Vidyarthi's works, which stresses "difference" in the British anthropological sense. The following, from the introduction of *The Maler: A Study in Nature-Man-Spirit Complex of a Hill Tribe*, displays the distinction Vidyarthi creates between himself (the anthropologist) and the Maler (his object of study).

> Our journey and stay in this inaccessible forested, hilly and wild areas of Rajmahal Plateau of the Santhal Parganas were really very challenging and full of adventures. Completely cut-off from the familiar world, I had to cover on foot even more than twenty miles on the hills to reach villages like Surjbera and Garsingla. At times, I had to carry my own luggage owing to non-availability of porters, and invariably our rations from the plains. Sometimes I had to go without bath for weeks and weeks together, and I had no alternative but to use muddy and dirty ditch-water for the drinking purposes at Deotikri. Fear from wild animals like bears and tigers was immensely great and on several occasions some of us could luckily escape their wild jaws. It was unusually tense moments for us, while some of us went to the mysterious "Kachná Surajberá" fort where numerous bears were lurking in the wild caves. Then, malaria and diarrhoea affected all of us at sometime or the other, and two of our students in the year 1956 had to return from the Maler villages without completing their assignments.
>
> With the flora and fauna, the people at times were also not less wild and inhospitable. Our arrival in their villages, at least in the beginning, used to create suspicions and anxiety in their minds. They used to interpret our identity and purpose in the light of their own experiences and we had to convince them that we were not one among them. We had the worst experience of suspicions in a very interior village, Nirbhitta, 12 miles from Hiranpur. The people, as I could gather, considered it very inauspicious to see a group of outsiders in their village. The headmen of the neighbouring villages met together to discuss the matter and decided to attack our camp violently, if we continued our stay there. In view of their aggressiveness and our complete isolation, we had no other alternative but to leave the village only after five days without completing our investigations. At Deotikri as well, when we were closing our camp, with the measurement of their heads and huts, they also turned to be very suspicious and summoned their Sardar from Bhatbhanga to deal with us. The frightening rumour that they would be taken down on the plain had completely made them suspicious towards the outsiders and we had

> to apply all devices to convince them that we were not one among them who wanted to take them down.
>
> Whatever may be the hazards, my satisfaction is that I could get a chance to live for a longer period in an environment, and with a people who are quite distinct from ours and who are very unfamiliar even to many anthropologists.
>
> (Vidyarthi, 1963 : 6-7).

Vidyarthi's distinction between "us and others" acquires a particularly definite connotation when he begins to propound the concept of "detribalization". Diane Lewis, in her article, *Anthropology and Colonialism,* states that the colonial anthropologists saw himself as a "detached scientific observer, objectively recording, "primitive" lifeways before they disappeared or became Westernized, or else as a buffer between two worlds, serving to soften the blow of Western political domination and economic exploitation" (Lewis, 1973 : 582). It seems quite ironic that Vidyarthi often speaks of reformulating the colonial experience through Indian eyes and yet, it appears that it is with a pseudo-colonial attitude that he approaches his own anthropological tribal studies. Certainly, Professor Vidyarthi recognizes the heterogeneity of Indian culture, i.e. a whole comprising many dissimilar parts. But, the posture adopted by Vidyarthi is one which reduces much of tribal culture to passing phenomenon. He underscores the evil effects of culture contact among the tribals, as he feels that it is such contact which results in the obliteration of traditional tribal ways of life. Tribal peoples are seen as being more acted upon than acting.

The urgency of contemporary circumstances in India has perhaps led Vidyarthi to neglect his own stance on historicism, with a resulting functionalist lack of "interest in the processes by which culture changes" (Murdock, 1951 : 468). Certainly, the fact of tragedies and injustices due to mismanagement of tribal administration makes this understandable. It is highly commendable that Vidyarthi advocates an administrative structure which takes into account the unique circumstances and problems of each tribal group. But, such a structure must also allow for self-determination on behalf of the tribal people. As Lewis explains of the colonial anthropologist,

> A great many anthropologists doubtless felt that their understanding of the native people placed them in the position to bargain on their behalf. Yet, as noted, these individuals rarely questioned the basic relationships of privilege and were, therefore, in the somewhat ambiguous position of many liberals in our society to reform a situation from which they themselves derive definite benefits.
>
> (Lewis, 1973 : 583).

It is unfortunate that a stance which stresses difference can unwittingly be implying inferiority and, hence, the need for jurisdiction and supervision.

The tendency towards a hierarchical stance, as depicted by Lewis' stereotypic colonial anthropologists, can of course stem from a caste upbringing as well. Béteille says of life in India, "We live in a society which is the most rigidly hierarchical in the world" (Béteille, 1972 : 1). In this hierarchy, Vidyarthi occupies a position in the upper echelon. Vidyarthi is a member of the Kayastha caste. Kayasthas were traditionally warriors and rulers. Vidyarthi could very easily find himself in the tenuous position of supporting the abolition of a hierarchical order which he helps to perpetuate. Even in modern India, caste signifies educational and financial privilege or deprivation, as well as social status.

The concepts of caste and class are of course not so utterly alien to one another, as Westerners would like to believe. As Dumont suggests,

> . . . caste has something to teach us about ourselves. . . . Anthropology by the understanding it gradually affords of the most widely differing societies and cultures gives proof of the unity of mankind. In doing so, it obviously reflects at least some light on our own sort of society.
>
> (Dumont, 1966 : 1-2).

Today, we find that caste inequalities are co-existing or continually being replaced by another type of inequality. Education, income, occupation and Western manners are in many respects becoming more important than caste in the traditional sense, particularly among urban, educated, professional groups. Béteille writes,

> The British in the nineteenth century wanted the new educational system in India to create a class of people who would be English in habits, tastes and culture, while remaining Indian only in blood. This is what it very nearly did. Among professional groups in India, the most significant difference is between those who have had an English education—whether in public schools, at home or in universities in Britain--and those who have not. Lawyers, doctors and engineers trained abroad have higher incomes than those who trained in India, and enjoy higher status. They also carry back with them elements of Western culture which give a distinctive character to their style of life at home. These elements can also be acquired directly in India, in public schools and in social circles dominated by people who have had contact with Western culture at first hand.
>
> (Béteille, 1969 : 232-233).

Hence, as suggested by Vidyarthi himself, the longevity of the caste system has been prolonged. Positions of privilege no doubt continue to be entrenched as well.

Murdock describes the British school as one which,

> . . . emphasizes certain highly refined canons of method and narrowly limits its range of theoretical interests . . . the entire corpus of writings constitutes a perfectly logical self-consistent system which provides answers, or techniques for securing answers, to a number of important scientific questions. It is obviously capable of giving intellectual satisfaction to a group of scholars who are content not to ask other questions, or who prefer to wait before doing so until they have answered most of those originally posed.
>
> (Murdock, 1951 : 470-471).

In numerous respects, Vidyarthi's research methodology carries an early British tinge. Vidyarthi advocates certain pre-conceived stands on theory be taught in the class and thereafter applied in the field. This could lead to the problem of presenting hypotheses which are relatively confined and simple and producing works which are not as widely problem-oriented and analytical as one would wish. Vidyarthi borders upon a position which tends to view the people of one's studies as means to an end, i.e. providing arguments and solutions to theoretical problems. Individuals are in danger of either being transformed into objects or lost amidst the generalizations.

Much of Vidyarthi's writing is of an encyclopedic nature, in that he presents historic overviews and broad survey information. Encyclopedic inventories were common among the British scholar-administrators who wrote about the tribes and castes. It is interesting to note that Vidyarthi's book, *South Asian Culture*, stemmed from a chapter written for the Encyclopedia Britannica. The book is a good example of Vidyarthi's tendency towards fact collecting, which one could suggest is derived from the father of fact collecting, Malinowski. But one thing to remember is that India is huge in diversity. Figures in a position to undertake writing anthropological works at all are relatively few. The job of reassessing such works is just beginning and Vidyarthi is in a position to be part of the solution.

In his article, Murdock claims that the British school is traditionally more akin to sociology than anthropology in perspective. It may be claimed that Vidyarthi's short fieldwork stints and heavy reliance on survey methods of research are not completely sufficient in understanding the concept of culture. Some of Vidyarthi's studies, such as those on caste, may be seen to lack depth and are of a synchronic rather than diachronic nature. Thus it is that in some respects Vidyarthi follows in the footsteps of the British structural functionalists who prevailed in the era between the World Wars.

VIDYARTHI'S ANALYTICAL PERIOD

In the light of events taking place after India's independence, Vidyarthi is of the opinion that the third phase in the development of social anthropology in India should be called the Analytical (1948-present) rather than Critical period. This period is characterized by an increased collaboration between American and Indian anthropologists. Ties were initiated by the Americans with Lucknow University and with the Central Ministry of Community Development. American scholars such as Morris Opler of Cornell University, Oscar Lewis of the University of Illinois and David Mandelbaum of the University of California came to India to do anthropological research. Also, Indian anthropologists visited American institutions of anthropology.

The influence of American scholars on Indian anthropologists is indeed far-ranging. Taking their cue from the Americans, Indian anthropologists began to engage in village and caste studies. (Robert Redfield was the first anthropologist to provide the model for village studies with his investigation of a Mexican village, Tepoztalan ; 1930) The publication of Srinivas' book, *Religion and Society Among the Coorgs of South India* (1952), was a landmark in these non-tribal studies and certainly of extreme value from an analytical perspective. Also of great importance during the Analytical period was Iravati Karve's book on the Hindu kinship system (1953). Dube, Majumdar and others engaged in theoretical studies of rural communities. Vidyarthi proclaims that, "in a real sense the literature of Indian anthropology began to be integrated with the world anthropological literature" (Vidyarthi, 1977 : 71).

Indian social scientists also found themselves studying change in tribal and rural India, as the Government of India had introduced community development programmes. In such programmes, the action anthropology of Sol Tax is seen to have somewhat replaced the applied anthropology of the British colonial administration. Later writings by Majumdar, Dube, Elwin, Vidyarthi and Jay display the whole-hearted acceptance of the principles of action anthropology by Indian anthropologists. Furthermore, the study of culture and personality found its way to the Anthropological Survey of India through S.S. Guha, a graduate of Harvard University. Psychologists Uma Choudhury and P.C. Ray made a study of racial differences, personality types, and other socio-psychological characteristics of tribal groups. Studies of the power structure and leadership in Indian rural society were initiated by the American, Oscar Lewis, and his Indian cohart, H.S. Dhillon.

The work of Robert Redfield, Milton Singer and McKim Marriott of the University of Chicago provided a theoretical appreciation of the folk and peasant communities in India as dimensions of Indian civilization. (This move also reflected the 1950's post-World War II changes in world configurations.) The "Great" and "Little Tradition" of India were re-evaluated and many studies of "great" and "little" (Vidyarthi, 1977 : 75) communities took place. The American influence caused an adoption of "network studies" and "part-whole" analyses, rather than a retention of "isolate studies" (Vidyarthi, 1977 : 76). Indian anthropologists began to study traditional and modern cities ; attempting to understand them as a part of Indian civilization and also placing them in terms of Redfield's folk-urban continuum. Studies of urbanization, industrialization and city planning were financed by the National Planning Commission. The importance of the study of cultural roles of cities was realized with Singer's study of Jamshedpur. As Vidyarthi states, "the scope of anthropology was broadened from the study of isolated primitive tribal communities to rural and then to urban and industrial centres" (Vidyarthi, 1977 : 75). The studies of Calcutta by Bose (1958), Kanpur by Majumdar (1961), Lucknow by Mukherjee and Singh (1961), and Gaya and Ranchi by Vidyarthi (ed. 1961 ; 1969) reflect both the influence of Chicago anthropologists and the support of the Planning Commission.

Evident in the study of religion in India are both the British and American influences. Majumdar initiated the "objective" study of primitive religion in India with his *Affairs of a Tribe* (1950). Srinivas was the first to study the religion of Indian villages with his *Religion and Society Among the Coorgs of South India* (1952). He proposed a theory of Sanskritization in explanation of changes in the Hindu village. Tribal and rural religions were further explored in *Aspects of Religion in Indian Society* (Vidyarthi, ed. 1961) and *Religion in South Asia* (Harper, 1964). The first, being the Majumdar memorial volume, opened with an essay on "Professor Majumdar and the anthropology of Indian religion" by Gopala Sarana. The Harper volume was the product of a conference on religion in South Asia, held in August of 1961. *Traditional India : Structure and Change*, edited by Singer and Cohn (1958), sought to "understand the image of 'New India' in the light of her rich and deeply rooted heritage" (Vidyarthi, 1977 : 74). Many of the papers touched upon the religious traditions of India. Vidyarthi approached his study of the sacred city of Gaya (1961) within the framework of the theories of Redfield and Singer. He presented Gaya as a dimension of the Great Tradition of Indian civilization. British and American influences are also apparent in the folklore research of India. The folklore work of Verrier Elwin was shaped by Franz Boas and Edward Tylor. Folklore research took a dramatic transformation from sporadic endeavours to in-depth examinations of the hidden social, historical and behavioural elements.

Due to the American example, Indian universities also sought to integrate the various branches of anthropology for training and research purposes. Furthermore, there was a stress for collaboration between social scientists, in order that a more complete cultural understanding of Indian communities could be obtained. Vidyarthi explains that with the recent constitution of the Indian Council of Social Science Research and with the reorganization of the Anthropological Survey of India by the Ministry of Education, interdisciplinary studies promise to be strengthened in the future.

Vidyarthi feels that it is quite "apparent that social research in India, which had originated and developed under British influence, is now mainly flourishing under the stimulation received from the United States and other countries" (Vidyarthi, 1977 : 76). British models for the study of kinship and marriage continue to be used. But, the British functional approach to tribal and rural studies has been overshadowed by the American cultural-historical view. The latter approach seems more appropriate for the study of a new India ; one emerging from its traditional structure. Vidyarthi proclaims that gone are the days of descriptive tribal studies. The analytical study of different communities and theoretical proposals are the aim of today's Indian anthropologists. Academic endeavours have replaced the administrative anthropology of the colonial era.

ANALYZING VIDYARTHI

After receiving his M.A. in anthropology from the University of Lucknow, Vidyarthi was accepted at the University of Chicago. He obtained his Ph.D. upon completion of his thesis on the priestly caste of Gaya. His teachers at Chicago were Robert Redfield, Milton Singer, Fred Eggan, McCown, Manning Nash and McKim Marriott. Vidyarthi claims that the work of Robert Redfield influenced him greatly. Of particular interest to him are Redfield's *The Primitive World and Its Transformation, Peasant Society and Culture, The Folk Culture of Yucatan, The Little Community*, and a number of his edited volumes on different civilizations. Vidyarthi felt encouraged to undertake historic appraisals of both complex and tribal societies. "Professor Vidyarthi still considers that with certain modifications Redfield's form of thought can prove to be quite important in understanding complex societies" (Sahay, 1981 : 5).

Robert Redfield has been criticized for holding an utopian view of folk community. According to Redfield, folk culture is dominated by a moral order, in which men are bound together through common conscience and convictions as to what is right. Members of folk societies are pursuers of "the good life". Lewis complains that, "When the anthropologist combines the idealization of primitive culture with the notion of cultural determinism, the result is an attitude that is both paternalistic and hypocritical" (Lewis, 1973 : 584). But, Redfield was far from being a romanticist. It would be correct to call him a humanist and Vidyarthi's works follow in this vein. Vidyarthi writes,

> As a human being, my heart also used to bleed to see the extent of starvation, disease, death, nakedness, illiteracy, helplessness, and then the "lack of complete refinement" prevalent among the Maler. I used to wonder, whether there could be a human group in such a state of affairs and yet they were optimistic and cheerful and not much willing to change. And with these I used to be emotionally disturbed and scientifically confused.
>
> (Vidyarthi, 1963 : 8).

Vidyarthi claims to be a supporter of Sol Tax's action anthropology, which seeks to accomplish practical action according to the desires of the people concerned. But, this calls for the difficult task of first of all defining who are "the people" and then realizing their goals. It is not known how much of what Vidyarthi has hoped to accomplish through action anthropology has been successful. But certainly, it is highly enviable to know that anthropologists in India feel they can move the Government by criticizing and studies, etc. Anthropologists in the West are generally forced to throw up their hands in despair when it comes to trying to influence government decisions.

Vidyarthi criticizes American scholars as sometimes engaging in "superficiality, inadequate fieldwork and indiscriminate application of questionnaire as a tool for data collection" (Vidyarthi, 1979 : 131-132). He himself could no doubt be accused of the same flaws. He often abvocates a statistical approach to anthropology. His support of Redfield's part-whole analysis may lead to a declaring of universal laws, simply on the basis of intensive study of a single society which is superficially related to its larger whole.

The American influence over anthropology in India is by no means met with enthusiasm in all cases.

> The over Americanization of the theory, methods and field expeditions were resented, as on occasion it fell short in explaining the complexities of the traditional societies of India, Japan and South-East Asia. To some, the Americanization was so overwhelming that it was considered a switch-over from colonial to neo-colonial anthropology. . . . Bose, while making a plea for the decolonization of Indian anthropology, commented that "the position of Indian Anthropology has, on the whole, been colonial in relation to schools which have dominated the European or American scene from time to time". . . A few scholars

> trained in America complained that "many of us still publish to gain approval from our patrons and mentors in the West" while some expressed the need to enquire into the extent of academic patronage which has continued to be a decisive factor in shaping the contour of scholarly enterprise in anthropology in India today. . . . In the light of his experience of South-East Asia, Alatas wrote about the dependence of developing countries on Western scholarship. He has systematically established that Western colonialism in the developing societies has created a class of imitative intellectuals or "captive minds"—a stage of intellectual bondage and a dependence on external groups through the operation of such media as books, institutions, radio, press, television, conferences, and meetings.
>
> (Vidyarthi, 1979 : 131-132).

Vidyarthi is of the opinion that Western types of analysis should not be entirely discarded in reaction against imitative conformity. Rather, where plausible, they should be integrated with indigenous theoretical modes and where not plausible, they should be readily abandoned. Such an attitude would be best in understanding the complex Indian culture and would allow for the emergence of Indianness in Indian social science, which Vidyarthi proposed as early as 1964. But, it is a difficult step indeed between what one would like to see accomplished and what one is able to actualize,

In Indian anthropology, Vidyarthi exists amidst numerous colleagues and consociates. The following are mentioned in the letter I received from Sahay : Professors S.C. Dube, Surajit Sinha, B.K. Roy Burman, P.K. Bhowmick, Gopala Sarana, L. K. Mahapatra, and the late Professor K.S. Mathur in the field of cultural anthropology, and Professors I.P. Singh, S. R.K. Chopra and S.C. Tiwari in the field of physical anthropology, which too is of considerable interest for Vidyarthi.

Vidyarthi has amassed a number of students. Mention may be made of Vijoy S. Sahay, B.N. Sahay, P.K. Mahapatra, Dilip Chakraborty, Saileshwar Prasad, Ambastha, Lakra, Sarkar, Sen, Edmund Toppo, Dilip Bose, Miss Devika Maitra, Manimaya Deogharia, Manu Das, S.B. Sahay, K.N. Sahay, R.B. Lal, Ramakant Prasad, Olive Toppo and P.N. Singh.

> Every year at least thirty-two students pass out with M.A /M.Sc. degress. And quite a good number of students enroll their names for Ph.D. under Prof. Vidyarthi. . . . Professor Vidyarthi observes that those who have acquired any degree under his name may be regarded his pupils. Ordinarily, in his opinion, however, they are his real

pupils who have made any contribution in the field of anthropology and are pursuing anthropological career.

(Sahay, 1981 : 3).

Vidyarthi's work, *The Sacred Complex in Hindu Gaya*, has been followed by Dr. M. Jha (1971, 1978, 1980), Sachindra Narayan, B.N. Saraswati, Manmohan Mahapatra, etc. Similarly, his work on the "Nature-Man-Spirit Complex" has been continued by Dr. Vijoy S. Sahay, Dr. G.S. Morab, Dr. A.N. Sandhwar, Dr. R.K. Prasad and Dr. R.K. Sinha. Vidyarthi's insights on culture change among the tribes of India have influenced Dr. K.N. Sahay and Dr. Bogaret (on Christianity), Dr. N. Mishra and Dr. S.P. Sinha (on Hinduization), Dr. V.S. Upadhyay and Dr. B.N. Sahay (on development programmes), etc. Vidyarthi's researches on industrialization and urbanization have been the forerunner to works by such pupils as Dr. Rajendra P. Singh, Dr. J.M. Sarkar, Dr. A.K. Haldar and Dr. Awinash C. Mishra. As well, Vidyarthi introduced linguistics and folklore studies to the Department of Anthropology at Ranchi University, which are being carried forth by several students, e.g. Dr. Ram Dayal Munda, Prof. Dulay C. Munda and Dr. Srivastava. "His pupils believe that Prof. Vidyarthi's manifold contribution in the field of anthropology in general and Indian anthropology in particular have prepared sufficient ground to establish the 'Ranchi School of Anthropology' " (Sahay, 1981 : 4).

It is indeed true that Vidyarthi has succeeded in creating an illustrious career for himself inside Indian anthropology. Vidyarthi was instrumental in the establishment of the department of anthropology at Bihar University. When the department opened in 1953, he taught anthropological thought, physical anthropology, prehistoric archaeology, research methodology and social anthropology. As the department expanded, he confined his teachings to anthropological thought, research methodology (primarily Redfieldian, based on his book, *The Little Community*), linguistics and folklore. He no longer teaches all the schools in anthropology, but, rather, concentrates upon "the Evolutionism" and "the Culture and Personality School". As well, he presents "New Trends in Anthropological Thought" and the rise and development of Indian anthropology.

Professor Vidyarthi is the first anthropologist of the "Third World" to be elected President of the IUAES (1973-78) and to host the ICAES. The Xth ICAES held at New Delhi in 1978 proved to be a success under Vidyarthi's guidance. Due to his devotion to action research, he was chosen by the National Planning Commission to act as Chairman of the Task Force on the development of tribal areas. The Task Force prepared the Fifth Five Year Plan, which is central to the planning process of tribal development. A glance at his curriculum vitae displays his expansive contributions to anthropology (note that his publications include 25 books, 130 papers and 36 edited volumes). In the light of his contributions,

Vidyarthi had been invited by the IUAES to co-chair the "Task on the Future of Anthropology". This symposium, along with numerous others organized by Vidyarthi, was presented at the XIth ICAES held in Canada in 1983.

Vidyarthi will indeed be revered by some of his successors as a great man in Indian anthropology. However, in India, as elsewhere in the anthropological world, there arise generational conflicts over how anthropology should be practised. Some emerging anthropologists are not pleased with what they feel to be the empiric, scientific and statistical tendencies in the anthropology of their elders. In the final days of the Xth ICAES, student anthropologists, in a session entitled, "Young Anthropologists Look at World Anthropology", declared that,

> Half-a-century-old tree of Anthropology could not yield much. It was, more or less, a waste in the sense that we could not do anything but borrow the ideas, concepts and methodology from other countries. . . . We were just a camera not even cameraman. . . . May be, the bureaucratic set-up of the administration is suffering from superiority complex and ignoring the vested interests and politics came as a hurdle in the total system
>
> (Sinha, 1978 : 1).

The student anthropologists complained that Indian anthropology was not of utility to man and society. They called for a "true" devotion towards action research. Furthermore, there was obvious resentment on behalf of the students, in being treated as "research labourers" (Sinha, 1978 : 3). Students are often required to collect as much data in as short a time as possible, so that their elders may mass-produce books and articles of a blanket and repetitive nature. Students claim that they receive little, if any, acknowledgement for their writing assistance. Too often, students are expected to follow the hypotheses of their supervisors. Thus, they have little freedom in conducting research. This problem is accentuated by the fact that government funding agencies (the Indian Government hires large numbers of anthropologists) are impressed by elitist prestige, rather than individual initiative. Sinha declares, "Our psychological dependence on the so-called academic guardians is so much high that we leave everything to be decided by them. Even our future is being decided by those whose future has already been sealed" (Sinha, 1978 : 4). In less dramatic ways, the same could be said of generational differences in Canadian anthropology as well.

The young anthropologists seek a new anthropology, but are careful not to destroy their elders. Lewis declares, "For the oppressed to be finally free, he must go beyond revolt, by another path, he must begin in other ways, conceive of himself and reconstruct himself independently of the master" (Lewis, 1973 : 588). In writing about the problem of student unrest in India, Dubé admonished,

> I began to sense, alongside the strong desire to work and make themselves a part of the dream for a beautiful future, a strong feeling of frustration. The fear that they might not be allowed to work for their dream made their eyes glisten. But these young, earnest and willing faces were India's future. The question was whether our leaders of today could ever become worthy of our leaders of tomorrow. And will the leaders of tomorrow have the maturity to control their own ambitions and energies ? A youth movement made too powerful too soon could be a very dangerous thing.
>
> (Dubé, 1978 : 133).

It can be seen from the reaction of the senior anthropologists to the session by their juniors at the ICAES (which the seniors did not even attend) that the young anthropologists are no longer fighting a colonial outsider. It is a case of the system fighting itself. The senior anthropologists are reported to have said, "The children should not disown their parents and warned, 'revolutions are not made out of slogans alone' " ("Young Anthropologists Clash With Old", Dec. 17, 1978). Vidyarthi has written of student unrest, but never with depth. He is perhaps not fully aware of the roots of student discontent. He has placed himself in the ambiguous position of seeking easy solutions, without realizing he is part of the problem. It remains for Vidyarthi to come to terms with existing student unrest.

A CONCLUSION ON VIDYARTHI

As anywhere in the anthropological world, there is no one model of doing anthropology in India. Professor L.P. Vidyarthi presents a particular way of doing anthropology and, therein, is engaged in particular concerns. Vidyarthi's struggle to reject the overriding colonial/Western influences upon anthropology in India have led to the difficult search for "Indianness" in a social science, which is itself a foreign invention. As well, circumstances in India have caused a need to socially justify much anthropological research, i.e. much research is development oriented. For purposes of reconsideration of some of Vidyarthi's perspectives I have used Lewis. But let me conclude by saying that, as Alfred Schutz would remind us all, this has been one person's experience of the other. It has been my experience of Vidyarthi. And, we must remember to always include that thinker in the thought, with all her/his limitations and influences and, certainly, my limitations concerning Indian anthropology are many.

References

Béteille, André, 1969 : *Castes Old and New.* Bombay : Asia Publishing House.
Béteille, André, 1972 : *Inqeuality and Social Change.* Delhi : Oxford University Press.
Béteille, André, 1974 : *Six Essays in Comparative Sociology.* Delhi : Oxford University Press.
Dubé, Rani, 1978 : *The Evil Within.* London : Quartet Books.
Dumont, Louis, 1966 : *Homo Hierarchicus : The Caste System and Its Implications.* London : Weidenfeld and Nicolson.
Hazlehurst, Leighton W., 1969 : Leadership in India (a review), *American Anthropologist* ; Vol. 71, American Anthropological Ass.
Lacy, Creighton, 1965 : *The Conscience of India.* New York : Holt, Rinehart and Winston.
Lewis, Diane, 1973 : Anthropology and Colonialism, *Current Anthropology* ; Vol. 14, The Wenner-Gren Foundation for Anthropological Research.
Malefijt, Annemarie deWaal, 1974 : *Images of Man.* New York : Alfred A. Knopf, Inc.
Murdock, George Peter, 1951 : British Social Anthropology, *American Anthropologist* ; Vol. 53, Am. Anthropological Ass.
Redfield, Robert, 1956 : *The Little Community and Peasant Society and Culture.* Chicago : University of Chicago Press.
Roy, Girish Chandra, 1976 : *Indian Culture : The Tradition of Non-Violence and Social Change in India.* Delhi : Ajanta Publications.
Sahay, Vijoy S., 1981 : Biographical sketch on Vidyarthi, March 10.
Schutz, Alfred, 1967 : *The Phenomenology of the Social World.* Northwestern University Press.
Sinha, Arbind K., 1978 : Young Anthropologists Look at World Anthropology.
Vidyarthi, L.P., 1955-1956 : Education in Tribal Bihar, *Man in India*, eds. B.C. Roy and N.K. Bose, Vol. 35-36, pp. 39-45.
Vidyarthi, L.P., 1959 : The Extensions of an Indian Priestly Caste, *Man in India*, ed. N.K. Bose, Vol. 39, pp. 28-35.
Vidyarthi, L.P., 1960 : In Memorium : Dhirendra Nath Majumdar (1903-1960), *Man in India*, ed. N.K. Bose, Vol. 40, pp. 320-321.
Vidyarthi, L.P., 1961 : *The Maler : A Study in Nature-Man-Spirit Complex of a Hill Tribe in Bihar.* Calcutta ; Bookland Private Ltd.
Vidyarthi, L.P., 1978 : *The Sacred Complex in Hindu Gaya.* Delhi : Concept Publishing Company.
Vidyarthi, L.P., 1961 : The Sacred Complex in a Maler Hilly Village of Santhal Pargana, *Aspects of Religion in Indian Society*, ed. L.P. Vidyarthi, Meerut City : Kedar Nath Ram Nath.
Vidyarthi, L.P., 1962 : The Seminar on Urbanization, Industrialization, and Social Change in India : An Introduction, *Journal of Social Research*, ed. L.P. Vidyarthi, Vol. V, No. 1, pp. 1-6, Ranchi Council of Social and Cultural Research, Bihar.
Vidyarthi, L.P., 1963 : Some Aspects of Tension Among Castes, *Anthropology on the March*, ed. Bala Ratnam, India : Social Sciences Ass.
Vidyarthi, L.P., 1964 : *Cultural Contours of Tribal Bihar.* Calcutta : Sankar Bhattacharya, Punthi Pustak.
Vidyarthi, L.P., 1965 : "Field Researches in Social Anthropology in India : Two Examples", *A Guide to Field Study*, ed. Sankar Sen Gupta, Calcutta : Indian Publications.

Vidyarthi, L.P., 1965 : *Leadership in India*, ed. L.P. Vidyarthi, Bombay : Asia Publishing House.

Vidyarthi, L.P., 1966 ; Social Science in India : A Social Anthropological Approach : Some Preliminary Observations, *Social Sciences Information*, Vol. 5, pp. 90-109.

Vidyarthi, L.P., 1968 : Conference on Urgent Social Research in India, *Current Anthropology*, Vol. 10, No. 4, pp. 377-379.

Vidyarthi, L.P., 1971 : S.C. Roy : The Father of Indian Anthropology : An Evaluation, and "Ranchi : Past and Present", *Souvenir : The S.C. Roy Centenary Celebration (1871-1971) : An International Symposium on Hundred Years of Indian Anthropology*, Ranchi : Indian Anthropological Association, Council of Social and Cultural Research, Bihar, and Ranchi University.

Vidyarthi, L.P., 1972 : Miscellaneous Notes : S.C. Roy International Centenary Celebration, *Man in India*, Vol. 52, pp. 87-90.

Vidyarthi, L.P., 1974 : Research Methodology in Anthropology in Indian Universities, *Social Science Information*, Vol. 13, Nos. 4-5, pp. 173-184, International Social Science Council.

Vidyarthi, L.P., 1974 : Tribal Development in Independent India and Its Future, *Man in India*, ed. S.C. Sinha, Vol. 54, pp. 45-72.

Vidyarthi, L.P., 1975 : Communications (IUAES and ICAES President's Second News Letter), *The Eastern Anthropologist*, ed. K.S. Mathur, Vol. 28, No. 1, pp. 291-297, Ethnographic and Folk Culture Society, U.P.

Vidyarthi, L.P., 1975 : The Future of Traditional 'Primitive' Societies : A Case Study of an Indian Shifting Cultivation Society, *The Eastern Anthropologist*, ed. K.S. Mathur, Vol. 28, pp. 313-326, Ethnographic and Folk Culture Society, U.P.

Vidyarthi, L P., 1976 : Applied Anthropology in India, *Anthropology in India, Vol. 1, Cultural Anthropology*, ed. S.C. Sinha, Calcutta : Anthropological Survey of India.

Vidyarthi, L.P., 1976 : *South Asian Culture : An Anthropological Perspective*. New Delhi : Oriental Publishers and Distributors.

Vidyarthi, L.P., 1977 : The Rise of Social Anthropology in India (1774-1972) : A Historical Appraisal, *The New Wind, Changing Identities in South Asia*, ed. Kenneth David, Paris : Mouton Publishers.

Vidyarthi. L.P., 1978 : *Rise of Anthropology in India : A Social Science Orientation, Vol. I, The Tribal Dimensions*; *Vol. II, The Rural, Urban and Other Dimensions*. Delhi : Concept Publishing Company.

Vidyarthi, L.P., 1979 : Communications (Presidential Address Delivered at the Inauguration of the Xth ICAES, Delhi, Dec. 10, 1978), *The Eastern Anthropologist*, ed. S.C. Varma, Vol. 32, No. 2, pp. 129-136, Ethnographic and Folk Culture Society, U.P.

Vidyarthi, L.P., 1979 : Foreword, *Process, Performance and Pilgrimage : A Study in Comparative Symbology*, by Victor Turner. New Delhi : Concept Publishing Company.

5

L.P. VIDYARTHI
A Dynamic Anthropologist

Ajit K. Singh

Lalita Prasad Vidyarthi, Professor and Head of the Department of Anthropology at the University of Ranchi, is, by common opinion, the most distinguished social scientist in general and anthropologist in particular. He has one of the outstanding influence in shaping Indian Anthropology. More than three decades have passed since the starting of his anthropological career and the time has come for an estimate of his contribution in understanding the human whole. (I feel, it is my noble duty as a pupil of Professor Vidyarthi to present an evaluation of his work on the occasion when he is going to receive "Distinguished Service Awards of 1983, with Sol Tax and Charles Wagley, Association of Anthropological Diplomacy Politics and Society and Association of Third World Anthropologists, U.S.A.)

Before me, it is a formidable task to evaluate the all work of Professor Vidyarthi—21 books written by himself, 9 books in co-authorship, 31 edited books and over 151 substantial articles (1954-1982). No one could survey such a vast landscape without committing distortion and I shall start from Vidyarthi's first writing.

THE SACRED COMPLEX

The anthropological approach to study the sacred centre as a dimension of Indian civilization, which was initiated by Vidyarthi in the early fiftees after studying the *Sacred Complex of Hindu Gaya* (1961), has now occupied an important place in contemporary Indian anthropology. This monumental work has attracted the attention of scholars of civilization and complex societies from all over the world. (Just after the publication of this book, scholars from all the spots of the globe expressed their opinions. Here mention may be made of Morris Opler, F.R. Allchin, Soneya Richmond,

Milton Singer, McKim Marriott, N.K. Bose, S.C. Dube, Surjit Sinha, and Malathi Sriram who have highly appreciated the book.) Apart from these social scientists, about two dozen daily newspapers of India and abroad published the review and gave the book world recognition. The main finding of his study is that the Sacred Complex of Hindu Gaya is formulated into three interrelated phenomena—sacred geography, sacred performances and sacred specialists.

Sacred geography

The sacred parts of Gaya constitute a heterogeneous complex of hundreds of sacred objects and places located within the "sacred ground" (*kshetra*), mythologically called Gaya *Kshetra.* Considered as a physical layout and as social organization, the sacred ground of Gaya may be subdivided into zones, and segments, and clusters of sacred centres. A sacred centre which is seen here as a minimal unit of Indian sacred geography is in Gaya as in other places, generally a temple, a tree or other natural shrine, or a bathing place. Some centres traditionally sacred to the Buddhists are also worshipped by the Hindus.

The spatial scope of social contacts, which Gaya's sacred centres have, is extremely various. A centre may have merely local importance ; it may have specialized connections with persons of the nearby districts ; or it may have ties by pilgrimage from certain regions or from all the Hindu majority regions of India. The greater and lesser scope of contacts or kinds of connections maintained with each sacred centre varies from centre to centre, and also according to the annual cycle of festivals and ceremonies. The sacred zone of Gaya, and with it several outlying sacred centres, furthermore, shows considerable change of scope through the centuries. They have grown from having merely local significance into having importance for all-India Hinduism.

Regarded both in space and time, the sacred geography of Gaya, thus, demonstrates the continuity of India's great and little traditions, and the processes of compromise and combination operating between them. Geographically, the sacred complex also demonstrates several kinds of combination between Hindu and Buddhist traditions of different levels.

In modern times, however, while the secular zone of Gaya is expanding in its population, area, resources and activities, the sacred zone is becoming more and more ruinous, desolate, neglected and disorganized. At some points in the sacred zone, ancient temples and former residential buildings of the priests have been replaced by parks, monuments and rest-houses constructed by secular agencies.

Sacred performances

The sacred complex of Gaya includes a set of sacred performances linked with the sacred centres. The various sacred performances observed by

Hindus at the sacred centres of Gaya may be analysed into floral offerings, meditational exercises, oblations, libations, artistic performances and religious donations. These elements are briefly described with a view to suggesting the diverse elements which exist side by side and in many cases as parts of one and the same sacred performance.

The main sacred performance for which Gaya is uniquely celebrated in the Hindu universe is an elaborate form of sacrifice to ancestral spirits, the Gaya Shrāddha. This form of sacrifice is described in detail, and appears to be an elaboration of and continuous with more common and widespread Indian forms of sacrifice to the dead.

Rules of Shrāddha found in certain ancient texts (Vishnu Sūtra, Vāyu Purāṇa, Manu Smriti) also offer some evidence as to how ritual practices traditional within folk and peasant societies have been continually accommodated and how through the textual medium some of these practices have received universal recognition, acceptance, and also modification. Perhaps such a process of combination and compromise on the textual level has helped in the past to develop the all-embracing Hindu civilization of today.

Sacred specialists

The various types of sacred specialists in the Gaya Complex are connected on the one hand with the sacred centres and performances of Gaya itself, and on the other with the "sacrificers" (singular, jajmān)—the pilgrims to Gaya and the patrons of Gaya Shrāddha—who belong to all parts of the Hindu universe. Among the sacred specialists of Gaya the most specialized group are the Gayawal caste of Brahman priests, who hold a traditional monopoly over the performance of Gaya Shrāddha.

The Gayawal is an orthodox Hindu priestly caste, ideally following a highly ceremonialized, sanskritic style of life much influenced by the great Hindu tradition. Internally, the Gayawal possess a complex caste organization and a strong group consciousness. Externally, their duties bring them into networks of social relationship extending throughout the Hindu universe. In relations outside their caste, the Gayawals appear as (1) disciples of their spiritual preceptors, (2) as priests acting for their patrons, pilgrims, sacrificers, (3) as masters of their ritual and domestic servants, (4) as partners with another caste of non-Brahman priests, and (5) as shrine priests for worshippers at certain shrines.

Three subcultural divisions may be distinguished today among the Gayawal-sanskritic, feudalistic and proletarian sanskritic priests are marked by orthodoxy, ceremonialism and strict adherence to the Brahmanic rules of priesthood ; the feudalistic priests are distinguished by their wealth and aristocratic way of life as well as by their employment of servants to perform their priestly and domestic work ; and the proletarian priests are noted for their commercial and mercenary orientation, for professional rivalry and group disorganization, while pretending to maintain priestly life.

The distinctive features of these three subcultures seem to characterize three probable phases in the development of the Gayawal through time. Earliest is the sanskritic phase ; it is followed by an intermediate feudalistic phase, and finally by the present proletarian phase brought on by the recent transformation of Indian civilization under the influence of Western industrialization, education and mass communication.

Another and still earlier formative phase can be conjectured, a phase in which the Gayawals would have been "folk priests". The Gayawals of today still reflect some of the characteristics of folk priests.

All four aspects of the Gayawal priesthood—folk, sanskritic,, feudalistic and proletarian—postulated above as successive phases, continue, of course, to exist among the Gayawal of today, three of them being very distinct. Since all are found together in the present, one may assume that each earlier variety of priesthood persisted along side each later type without replacing it entirely. These subcultures and phases of Gayawal cultural development may be understood, in part, as an effect of the impact of the larger Hindu universe upon the sacred complex of Gaya.

In the "Foreword" of his book, ***The Sacred Complex of Hindu Gaya***, Professor D.N. Majumdar, who had been also the teacher of Dr. Vidyarthi, wrote that "he has done a good piece of original work, and has not followed the traditional path that anthropologists in India have so long preferred to follow, which has been uptil now the "great tradition" of Indian Anthropology, viz. the study of tribal cultures or rural life. He has pointed to the new foci of anthropological interest, the study of cities and centres of culture (1961 : xiii-xiv).

The methodological orientation is the unique feature of Dr. Vidyarthi's contribution. The theoretical stand and the rich material on which he elaborates provide an excellent analytical study of a levitical sect that faces evil days. He has coined and used terms like sacred centres, sacred segments, sacred cluster, sacred zone, sacred ground and sacred geography to describe the social organization of the temples. He describes the sacred complex of a place of pilgrimage, and thinks that such a concept is applicable even to tribal religions in India, with their sacred groves, sacred performances and sacred rituals. However, he does not use "sacred" in the sense in which E. Durkheim had used it, i.e. "sacred" as distinguished from profane. He has used "sacred" as distinct from 'secular' and has shown the possibility of a reorganization of the sacred complex, which might show the way to rehabilitate the sacred community of the Gayawal.

The scholars of civilization and complex societies found this study useful in understanding the cultural roles of a traditional town in context with the complexity of Indian civilization. The description, terms and concepts used in this study were found rather useful by other researchers in this little explored field and their researches have further established the wider applicability of the terms and concepts proposed in this book (Vidyarthi, 1961 : xv).

Morris E. Opler (1961) writes that Dr. Vidyarthi tries to give as much time depth as possible to his discussion of Gaya and the Gayawal. He produces evidence to show how various shrines and centres of Gaya have become more prominent or have lost favour with pilgrims over the centuries. He suggests that symbols and images which once were associated with Buddhism or with local folk belief have gradually been absorbed into the *shraddha complex*.

Opler further says that "... whether or not we accept all of Dr. Vidyarthi's terminology and theory, we are sure to be impressed by the amount of information and illumination he has provided in this pioneering effort. We have been sadly in need of some analysis of the internal organization of the religious centres which dot India, and Dr. Vidyarthi has so well demonstrated how rewarding studies of this kind can be that others are sure to follow. Another happy feature of the book is the personal life histories of Gayawal informants which are included in an appendix. They reveal more about Brahmanical family life than anything else I have seen in print."

Thus, analysing the "Sacred Complex" of a traditional city of India, Dr. Vidyarthi not only brings to our light concrete data on Gaya and the Gayawal but opens up a large area for scientific research on priestly groups, on Indian towns and cities, and on evolution and change within Hinduism as such.

B.N. Saraswati in his paper "Studying Sacred Complex in Kashi" (1974) remarked that Gaya being one of the Pauranic Tirthas has acquired an all-India character. And it is in this context of understanding a wider cultural tradition that Professor Vidyarthi's contribution to Indian Anthropology in general and the study of Indian sacred tradition in particular is both original and fundamental. But at any rate, in such a vast field of knowledge his work was of exploratory nature. He was concerned mainly with the organization of the Gayawals—a priestly community—and was obviously influenced by Robert Redfield, Milton Singer and McKim Marriott in his approach to the understanding of cultural phenomena. Nevertheless he examined the structure of the "sacred" anew and described it as a sacred complex composed of three elements : (1) Sacred geography, (2) Sacred performance, and (3) Sacred specialists.

Thus one can notice that how Dr. Vidyarthi has blazed a new path in Indian anthropology by undertaking a study of the sacred complex of a place of Hindu pilgrimage such as Gaya which served as means to gain understanding of the structure and characteristic processes of Hindu civilization. Applying the same terms and concepts but obvious awareness to refine, expand or modify them, several other great traditional towns have been studied and anew are in the process of study (Jha : 1971, 1978, 1982 ; Narayan, 1970 and 1972 ; Mahapatra, 1971 ; Sahay, 1972 ; Upadhyay, 1972 ; Shrestha 1972-73 ; Vidyarthi & Jha, 1974 ; Vidyarthi *et al.* 1979 ; Sahu, 1983). Dr. Vidyarthi's anthropological approach to the study of civilization has made a considerable headway and envisages a great promise in the future.

THE NATURE-MAN-SPIRIT COMPLEX

Anthropologists have suggested a variety of approaches as part of their research methodology to understand the man, his society and culture. Among the more important of these, in the twentieth century, pure functionalism (Branislaw Malinowski), "structure functionalism" (Radcliffe Brown), "Structuralism" (Claude Levi-strauss), "ethnolinguistics" (F.C. Wallace ; Strutevant), "neo-evolutionism" (Leslie White) and "Cultural ecology" (Julian Steward) can be included. "Cultural ecology" in association with "Spirit" forms the soul of this Concept of the Nature-Man-Spirit Complex (Vidyarthi). In the context of the Indian tribal situation, the world of spirits is also found to have a very close interaction with man, his social structure and the natural environments. Professor Vidyarthi's concept of 'nature-man-spirit complex' provides a sharp tool in exploring, analysing and describing the cultural matrix of Indian tribes.

Just after two years of the publication of his famous book on Gaya and Gayawals Dr. Vidyarthi published his another theoretically oriented book in 1963 "on the Maler"—a most primitive shifting cultivator tribe of Rajmahal Plateau of the Santhal Parganas in the Eastern district of Bihar. Dr. Vidyarthi presented a competent account of the anatomy of Maler culture in the line of Malinowski's Trobriands (1922) and Evans Pritchard's Nuer 1940). The culture of the Maler community has been described in such a meaningful manner that not only the different "items" of culture but the very "configuration" of culture is discerned.

Dr. Vidyarthi's book on Maler tribe fits within the broader purview of cultural ecology in terms of its attributes of interrelatedness, adaptation and interaction between socio-cultural phenomena and environment. An added dimension of his work is the analysis of spirits and other religious attributes, in their relationship to man and his culture on the one hand and nature on the other. Dr. Vidyarthi (1963 : 175-176) writes that "keeping the focus on "Nature" thus, I could further see its interactions with the "Maler Man" and in the light of these data, I could realize the importance of the "Nature-Man" approach in analysing a primitive culture (Evans-Pritebard, 1940 ; Redfield, 1955 ; Thomas, 1956). But, as I proceeded ahead from the level of observation to the level of logitation, it became more and more clear to me that this Nature-Man relationship was not only confined to the ecological or subsistent level alone. I noted an "environment" of supernatural beliefs and rituals modifying and influencing the "Nature-Man-interrelationship".

A large number of scholars tried this approach of Nature-Man-Spirit Complex to understand the validity of the concept as well as to analyse the tribals' style of life. Here mention may be made of Rai (1967), Prasad (1968), Sandhwar (1973), Sinha (1977), Singh (1979), Sahay (1979), Morab (1980), Borbora (1981), Sahoo (1981), Das Gupta (1982), etc. who found this concept useful in analysing the life-styles of simpler communities. Mann (1981) edited a book on "Nature-Man-Spirit Complex in Tribal India" in which different scholars contributed their papers in the context of nine tribes of India, namely, the Maler, the Ho, the Parahaiyas, the Pando, the Bhil, the Soliga, the Nicobarese, the Kinner and the Onge. This work gives an exhaustive account of socio-cultural-environmental phenomena in the case of Indian tribes. It is evident from the book that where ecological variation, as broad as sea, forest, hills, plains, high altitudes, etc., mark the Indian tribal scene with deep-rooted religious organization, the method of "cultural ecology" is of a unique significance in exploring the tribal cultural nexus.

Work on urban-industrial anthropology

The urban population in the different States has continued to increase and during the last two decades there has been a considerable growth of urban centres in the geographically isolated hilly and forested regions. The growing towns, cities and industries attracted the attention of Dr. Vidyarthi. He took up the large-scale research projects from the various government sources and published a series of books on Urban-industrial population. His books *Bhartiya Nagar* in Hindi (*Indian Cities* 1966), *Cultural Configuration of Ranchi : Survey of an Emerging Industrial City of Tribal India* (1969), *Socio-Cultural Implications of Industrialization in India : A Case Study of Tribal Bihar* (1970), *Uttar Bharat Ka Ek Sanskritic Nagar : Gaya* in Hindi (*A Traditional City of North India : Gaya*, 1970) etc., are worth mentioning here. The other traditional towns like Deoghar and Janakpur, have been studied by his students.

At the end of the sixties, Dr. Vidyarthi's two books (1969, 1970) marked a new trend in the study of urban and industrial society. His book *Cultural Configuration of Ranchi* presents a detailed account of growing up of Ranchi to a regional centre for administrative, commercial, transportational, cathedral, military, and educational activities, from a cluster of tribal villages. From methodological point of view the study of Ranchi town is significant and timely while it was at the threshold of industrial urbanization as Heavy Engineering Corporation (Hatia) and its other associated ancillaries had just started their construction.

A vivid account of Ranchi city has been reflected specially its history, demography, migration, occupation, housing conditions, leisure and recreation, religion and festivals, tribal leadership, rural-urban continuum, etc. Dr. Vidyarthi has ably traced the process of transformation from primitivism to industrialisation. Dr. S.N. Sen in his "Foreword" for the book remarked that it reveals like a story of the evolution of folk and peasant culture to pre-industrial urbanization, and then to rapid industrialization.

Dr. Vidyarthi's other study on "Socio-cultural Implications of Industrialisation in India : A Case Study of Tribal Bihar" is based on a sound footing from the methodological point of view. The whole study has been conceived into four stages : the bench line society, the emerging industrial complex, reorganisation of the old to the new social system and preservation of some elements of the old order. The problem of social adjustment has been studied through the formulatory, constructive, productive and elaborative phases of the industrial complex. At the spatial level, it discerns three concentric regions of expansion and influence : the core, within a radius of five miles covering the industrial, urban and communicational network ; the fringe, within a radius of 10 miles covering 150 villages ; and the margin, upto 20 miles from the industrial core covering 200 villages. In this way the study envisages sophisticated approaches for microcosmic and longitudinal analysis of various phases of industrialization.

Dr. Vidyarthi has made a positive contribution to both academic and applied aspects of the study of the industrialization in India. This richly documented ethnographic study provides a very sound bench line data for the future historical perspective. Initiated by Dr. Vidyarthi, a number of scholars from anthropology and other disciplines made significant studies on his approach to study the heterogeneous population of industries and mining complexes. Singh (1967), Sarkar (1970), Sharma (1978), Roy (1974), Choudhary (1978), Halder (1978) and Srivastava (1979) studied a large number of different urban-industrial towns like Hatia, Bokaro, Patratu, Jharia, Jhinkpani, Jamshedpur and Rourkela, Gua and Noamundi. They found the methodology applicable and the concept befitting. (Besides this, he has also written about a dozen articles on industrialization in national and international academic journals.) A large-scale research project on "Socio-cultural Implications of Industrialization in Middle India" is in the process of completion.

Work on applied and action anthropology

The colonial concept of applied anthropology has been partly replaced by the concept of Action Anthropology, as developed by Sol Tax and his associate, Dr. Vidyarthi who conceptualized it as "Developmental Anthropology". In the democratic set-up of the nations this realization has marked the beginning of a new phase in planning and implementation, where administrators and anthropologists have been working together to induce social and economic development and solve other problems of modernization. According to Dr. Vidyarthi, "The position of action anthropologists, from the point of view of both science and action, seems to be the best. As a social doctor, an action anthropologists combines in himself the responsibility for diagnosing the disease, prescribing the medicines, following up the treatment, changing the prescription, if needed, and finally bringing about health and happiness in the society. Having this idea into his mind Dr. Vidyarthi published a number of books and articles on applied and action anthropology. Here mention may be made of Anthropology and Tribal Welfare in India (1959), Indian Anthropology in Action (1960), Applied Anthropology in India (1980), Applied Anthropology and Development in India (1980), Tribal Development and Its Administration (1981). Dr. Vidyarthi also wrote a large number of papers on development of the different tribal ethnic groups. Initiated by Dr. Vidyarthi, A.K. Singh, V.S. Upadhyay, A.N. Sandhwar, etc., also conducted their studies on applied research.

Dr. Vidyarthi has achieved such a position in tribal context in India that it is now impossible to think about tribal development or action programme without him and his ideas. He has been closely associated and envolved with the voluntary organizations of Chotanagpur like Operation Self-help (Lamkana), Kamre, Adimjati Seva Mandal (Kharsidag) and Vikash Bharati (Bishunpur). He is the President and Chairman of these last two voluntary organizations. He was also the director of the Birhor Action Research Project (1975). Now he has been director of a Social Forestry Project in Netarhat area sponsored by the Swedish International Development Agency and Government of Bihar (Forest Department). Thus he follows the trends—Research and Action—Action and Research.

The Government of India appointed Dr. Vidyarthi as the Chairman of the Task Force on the Development of the Tribal Areas (1973). The Report of the Task Force is considered a valuable document on tribal development and reflects the mature thinking on this vital national issue. In the light of the report the Fifth Five Year Plan has devoted an exclusive chapter (Chapter 13) on the backward classes which highlights the fond policy of the Government of India regarding tribal development. It adopts an integrated development approach for the tribal areas and makes a plea to identify needs of specific groups of tribes in specific areas and strives for coordinated planning and coordinated execution of programmes for maximization of desired results.

Dr. Vidyarthi (1972) makes certain general recommendations for the tribal development in India. Basing his materials on tribal Bihar he points out seven principal deficiencies in the earlier plans and spells out the diagnostic features to carve out micro and meso areas within the macro development region. In addition to lending support to the area development approach later adopted by the Government of India, he also suggests to take up the problems of the least development primitive pockets and isolated tribes on an urgent and priority basis as the part of new national strategy for tribal development.

Village studies

For the systematic study of Indian villages, with a view to testing certain hypothesis and for refining some of the methodological framework development elsewhere a number of foreign scholars like Morris Opler, Oscar Lewis, David Mandelbaum and McKim Marriott confined themselves to village as a unit of study. Along with these American anthropologists, Dube (1955), Srinivas (1955), Majumdar (1958), Vidyarthi (1966) and a few other Indian anthropologists were stimulated to take up analytical study of rural communities in India.

Dr. Vidyarthi's book *Ghaghra : A Village in Chotanagpur* has been studied in the light of Robert Redfield's "Little Community". The various social institutions have been studied in depth and a good analysis of the working of these institutions has been presented. Later on Dr. Vidyarthi studied a number of villages of Bihar and focused the village as a unit of study. (Here mention may be made of study of Maler villages (1966). In his book *Cultural Configuration on Ranchi* (1969), Dr. Vidyarthi studied a number of villages in and around the Ranchi town.)

A study, which is in the final stage, on 'Life and Culture in Bihar' constituting several villages of the culture linguistic zones such as Bhojpuri, Maghai, Maithil and Chotanagpuri have been studied by Dr. Vidyarthi and his research team. Besides, village studies, region and civilization study has also been stressed in this book. The approach of Dr. Vidyarthi's village study was followed by different scholars like Purnima Verma (1971) who studied "Social Structure of Chotanagpur villages" and N.K. Shukla (1968) who studied the Bhagalpur villages. Recently, in December 1982, five villages of Netarhat plateau were subjected to a detailed and microscopic study by A.K. Singh.

Study on scheduled caste

As Dr. Vidyarthi is interested for the upliftment of the weaker sections and the poorest among the poor he always tried to understand their problems to bring the national resources for their help. His book *Harijan Today* (1977) earned the national repute. His another edited book *Scheduled Castes in India* (1975) is also of great interest for social workers and social scientists.*

* His articles on "Thinking about the Problems of the Scheduled Castes" (1976) is also of immense value.

Work on folklore researches

Folklore has provided man with a method for orally transmitting not only the customs but also the ethical, moral and world views of his particular culture from one generation to the next. Among the anthropologists Dr. Vidyarthi has done considerable work on "Folklore". In his long article on "Folklore Research in India" (1978), the trends of development and the various approaches and areas of research in Folklore have been analysed in minor detail. Besides these, he wrote more than a half dozen articles on folklore in different national and international journals.

Study on leadership

The study of leadership, public acculturation, voluntary organization as an effective machinery of change in the rural and urban communities has also attracted the interest of Dr. Vidyarthi's books on *Dynamics of Tribal Leadership in Bihar* (1970) and *Student Unrest in Chotanagpur* (1976). On the working of a voluntary organization he wrote a book on *The Peasant Organisation in India : A Case Study of a Voluntary Organisation in Tribal Bihar* (1977).

Major fieldwork

Dr. Vidyarthi has covered a wide range of geographical, cultural and ecological area of fieldwork since 1953 till date. He followed the Malinowskian style of fieldwork during his researches among the Maler of Santhal Pargana. He conducted fieldwork among the most primitive tribe like hunters and food gatherers Andamanese, Jarwas, Sentinalis, Birhors, etc. ; primitive agriculturist, i.e., hill cultivation type tribals like the Maler ; agriculturist tribes such as the Munda, Oraon, Kharia and the artisan tribal groups like the Asur, Mahli, Chik Baraiks, etc. He also did his fieldwork among the Todas, a pastoral community of South India. Town, mine and industrial areas have also been covered extensively and intensively by him during his fieldwork.

Work on anthropological theories

In his Presidential address at the XII Annual and V Special Conference of the Indian Anthropological Association, Dr. Vidyarthi made an extensive lecture on "The Current Trends in and Future of World Anthropology". During his speech he dealt with Anthropological Theories and Their Internationalization, Cultural Evolutionalism, Diffusion, Culture Area and Innovation, French Structuralism of Levi-Strauss, Ethnoscience, Systems of Symbols, Interaction Theory, Ecological Anthropology, Human Ethnology, Psychological Anthropology and Application of Anthropology (1977).

During his Presidentship of the Xth International Congress of Anthropological and Ethnological Sciences held in New Delhi (1978), Professor Vidyarthi brought out two books : ***Rise of World Anthropology*** (1978) and ***Trends in World Anthropology*** (1978). The first book deals in brief, a summary of the History of International Anthropology over the period from 1934 onwards, commenting upon its trends, its achievements and its efforts to take shape as the true Science of Man.

This book provides a brief survey of the nine international congresses of anthropology, from the first Congress in London in 1934, through the Copenhagen (1938), Brussels (1948), Vienna (1952), Philadelphia (1956), Paris (1960), Moscow (1964), Tokyo (1968) to the IX Congress in Chicago in 1973, including a brief account of the 1978 Congress in India.

It reflects upon the major trends in the genesis and development of this science through these congresses, particularly the amalgamation of the two main trends of internationalization and localization which has greatly contributed to the tremendous growth of anthropology and made it possible to hold its X Congress in a developing country. The fast growth of science and the needs of its increasing international spread, have also brought about a number of meaningful concommittal organizational changes and functional improvements making it more sensitive and receptive in search of knowledge. This work includes information on the organizational growth as well.

The second book presents an overview of the development of anthropology in the various parts of the world, particularly the Asian countries since 1950. The content of this book is the revised and detailed version of a paper submitted by Dr. Vidyarthi to the International Social Science Council on its Silver Jubilee celebration in Paris in 1977. Dr. Vidyarthi was commissioned, along with Prof. F. Eggan, by the Council to review the development of anthropology during the third quarter of this century. The work reports not only on the various major international trends and methodologies in anthropology, like the initial British tradition of studying tribes and castes in their colonies for the purposes of better colonial administration, the American tradition of village studies, ***Levi-Strauss' Functional Structural Principle***, etc., but also on particular national and regional styles of anthropology and situations peculiar to various countries.

Dr. Vidyarthi's contribution (*Rise of Anthropology in India*) in two volumes to the literature of "Theory and Thought" in Social and Cultural Anthropology is pioneering in nature. Based on the review of the literature, the volumes themselves speak for the quality of the vigorous library work and analysis. Through a meaningful classification of the tribal, rural and urban studies, Dr. Vidyarthi has successfully attempted to bring out the genesis, philosophy and the gradual development of anthropological research concepts.

The first volume is devoted to a review of the ethnographic researches on tribal culture of the different parts of India and includes a theoretical and methodological appraisal of the studies of social change among the tribes of India. The second volume evaluates the researches of Indian and foreign scholars in the field of village, urban and industrial complexes and caste, psycho-social-religious as well as folklore studies. Biographical sketches of eminent anthropologists have also been included in the second volume. The comprehensive coverage provides a rich treasure for social scientists in general and anthropologists in particular.

Dr. Vidyarthi not only studied the culture of the primitive or non-literate but brought into light the life-style of the priestly community, urban, industrial, island village and the so-called untouchables. On the basis of his fieldwork and contextual analysis, Dr. Vidyarthi builds up the picture or general outline of the social system or culture of different societies. His theory of Sacred Complex and Nature-Man-Spirit Complex which has earned wide recognition, is taught in different universities at a higher level of education.*

The tribal culture of India

It seems difficult if not impossible to evaluate or review all the books (about 60) and research papers (151 in number) due to more than one reason. Here I am mentioning only two books of importance, one in English and the other in Hindi. During 1977, Dr. Vidyarthi along with Dr. B.K. Rai published *The Tribal Culture of India* which fills a long-felt gap in the study of tribal societies in India. It provides at one place most of the significant information on tribes. One cannot but admire the meticulous care with which the authors have culled information and ideas from studies, some of which are rarely available. The contents have been treated at two levels. At one level the various aspects of life have been described in detail, at the other, some of the institutions like matriliny and polyandry have been taken up for a more intensive discussion.

Though the discussion of the economic system and social organization of the tribals has been by and large confined to micro-level studies, one can see glimpses of the macro-context provided by the colonial rule in the pre-Independence period and the functioning of the welfare democracy after Independence. It is this awareness of the macro-context that leads the authors to conclude that a transition marking the meeting of the two worlds, traditional and modern, is in process. What is particularly praiseworthy in this monograph is that it has avoided the usual cliches about

* Presently, Professor Vidyarthi is writing a book on "Theories and Methods in Anthropology" under the University Grants Commission Quality Book Writing Scheme. His more than 20 books are prescribed in different colleges and universities of the country. These books are not only on anthropology but on other sister disciplines also like sociology, psychology, etc.

the meaning of modernization. Modern is ever modernizing itself. It is neither Westernization for ever, nor Sanskritization for ever. It is man's capacity always to have a fresh look at himself and at his surroundings. This book has brought out this abundant capacity of the tribals. They respond to various influences, they change ; but "the identity and variety of tribal culture" persist. The tribals carry the traditions with them ; but do not wallow in traditions.

Published under the auspices of the Hindi Samiti, Government of U.P., Lucknow, the other book, *Bhartiya-Adivasi* (in Hindi), is another outstanding contribution of Dr. Vidyarthi. Besides Dr. Vidyarthi has to his credit three other standard books in Hindi : *Bihar Ke Adivasi* (1960), *Manav Shastra Ki Rup Rekha* (along with I.P. Singh & K.S. Mathur, 1963), and *Bhartiya Nagar* (1966). These books on anthropology have been so widely read by the students, researchers and teachers, specially of the Hindi-speaking States like Bihar, Uttar Pradesh, Madhya Pradesh, Rajasthan, Gujarat, Haryana, etc., that the first editions of these books were sold out long ago and since then a few are out of print. However, through the *Bhartiya-Advasi* Dr. Vidyarthi has fulfilled the long-felt need for a book in Hindi which could cover the whole tribal India, instead of any particular tribal region.

At the end, I must admit that it is very difficult to assess or evaluate all the works of Dr. L.P. Vidyarthi who has contributed a vast treasure of knowledge to the service of man in general and anthropology in particular. To understand the human whole, he has viewed it from different angles, viz., social, cultural, political, economic, religious and psychological. He has always endeavoured to know man in tribal, rural, urban, industrial and ecological setting. In a few words, he has endeavoured to study man in every setting.

Professor Vidyarthi, Dean, Faculty of Social Sciences of Ranchi University, has received about 11 distinguished fellowships and awards from national and international organizations. He has been President, Vice-President, Chairman, Local Secretary, Member and Director of different committees, organizations, seminars and symposia. He was the Vice-President of the International Social Science Council, UNESCO, Paris, during the years 1979—82. He is Chairman, Secretary, Director and Member of various institutes, organizations, Government commissions and various committees. He achieved the highest position in his discipline (anthropology) after becoming the President of the Xth International Congress of Anthropological and Ethnological Sciences. Being a successful Teacher, President, Vice-President, Chairman, Secretary, Director, Editor, Associate Editor, Assistant Editor, Dean of Social Sciences, and Social Worker proves his dynamism. After reviewing his all academic work one can easily conclude that he is one of the top anthropologists of the world.

References

Allchin, F.R., 1960 : *Bulletin of the School of Oriental and African Studies,* University of London, Vol. 25, Pt. 2.

Borbora, S., 1960 : *Cultural Ecology and the Nature of Transformation* : A Study of the Asur of the Netarhat Plateaus. Ph.D. Thesis, Ranchi University.

Choudhary, G.N., 1978 : *Socio-Cultural Impact of Industrialisation on the Tribal Villages around the H.E.C.,* Ranchi. Ph.D. Thesis, Ranchi University.

Das Gupta, A., 1982 : The Symbols and Rituals among the Ho of Singhbhum. Ph.D. Thesis, Ranchi University.

Dube, S.C., 1955 : *Indian Village.* Ithaca, Cornell University Press.

Evans-Pritchard, E.E., 1940 : *The Nuer.* Oxford.

Halder, A.K., 1978 : Mining Labourers of Chotanagpur, A Study of the Coal and Iron Ore Mining Labourers. Ph.D. Thesis, Ranchi Un versity.

Jha, Makhan, 1971 : *The Sacred Complex in Janakpur.* Allahabad : The United Publishers.

Jha, Makhan, 1978 : *Dimension of Indian Civilization.* New Delhi : Classical Publication.

Jha, Makhan, 1982 : *Mithila & Mahakoshal.* New Delhi : Capital Publishing.

Mahapatra, M., 1971 : Lingaraj Temple, its Structure and Change, 1900-1962. A Doctoral Thesis submitted to Utkal University, Bhubaneshwar, unpublished.

Majumdar, D.N., 1958 : *Caste & Communication in an Indian Village.* Bombay : Asia Publishing House.

Malinowski, B., 1922A : *Argonauts of the Western Pacific Studies in Economics & Political Science,* No. 65, pp. xxxi+527, London.

Mann, R.S. (ed.), 1981 : *Nature-Man-Spirit Complex in Tribal India,* Ranchi Anthropology Series-3. New Delhi : Concept Publishing Company.

Morab, S.G., 1980 : The Soliga : A Study in Economy, Ecology, Society and Religion of a Hill Tribe. Ph.D. Thesis, Ranchi University.

Narayan, S., 1983 : *The Sacred Complex of Deoghar and Rajgir.* New Delhi : Concept Publishing Company.

Opler, Morris E., 1962 : *American Anthropologist,* Vol. 64, No. 2.

Prasad, R.K., 1968 : Economic & Social Change among the Parahaiya of Palamau : A Study in Tribal Dynamics. Ph.D. Thesis, Ranchi University.

Pusalker, A.D., 1961 : *The Sunday Standard* dated 27-8-61.

Rai, B.K., 1967 : Nature and Man : A Study of Interaction between Man and Forest in Chotanagpur. Ph.D. Thesis, Ranchi University.

Redfield, R., 1955 : *The Little Community.* Chicago : University of Chicago Press.

Richmond, Sonya, 1961 : *Burant's Press Cuttings* : 29-39. Mount, Pleasant, London, W.C.I., dated 16-8-61.

Roy, P.K., 1974 : Socio-Economic Impact of Industrialisation on the Indian Family : A Case Study in Hatia, Ranchi. Ph.D. Thesis, Ranchi University.

Sahay, K.N., 1972 : The Sacred Towns of Rameshwaram & Tirupati, Fieldwork with Student.

Sahay, Vijay S., 1979 : The Nicobaries : A Study in Nature-Man-Spirit Complex. Ph.D. Thesis, Ranchi University.

Sahoo, A.C., 1981 : The Changing Bondo Highlanders. Ph.D. Thesis, Ranchi University, Ranchi.

Sahu, R., 1983 : The Sacred Specialists of Kashi. Ph.D. Thesis, unpublished. Submitted to Ranchi University.

Sandhwar, A.N., 1973 : The Korwa of Palamau : A Study of Their Society and Economy. Ph D. Thesis, Ranchi University.

Sarkar, I.K., 1970 : Socio-cultural Implication of Industrialisation in Bokaro. Ph.D. Thesis, Ranchi University.

Saraswati, B.N., 1974 : Studying Sacred Complex in Kashi : Symposium on the Sacred Complex in India. Reprinted for *Journal of Social Research*, Vol. XVII : 1, p. 6.

Sharma, G.R., 1971 : Living Conditions of Colliery Workers in Jharia Coal Field. Ph.D. Thesis, Ranchi University, Ranchi.

Shrestha, T.P.S., 1972-73 : The Sacred Complex of the Valley of Kathmandu. ICSSR Research Project.

Shukla, N.K., 1968 : Social Structure of a Village in Bihar. Ph.D. Thesis, Ranchi University.

Sinha, R.K., 1977 : A Study of the Nature-Man-Spirit Complex among the Pando of Chhatisgarh. Ph.D. Thesis, Ranchi University.

Singh, R., 1967 : Impact of Industrialisation on Patratu and Four Oraon Villages. Ph.D. Thesis, Ranchi University.

Singh, A.K., 1984 : *Tribal Development in India.* New Delhi : Classical Publishing Company.

Singh, Jitendra, 1979 : Religion & Society among the Tharus of the Cis-Himalayas. Ph.D. Thesis, Ranchi University.

Sriram, Malathi, 1961 : *Sunday* dated 21-5-61.

Sriniwas, M.N., 1955 : *India's Village*. Calcutta : Asia Publishing House.

Srivastava, M.P., 1979 : The Coal Miners of Chotanagpur. Ph.D. Thesis, Ranchi University, Ranchi.

Thomas, William L., 1956 : *Man's Role in Changing the Face of the Earth* (ed.). Chicago : University of Chicago Press.

Upadhyay, V.S., 1972 : The Sacred Towns of Dwarika, Fieldwork with Students.

Verma, P., 1971 : Social Structure of Chotanagpur Village. Ph.D. Thesis, Ranchi University.

Vidyarthi, L.P., 1961 : *The Sacred Complex in Hindu Gaya*. Bombay : Asia Publishing House.

Vidyarthi, L.P., et al. 1963 : *Manav Shastra Ki Rup Rekha* (Hindi). Meerut City : Kedar Nath Ram Nath.

Vidyarthi, L.P., 1963 : *The Maler : Nature-Man-Spirit Complex in Hill Tribe of Bihar.* Calcutta : Bookland Pvt. Ltd.

Vidyarthi, L.P., 1966 : Ghaghra : A Village in Chotanagpur. Census of India, Monograph No. 2, Office of the Registrar General, India, Ministry of Home Affairs, New Delhi.

Vidyarthi, L.P., 1969 : *Cultural Configuration of Ranchi* (A Survey). Patna : Bookland Pvt. Ltd.

Vidyarthi, L.P., 1970 : Dynamics of Tribal Leadership in Bihar : Planning Commission Report, Kitab Mahal, Allahabad.

Vidyarthi, L.P., 1970 : Socio-cultural Implications of Industrialisation in India : A Case Study of Tribal Bihar, Council of Social & Cultural Research, Bihar.

Vidyarthi, L.P., 1972 : Problems and Prospects of Tribal Development in India in *Indian Anthropologist*, Vol. 2, No. 2.

Vidyarthi, L.P., 1973 : Report of the Task Force on Tribal Developments. Planning Commission, New Delhi.

Vidyarthi, L.P. & Jha, M. (ed.), 1974 : Symposium on the Sacred Complex in India, Reprinted from *Journal of Social Research*, Vol. XVII, No. 1.

Vidyarthi, L.P., 1976 : *Student Unrest in Chotanagpur*. Calcutta : Punthi Pustak, 34 Mohan Bagan Lane.

Vidyarthi, L.P. & Rai, B.K., 1977 : *The Tribal Culture of India*, New Delhi : Concept Publishing Company.

Vidyarthi, L.P., 1977 : *Harijan Today*. New Delhi : Classical Publishers.

Vidyarthi, L.P., 1978 : *Rise of Anthropology in India*, Vols. I & II. New Delhi : Concept Publishing Company.

Vidyarthi, L.P., 1978 : *Trends in World Anthropology*. New Delhi : Concept Publishing Company.

Vidyarthi, L.P., 1978 : *Folklore Researches in India : In Varia Folk-lorica* (ed.), Alan Dundes. The Hague : Mouton.

Vidyarthi, L.P., 1978 : *Rise of World Anthropology*. New Delhi : Concept Publishing Company.

8. Prof. Vidyarthi at a party after receiving the Distinguished Service Award at Chicago in 1983. Prof. Sol Tax (extreme right) and Mrs. Sol Tax are also in the picture.

9. In a fighting mood ! Prof. Vidyarthi with his fellow investigator (of Chicago University) at the Fair of Red Indians in 1957.

10. Prof. Vidyarthi congratulating Mr. Ushiyame after he received the Award at the Japanese Press Club in Tokyo in 1984.

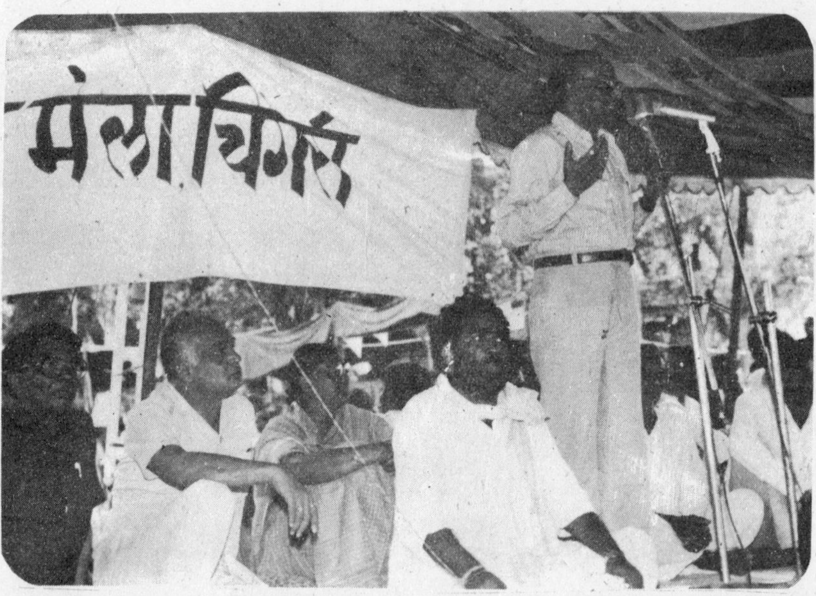

11. Prof. Vidyarthi addressing a tribal gathering on October 2, 1984, at the birthplace of Jatra Bhagat, father of Thana Bhagat, in the village Chingri near Bishunpur in Ranchi district. Sitting (on his right) are Mr. R. M. Bhagat, Mrs. K. Oraon, Dr. Biswanath Prasad, Vice-Chancellor, Ranchi University, and Mr. Bandi Oraon, a State Minister.

6

VIDYARTHI'S CONTRIBUTION TO HISTORY, POLITICS AND ADMINISTRATION

L.M. Prasad

Among the innumerable Third World social scientists, Vidyarthi is, perhaps, the most dynamic and interdisciplinary. In view of the above, I refuse to call him merely an anthropologist. As a matter of fact, Vidyarthi is like a scholar whose ideas can irrigate almost all branches of social science. A serious student of Vidyarthi will find his writings on history, politics, public administration, sociology, psychology, geography also. Anthropology being the study of man in totality, he could write with authority on all disciplines alike which concern man. As such, it is difficult, if not impossible, to evaluate the contributions of Vidyarthi and reach a definite conclusion. As a student of political science and public administration, I shall, therefore, keep myself confined to the historical, political and administrative contributions of Vidyarthi to the world anthropology and social science.

HIS CONTRIBUTION TO HISTORY

History for history's sake is the exclusive privilege of the historians. Vidyarthi, in his attempt to understand the dynamics of tribal leadership and tribals in their totality, has gone into their antiquities and has searched their hoary past. While searching for their antiquities, he has consulted the Rig Veda, Manu Sanhitas, Aitareya Brahmana, Bhagwat Purana, Brahma Vaivarta Purana, Parasara Sanhita, Harivansha Purana, Vayu Purana besides consulting the Ramayana and the Mahabharata.[1] These studies convinced him that the tribals are an integral part of the Indian civilization.[2] Incidentally they were the earliest among the present inhabitants of the country. He further finds that the ancient literature and scriptures of India name them as (i) Nishadas, Sabaras, Bhils and Kollas,

(ii) Kiratas and (iii) Dasas, Dasyus, Sudras,—Dramidas and Dravidas. This opinion of Vidyarthi contrasts with those of the English scholars who say that historically the tribals were a separate entity.[3] He opines that despite the "long centuries of Hindu rule and Hindu neighbours, the tribals find themselves assimilated to an extent with the Hindu culture."[4]

Vidyarthi took pains for finding references for these Indian tribes. We know that their references are widely scattered during the long Hindu period of Indian history. No single work of any author depicts the history of all the major tribes of India in one volume. In the absence of any written history on them even in the historical period, Vidyarthi created history by searching their wandering conditions. He found the antecedents of the Mundas before their settling in Chotanagpur. By searching the parting of the Santhals from the Mundas and the Mundas pushing the Asuras westward, Vidyarthi tells the antecedents of these tribes of Chotanagpur.[5]

Vidyarthi has also searched the antiquities of the Oraon's, another major tribe of Chotanagpur. He mentions the Oraon legends of taking part in the Ram-Ravan Yudha. By mentioning their wanderings from Bhojpur, Rohtas, and then Ranchi he established the antecedents of the Oraons also.

He, however, did not remain confined to Chotanagpur tribes only. He also searched the wanderings and antecedents of the Kolarian tribe, the Saoras, and of the Bhils, another major tribe of middle and western India. Regarding south India, he says that in ancient days the ancestors of the Urali Kurumbas of Kerala were the Kurumans or Kurumbas who were supreme till the beginning of the 8th century A.D. when they were repeatedly defeated by the Kongas, the Cholas and the Chalukyas and finally overthrown and scattered by a Chola king. Likewise, Vidyarthi has explained the antiquities of north-eastern Himalayan tribes—the Bodos and Ahoms of Assam. Further, he has also explained the historicity of the Koltas of Jaunsar and the Bawars of central Himalaya and the Tharus. Having explained these facts, he concludes that the tribals in the early historical period appeared to have lived in a state of internal movement cutting across the country, their movements were generally guided by the river valleys, and destinations were the hills and forest regions of the country.[6]

The position of the tribals in the medieval period has been well explained by Vidyarthi. He explains how by the end of the 16th century they were harassed by the Mohammedan rulers and gradually lost their status. He explains how the Nagbansi Raja of Chotanagpur was reduced to a Malguzar or tributary (1585 A.D.).[7] The copying by the Nagbansi Raja of the Mughal court and gradually being fully Hinduized and making his own brethren his serfs has been well explained. Here again, Vidyarthi did not remain confined to Bihar only but explains how the

Bhils of western India felt disturbed due to Mohammedan and Maratha invaders, how they were mercilessly treated by the British.[8] Likewise, the position of the Gonds of middle India, the Banjaras of north and western India, Khasa area of the Himalayan region in the Muslim period has been well explained. Reviewing the whole Indian situation, Vidyarthi concludes that during the medieval period the tribal people inhabiting different parts of India were either disturbed by the then Mohammedan rulers or the regional rulers or by both.[9]

A compact history of modern period also has been presented by Vidyarthi. He explains how the tribals of Chotanagpur (then known as Jungal Mahal) protested vehemently the incursions of the Britishers in 1795, 1800, 1801, 1807, 1808, 1816, 1821 and Chaur or Paik rebellion in Bengal between 1787 and 1830, and the great Kol rising of 1831-32. The passing of Regulation XIII of 1833, the Scheduled District Act of 1874, etc., have been explained in a chronological manner. Passing of various Acts by the British Government and concessions given to the tribes in the Act of 1919, Simon Commission (1928), and in the Act of 1935 have been well explained. The coming of the Christian missions and various problems arising from this (both for the tribals and the Government) have also been well explained. As such Vidyarthi has presented a well-documented history of tribal India though he is not a professional historian.

Tribal rebellion and leadership study

Rebellion study is normally the task of a historian or a political scientist. Vidyarthi has studied in detail the tribal rebellion in a bid to search the dynamics of tribal leadership. This, again, is the privilege of a political scientist. As such, Vidyarthi has successfully and creditably performed the role of a political scientist when he studied the evolution of tribal leadership in Bihar in his synchronic and dychronic study *Dynamics of Tribal Leadership*. In this celebrated study an attempt has been made to present the details of all the major rebellions and uprisings in tribal Bihar in an almost chronological sequence which helps us to understand the leadership situation and the nature of tribal leadership involved therein. We find that the freedom-loving tribals fought relentlessly against the British overlordship. Especially the period of 1795-1800 witnessed the trial of strength between the British forces and the tribal people. Vidyarthi has explained all the rebellions of Bihar in detail like Chauri Larai, Ho Rebellion of Singhbhum, the Great Kol Rising, Bhumij Rebellion of Manbhum and Singhbhum, Maler Revolt, the Santhal Insurrection (1855-57), 1857 Rebellion among the tribals in Chotanagpur, Raja Arjun Singh's Rebellion at Singhbhum, the Bhogta Rising at Palamau, Bhagirath Kherwar and Saphahor Movement, Rai Movement, Sardari

Larai, Birsa Rebellion, the Christian Movement, the Tana Bhagat Movement, the Bhumij Kahatriya Movement, the Jharkhand Movement and so on.[10]

The studies in the rebellion beautifully explain the leadership position, power structure and decision-making in Indian rural society. I do not mean that Vidyarthi was the first scholar to study these problems. A beginning of such studies in India dates back to 1891 when Sir Henry Maine brought out the role of the Council of Elders in an Indian village. The social anthropologists thereafter did not pay much heed to these studies. Oscar Lewis and his Indian collaborators initiated the study of factions and leadership with their two volumes on north Indian and south Indian villages respectively. But it is to the credit of Vidyarthi to make the leadership study empirical. In fact he initiated a new era of empirical research on leadership studies. Of late some political scientists like Rajni Kothari, Iqbal Narain, U.M. Sirshikar have initiated leadership studies. Sociologists and social anthropologists like Srinivas, N.K. Bose, A.P. Baranabas, Yogesh Atal and others have published works based on their empirical studies. The need for bringing about an alround transformation in the villages further accelerated the need for understanding the dynamics of tribal and rural leadership. Vidyarthi opines :

> Leaders are inseparable from any political network. They have the same importance, purpose and place as the head has in the case of a human body. A political network without a leader is like a rudderless ship. The leaders provide the means to attain the objectives of a political network. In the simpler communities like the tribes of India, they are more important as the tribal people have a staunch belief and faith in them. Tribal leaders are not only helpful in achieving the objective of a political institution but also provide numerous other activities for the community. They determine the course of action in the interest of a group and its members follow it.[11]

In the field of tribal leadership, Vidyarthi has presented the most comparative work which studies the pattern of tribal leadership in Bihar both in terms of dichronic and synchronic levels, sponsored by the Indian Council of Social Science Research. This large-scale study highlights the dynamics of traditional, modern as well as transitional leadership among the tribes of various cultural types. To fill in the void of an integrated and analytical study of tribal leadership on an all-India level, an attempt was made under the leadership of Vidyarthi during an All-India Seminar on Tribal Leadership, held at Ranchi. He is of the view that a detailed and systematic study of tribal leadership is of great significance for various reasons.

First, tribal communities are relatively simpler societies and they provide laboratory situations for understanding those basic features or origin and development of leadership which get complicated in more advanced communities. When conducted with more theoretical and methodological sophistication, studies of tribal leadership might even help elucidate many concepts of leadership. Second, tribal societies are the weakest section of India's population and efforts are being made to "uplift" them and integrate them with the advanced section of the Indian population. Consequently the sensitive problems involved in promoting induced culture change among the tribals need careful understanding of the traditional and transitional tribal leaders. Third, detailed tribal studies are highly significant because the tribals have their own village councils with traditional heads. Their offices are more or less hereditary and, in each village, they wield tremendous influence. During the last few decades, however, the traditional institutions and their hereditary leaders have sustained a setback owing, firstly, to conversions to Christianity and, secondly, to the introduction of the Bihar Panchayati Raj Act. The converted tribals have since had nothing to do with the traditional officials and look to the priests for leadership. Functioning of the two types of village councils in the tribal areas of Bihar and Orissa have made the nature of conflicts, compromise and coexistence of two types of leadership. As such, he opines :

> While plans are being made for the introduction of Panchayati Raj in the tribal area, a systematic study of the traditional pattern of leadership should be made and the course of emerging leadership smoothened.[12]

Fourth, a significant point is that the whole of the tribal belt in middle India is exposed to the process of industrialization and urbanization. With these developments, new crises in the tribal societies have arisen and many more are likely to arise in future. The tribals have to face these new situations with their new leaders. Such leaders are bound to be urban-bred, rational, secular, educated and materialistic and thus in a position to tackle the problems arising out of industrialization. Fifth, a study of the dynamics of change implies a study of the emergence of leadership from time to time. While traditional leaders at the village and regional levels played an important role in tribal India, there was scope for the growth of new leaders in moments of crises. Sixth, a historical study of the political parties of the tribals like the Jharkhand party, Naga National Council, Adivasi Maha Sabha should be undertaken with a view to understanding their social, cultural and political roles and to analyse the pattern of leadership. And finally, along with the study of the sociopolitical parties of the tribals, biographical study of the modern tribal leader and the elite also deserves to be undertaken to acquire an insight into the felt needs and aspirations of the leaders. Through biographical studies one can also analyse the nature of change in the tribal leadership that has occurred from the time of Birsa Bhagwan to Marang Gomke.

Vidyarthi opines that tribal leadership is changing fast. Birsa and the other traditional leaders of the tribals were rural bred, charismatic and religious in their approach. They had little education, but they derived power through dreams, divinations, etc., to lead the masses. The leadership in these movements was religious, economic, social as well as political. After the death of Birsa, says Vidyarthi, it appears the leadership of the Mundas went into the hands of Western-educated Christian tribals who were essentially rationalistic in interpreting and tackling political situations. Most of these leaders were urban-bred. He, however, opines that later on the Christian-oriented, Western-educated model is losing its exclusiveness. The organization which essentially started for the consolidation of Christian converts is fast expanding its scope and a number of Hindus have also joined the Christian-sponsored Jharkhand Party. He says that a new model of leadership is emerging under the increasing impact of urbanization and industrialization in Ranchi.

Vidyarthi opines that the character of leadership has changed a great deal since the days of Birsa Bhagwan and Jatra Bahagat. The most significant and obvious fact is the switch-over from religious leadership. This change corresponds to political leadership. It corresponds to a difference in method. The modern leaders are representing the tribal people to an outside, political world. They are not concerned primarily with raising the social status of the tribals by making their ritual practices resemble closely those of the Hindus. Their chief task is to improve the material conditions of the tribals and to obtain government funds and services. Their activities are more within the realm of the civil and the political and less within the realm of the religious and the social. Vidyarthi thus is of the view that the emergence of India's tribal societies into the modern world is marked by some basic changes in the character of their leadership, and in their self-image as a people.[13]

Regarding classification of a leader Vidyarthi says that there may be many criteria for the classification of a leader. However, he classifies it on four definite criteria : (1) Social position held by a leader, (2) Personal qualities of a leader, (3) Functional achievements of a leader, (4) Spatial influence of a leader. Nevertheless, he opines that each criterion is not isolated from the other ; it has always overlapped.[14]

On the basis of the social position, leaders have been classified as (1) Formal leaders, (2) Informal leaders, and (3) Exploiter leaders.

Formal leaders are such tribals or non-tribals as hold a position in the formal hierarchy or organization, or hold some kind of formal designation and enjoy the privilege of leadership because of their position. These leaders include the traditional and institutional religious leaders like Pahan, Baiga, Deori, Nayke, Manjhiye and their assistants or the traditional and institutional secular leaders like Mahto, Munda, Pradhan, Manjhiye, Patel and their assistants or the inter-village chief and his subordinate officials. They also include various magicians like Ojha, Mati, Bhagat, Guru Demano, Witch, etc. Modern institutional leaders like Mukhiya, Up-Mukhiya, Sarpanch, Gram Sevak, Panch and the like also constitute this category of leaders. Teachers, Block Development Officers, Village Level Workers, Clerks, Welfare Inspectors, Members of Legislative Assemblies and Parliament, Christian priests, catechists and missionaries further constitute this category of leaders.

Informal leaders are those who are not associated with any type of formal hierarchy or organization nor hold any kind of formal designation, and yet have influence over the people or people come to them as they possess some leadership qualities. This category may also include such persons as held some position in a formal organization or held some designation, but are now leading a retired peaceful life.

Exploiter leaders are those leaders who had once been exploiters of the tribals or are still so in some measure, like the ex-landlords and Mahajans or moneylenders and who, because of their privileged position, were in a position to win the following of the tribals. Though the Mahajans and landlords are said to have exploited the tribals for a long time, they have also been helpful to them in times of dire need and guided them in many matters.

Secondly, on the basis of attributes of leaders, Vidyarthi has classified them into four types : (1) Ideal Leaders, (2) Institutional Leaders, (3) Benevolent Leaders, and (4) Socially privileged leaders.

Ideal leaders are called those leaders who possess such attributes as are considered ideal by the people and which they (leaders) must possess for the sake of leadership. They must be "good of character", "honest", "sincere", "good judges", "sober", "good advisers", "powerful and influential", "active", "gentle", "faithful", "frank", "innocent", and "wise".

Institutional leaders, the second type, include all such leaders whose attributes are said to be their affiliation with some institution or some position in any formal organization, viz., the religious or secular village or inter-village leaders, Magician, Sarpanch, Panch, Mukhiya, Up-Mukhiya, Gram Sevak, Village Level Worker, Block Development Officer, Welfare Inspector, etc.

The third type, i.e., benevolent leaders, are those who are basically benevolent in their character and attributes and possess four qualities like "welfare of the people", "helpful", "kind" and "well-wisher of the people", and have eight attributes—"businessman", "wealthy and rich", "old", "singer", "educated", "medicine man", "important and experienced", and "good cultivator". Under the category of socially privileged leaders, according to Vidyarthi, come persons who are or were holding traditional posts like village head, village priest, elder villager, etc. School teacher or a well-educated or travelled villager is also considered as their leader.

Thirdly, according to Vidyarthi, tribal leaders may be classified from the point of view of the function they perform or the needs they serve. Usually there are two types of needs—traditional and modern. Hence the leaders may accordingly be classified as (1) Traditional Leaders, and (2) Modern Leaders. He, however, adds a third type in view of the impact of modernity on the tribals, i.e., Transitional Leaders, who come in between the two, from the point of view of their function. Traditional leaders are those who have been operating in the traditional social structure, standing for the old traditional values and institutions and satisfying various traditional needs of the tradition-oriented tribal society. Here he gives the names of the traditional religious leaders like Pahan, Baiga, Deori, Manjhiye, Naiki, the traditional secular leaders like Mahto, Munda, Manhji, Manjhiye as well as various inter-village regional chiefs from different tribal areas like Parha Raja, Manki, Parganait and Sardar along with their subordinate officials as well as most of the magical specialists like Ojha, Mati, Bhagat, Demano, Guru, etc.

The tribal leaders who operate in the new social structure in free India associated with the newly introduced associations, institutions or organizations and who stand for new innovations and ideas in their society, thus satisfying the needs of the modern wider social system, according to Vidyarthi, are called modern tribal leaders. This category includes leaders like the Christian catechist, priests, Christian missionaries and various denominations of authorities in the Church hierarchy (for the Christian converts), Mukhiya, Up-Mukhiya, Sarpanchs, Panchs, Gram Sevaks, Welfare Inspectors, teachers, Members of Legislative Assemblies and Parliament of the region, religious reformists, trade union leaders and the like.

But besides the tribal leaders who operate in the traditional social structure, and those who work in the new social structure satisfying the traditional and modern needs of the people and go by the name of traditional and modern tribal leaders, according to Vidyarthi, there are a few tribal leaders who operate both in the traditional and modern or emergent social structure. Such leaders fulfil the traditional as well as modern and emergent needs and have been termed as transitional leaders. They usually come from the traditional leadership set-up or are inspired by traditional leaders.

Fourthly, Vidyarthi opines that tribal leaders may be viewed in terms of their spatial influence and are classified into four different categories : (1) Village level leaders, (2) Sub-regional leaders, (3) Regional leaders, and (4) Urban leaders.

Village-level leaders as those who belong to a particular village, who have been normally born and brought up in the village and whose influence and following are exclusively confined to the people of that village. This category includes leaders like the village religious head, secular head, their various assistants, village catechist among the Christian converts, village medicine man, and village magician who operate on the village level.

The leaders of the sub-regional level are those who are also normally born and brought up in the village but who have their influence, following and operation extending to a group of villages in an area. These leaders include the head or chief like Parha Raja, Manki, Parganait and Sardar of an inter-village ring and their subordinate officials who operate within a sub-region. Among modern leaders it includes such Christian leaders as the religious authorities of a Parish, Bhikahariate Illaka, or Block Development Officers, Village Level Workers, Welfare Inspectors, teachers, Mukhiyas, Up-Mukhiyas, Sarpanchs, Panchs, Gram Sevaks and the like. When it comes to the modern sub-regional level leaders, they may be urban bred and belong to a different social system such as the Block Development Officer, Welfare Inspector, Village Level Worker and the like.

Regional-level leaders include such leaders as wield influence and have a following even outside and inter-village ring. These leaders are well known to the tribals of a particular region or are generally coinciding with an Assembly or Parliamentary constituency or sometimes (in a few cases) are known by a whole tribal group or even by those living in contiguous tribal areas. Vidyarthi says leaders like Jaipal Singh who usually won from a particular Parliamentary constituency, and yet had been known as an important leader of the whole of tribal Bihar, belong to this category. Besides Members or Legislative Assemblies and Parliament, it includes those who become Ministers or important leaders of a political party or are ex-men, or those defeated in the General Elections. The leaders of regional level may be rural as well as urban bred as those who become leaders of a particular tribal region develop frequent contacts with urban areas, stay there for most of the time and, in most cases, settle in towns and cities or show an increased tendency towards them.

Urban leaders are those who are born and brought up in urban areas or are domiciled there or are living there in connection with their professional activities. They include those Members of Legislative Assembly, Legislative Council or Parliament who fulfil this condition, or those engaged in business, those practising in law courts, office-bearers of political parties, of Church authorities who live in the headquarters of a

Synod, Anchal, Diocese or Archdiocese, who are in effective contact with the tribals. The urban leaders may also be regional leaders because their sphere of influence extends to a definite area though they stay in and operate from a city or town.[15]

It is significant to note that these ideas of Vidyarthi still hold good. In fact his views on tribal leadership can be regarded as concept.

Voting behaviour study

The study of elections by political scientists and political sociologists came into vogue in the post-World War II period. It was a new attempt to understand and explain the social reality. The behavioural approach opened up vast areas to fruitful empirical research. In India the first election study was produced by Kogekar and Park in 1952. Studies were made in Punjab, Bombay city, Poona, Kerala, Gujarat, Goa, etc. However, the first major steps in voting behaviour studies were taken at the time of the fourth General Election in 1967. This was organised by Rajni Kothari on an all-India basis, employing a highly sophisticated research design. None of these studies, however, dealt with voting behaviour with special focus on the tribals. It was Vidyarthi who highlighted the importance of such elections for the tribals. He emphasized,

> "It is highly significant and interesting to know the concept of franchise and the way in which the preliterate folks utilize it, their over-all political consciousness, political interests, the manner in which they are approached and wooed, or exploited by political parties, the considerations which guide them to vote for a particular candidate, whether rational or sentimental and the like. . .[16]

As such, among the tribes of Bihar, the first attempt was made by Vidyarthi during the second General Election in 1957 under the auspices of Culture Change Research Project sponsored by the Research Programmes Committee and conducted by the Department of Anthropology, Bihar University, but it remained mainly confined to casual observation and interviews among the Munda and Oraon tribes of Chotanagpur.

Motivated by these considerations, an intensive and detailed study of the fourth General Election among the tribals of Bihar during the 1967 General Election was taken up by Vidyarthi. In contrast to the studies mentioned above, the present study is more broad-based, systematic, representative and substantial than the previous one. It is also the intention that it could bring out qualitative and quantitative data on the topic.

The period intervening the 1967 General Election and the mid-term poll of 1969 marked an important epoch-making development in the politics of Bihar in the form of collapse of the twenty-year-old Congress Ministry followed by tumbling down of its successor United Front Ministries. Hence it provided a unique opportunity to study its reactions on the tribal mind as it got reflected in the voting pattern of the tribals and, consequently, electoral results. In this background the data obtained from the two election studies were computed and compared by Vidyarthi for a meaningful analysis of election situations.

He divided the election study into two parts : firstly, pre-election study of the tribals regarding their concept of election and other general information related to it which was obtained from the tribals about two weeks before the election and, secondly, the study of elections proper including the election campaign of political parties, voting behaviour of the people in the tribal reserved constituencies and an analysis of electoral results.

This is a well-digested study in which a voter's understanding of the General Election, the sources through which he knew about it as well as his degree of acquaintance with certain modern means of communication were the first few items on which his reactions were recorded.

After studying the pre-election situation of the tribals, Vidyarthi analyses the actual leadership process involved in the General Election by studying the election campaign of the various political parties in tribal areas, voting behaviour of the tribals during election and, finally, by making a comparative analysis of the electoral results of the 1967 General Election and the mid-term poll of 1969. In fact dynamics of tribal leadership is a vast study which explains : Slogans and allegations, socio-cultural aspects of canvassing, role of "Jharkhand" in canvassing, attachment with party symbols and its role in canvassing, percentage of polling in the city area, polling in the interior areas, lack of political consciousness, ignorance about the procedure of voting, difficulties of illiterate voters, canvassing at the booth, ethnic affiliation of the winning and contesting candidates, religious affiliation of the winning and contesting candidates, etc.

While doing the post-election study he inquired about the following points : Source of knowledge, reading of newspapers and listening to radio, representative's help during periods of crises, consultation with people during development work, opinion on election, expectations from representatives, voting experience and their awareness of the problems and events, past experience of voting, parties for which voted, development works by the candidates, their latest belief in the party, qualities of a leader, qualities of the candidates voted for, problems of the area, contact with contesting candidates, reaction to candidate's failure to keeping his promise, pressure tactics of the candidates, likeness for election system, opinion on uncontested election, type of representatives they like, likeness for the method of election, seeking advice regarding election, information about the candidates seeking election from Jharkhand, knowledge about

Congress-Jharkhand merger, information about Jharkhand, and so on. From the above-mentioned study, Vidyarthi drew several startling and interesting conclusions which deserve mention. They are :

Firstly, the nomadic Birhor and the hill-dwelling Maler who remain socially and physically isolated from the "outer world" because of their nomadism and hill dwelling respectively are politically least conscious or informed in comparison to those tribal communities who are settled agriculturists and exposed to external influences through their contact with neighbouring Hinduism, Christianity and the like.

Secondly, the settled agriculturists who were more exposed to the agencies of modernity had in majority of the cases a liking for elected leaders but the responses of the Birhors and Malers who live in comparative seclusion, in majority of the cases, voted in favour of traditional and hereditary leaders.

Thirdly, on some important issues like the choice of leadership or problems faced by the people, a considerable number of city dwellers showed a rural and traditional bias and voted for the traditional tribal leadership.

Fourthly, as regards opinions and attitudes of the people, on many points, the rural folk showed uniformity of thinking. In several cases, whether it was regarding the choice of qualities of a leader, about the understanding of general election, opinion about traditional leadership, choice of representatives or the method of election, by and large, the responses of majority of the rural folks generally on village level, and, in some cases, on inter-village level were similar, but responses to the same set of questions obtained in the city area of Ranchi showed a greater tendency towards diversity.

The fifth point which emerged is that, on the whole, there was no general and essential correlation between the education of the informants and the type of responses obtained among the settled agriculturists.

The attachment of the tribals to the Jharkhand party was also because of the deep symbol-orientation of most of the tribals. The cock which was the symbol of Jharkhand was the object of great ritualistic importance and it symbolized their "Supreme Being". Again it had a great utility in their day-to-day life. So it had the greatest appeal for the preliterate folk. As such, besides other things, the election was a psychological battle—a battle of symbols. The tribals in general cared less for the details of manifestoes or critical evaluation of the political activities of a party.

Among the booths situated in the city area, the percentage was greater at the booths dominated by Christian tribals which can be interpreted in terms of greater civic consciousness and a right type of leadership which the Christian tribals got from their missionaries or church leaders. It also reflects the psychology of a minority community who will be naturally more conscious of its rights and privileges. Again in the same booths in city areas dominated by Christians the number of women voters was greater. The voters usually come along with their family members.

The sixth significant point which emerged was that the non-tribal voters of the same area, in general, were politically more conscious than the tribals. This fact also got substantiated with the comparative electoral figures of the tribal reserved constituencies or general constituencies. Percentage of polling, if it reflects the extent of political consciousness of the people, was the smallest in the tribal reserved constituencies.

The next important feature to be noted in the tribal politics of Bihar, however, was the loss of monopoly of the Christian tribals in winning most of the Assembly and Parliamentary seats which reflects the awareness of 90 per cent non-Christian tribals to elect non-Christian tribals as their leaders. Vidyarthi found implicitly the revival of the Hindu model among the tribals. This also reflected the stronger sense of identity with the major regional culture and a will for establishing regional identity in the wider frame of national integration.[17]

The above-mentioned findings of Vidyarthi are still quite valid. They are very comprehensive and the first study of this kind. We are yet to find a wider study on tribal politics.

Political life of the tribals

Regarding political life of the tribals, Vidyarthi opines that the political life of the tribals of India reflects a paradoxical situation in which democracy and monarchy co-exist. He opines that every head of a community at different levels like clan, village and territory is generally honoured, obeyed and accepted as the head of the group. His office is hereditary. The supreme and final authority is in the hands of a single person. The Nagas of the north-east Himalayas have chieftainship. The entire population of a specific area, mostly confined to a village or a small territory, is knitted together in either kinship, religion, natural social instinct or economic or small activities. Every tribal has a share in the political ties of the village and the region. It exists for the majority, it is born of it and embodies it. The tribal leader governs the community only because he is backed by the majority or the whole of the group. The Mundas of Chotanagpur elect their head. It fits in with the philosophy of a local saying of the tribals of Chotanagpur that Munda Gaon Chalata Hai (Munda, the head of the village, runs the village).

Aristotle believes that man is a political animal. Likewise, Vidyarthi believes, "there seems to be no society where political activities are non-existent". He is of the view that even the smallest community requires some form of government. He substantiates it by the small wandering bands of the Birhors of Bihar who lay claim to distinct territories, and thus recognize the bond of a common homeland and are governed by a headman. Likewise the forest dwellers, Juangs of Orissa, are also governed by a combination of secular and religious heads. The Dihuri or Bhuihar and Padhan who are the sacred and secular heads respectively hold the office for generations together as the posts are hereditary. The Padhan sometimes combines in his person the function of a Dihuri. The forest-hunting type Chenchus of Andhra Pradesh have Peddamanchi, a leader, for every local group who functions as the spokesman when dealing with outsiders. When there is any dispute the elders of the group along with the Peddamanchi may try to mediate. The Kadarelders in Cochin also act in the same manner. They have the Muppam as their headman. Among the Mal Pantarams or Malai Pandarams of Travancore hills in Kerala the political control lies in the hands of the Muttu Kani, headman, and council of elders.[18]

Vidyarthi believes that it is difficult to distinguish political affairs from domestic affairs. He says, "as a rule the tribals, living in small groups, are united by kinship, marriage and frequent individual contact, and with them it is difficult to distinguish political affairs from domestic affairs". Regarding tribals' political associations, Vidyarthi says, "Tribals political associations, are of various kinds and incorporate individuals, elders, families, a clan group, a village and a tribal territory. Still they are micro-political in nature. The simple tribal communities of India have their own political influences which may spread quite beyond the confines of the small territory. The political characteristics of tribals may broadly be looked at through their social organization. They are : (i) Political association based on clan lineage ; (ii) Political association based on the village as unit ; and (iii) Political association of a group of villagers of a territory".

He says, "lineage segmentation is particularly important as a principle of political structure where central authority is weak or unknown and where, therefore, lineage members have to provide their own security against others of the same tribe, as well as against outsiders".

The political functioning of the lineage system among the tribes like the Santhal, Oraon, Bhil and Gond has been illustrated by Vidyarthi diagrammatically by what happens when a member of one lineage agonizes a member of another in the clan.

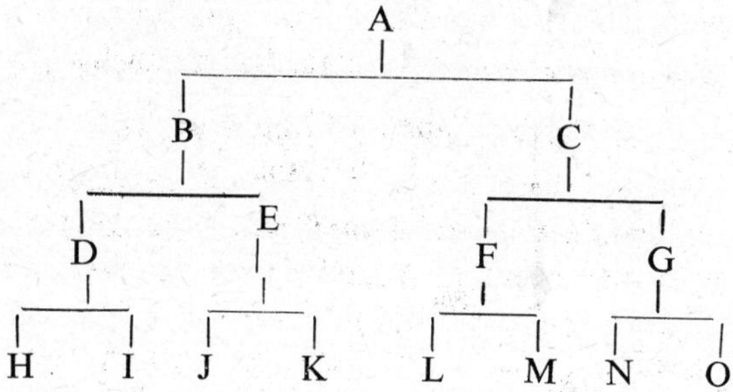

Here the letters represent lineages of different orders, all claiming descent from A, and thence, in the male line, through B, C, D, E, and so on. If a member of lineage H has enmity with a member of lineage I, then all members of H and all members of I are potentially at enmity with one another. Others are not necessarily involved. But if a member of H or I does harm to a member of J or K, then all H and I (now regarding themselves as members of D) may be engaged in hostilities with all J and K (now united as E). So also all B lineages will tend to unite against all C lineages if a man from one lineage kills a man from the other ; and finally the whole of A will be united - in theory at least—against outsiders who have injured any one of their members.

Vidyarthi says, "the tribal village works actively as a political unit. The village officer and village administration in tribal areas regulate and work for the tribal life. The mechanism functions through its officers who are known by different designations among the various tribes under review. For example in the minor tribes like the Birhor, Juang, etc., the ordering of the social, political and ritual relations of the village is in the hands of one man. The Malers and the Kamars have Manjhi and Biga as their respective heads. But among major tribes like the Santhal, Bhil, Munda, etc., we find a differentiation of function and authority vested in two headmen each with his own field of interest and prescribed duties. A primary differentiation of function splits village affairs into secular and sacerdotal spheres of activity with a headman responsible for each. Among some tribes, this differentiation is further emphasized by the appointment of assistants to help each headman in the discharge of his duties".

Vidyarthi also describes the judicial machinery of a village. He says,

> most of the tribes have a judicial machinery to deal with disputes, breaches of peace and social offences at the village level. It is usually a village council or assembly of elders known as Panchayat. Some settlements like the Hill Kharia are so small that they do not have any organization at the village level. Among the Malers, the Council of Elders of the village is presided over by the Manjhi and the Gorait acts as the public prosecutor. The Panchayat is called at the instance

of the Manjhi by the Gorait. Among the Mundas, Santhals, Hos, Oraons, Gonds, Bhils, etc., each village has a Panchayat.

He also sees some negative sanctions herein. He says,

> among all the tribes there are a number of negative sanctions that follow on misconduct or misdemeanour. The village people meet quite often in the evening around a fire in the village street or ground (Akhara) to watch dancing of the village youth or just to smoke or gossip. At such informal gatherings, the behaviour of individuals within the community is discussed, commented on and criticized. In a tribal village the behaviour of every tribesman is a matter of public concern and a man or a woman can gauge the effect of his or her behaviour by watching the reactions of the village community. Thus even without the direct exercise of the social prerogative, the village community exercises a limited control over public behaviour.

However, Vidyarthi believes that in the tribal village politics are not limited to the village boundary. . . . For example, the third type of political association is the territory in which the tribal political affairs go further to form a group of villages or a territorial group and in some cases the tribe as a whole. Among the Kumars Kurha is the chief of a group of villages. The Maler villages combine to form a Sardari region and the Sardar heads the union. The village of the Sardar is called the Sardari Village. Parha Raja heads the Parha, a union of a number of Oraon villages, whereas Manki heads of Ho Pirh (regional Panchayats of the Hos). The Pavagana of Gonds, a union of villages, is headed by Paraganamanjhi. Deshmukh is the head of 10 to 12 Bhil villages.[19]

The political structure

Vidyarthi believes that the political field of activities is broadly of two types with further sub-types : (a) Traditional Political Field, and (b) Contemporary Political Field.

The first type is the product of their traditional political life which at the same time combines political affairs with social and religious affairs. The second type has come out as the precipitate of culture change, culture contact and alien way of life, the mode of electing the Mukhiya, Pramukh, Adhyakh, Vidhayak and Sansad Sadasya in the present democratic set-up.

The condition throughout tribal India, at first instant, reveals the regionwise picture of the tribal political structure. The verdict of the tribal Panchayat or headman of the village is law to the tribal people. The sanction behind it is the great faith in the elders and village leadership. Every tribal village has some type of political machinery to look after the village affairs.

12. Prof. Vidyarthi responding to the felicitation address after the announcement of his being chosen for the Distinguished Service Award. Also seen in the picture (facing the camera) are Dr. A.K. Dhan, Vice-Chancellor, Ranchi University, and Dr. A.K. Singh.

13. Prof. Vidyarthi with the Ainu leaders and a local Japanese Professor near Sappro in Hokkado (Japan).

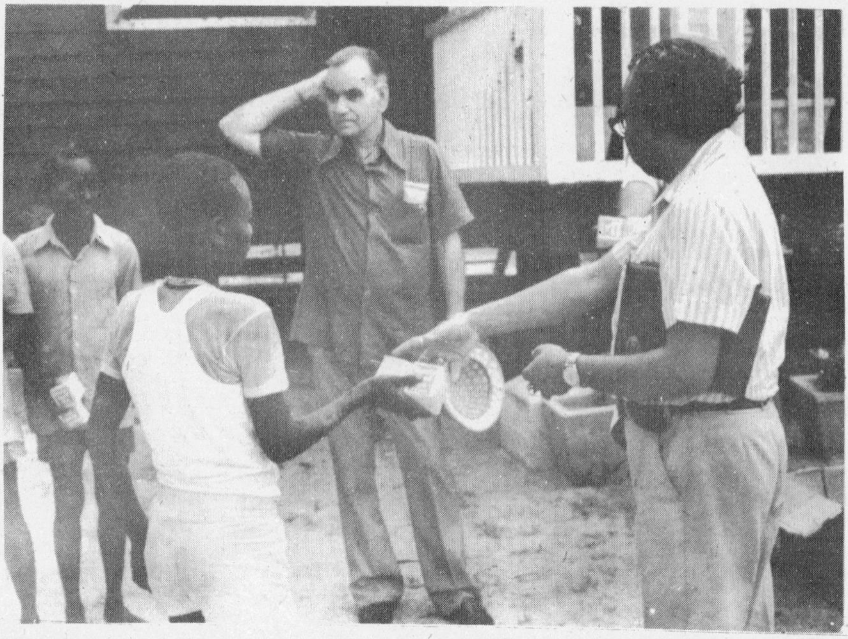

14. Prof. Vidyarthi distributing gifts to the tribals on the Andaman Islands in 1978. Also seen in the picture is Mr. S. N. Krishnarthi, the then Commissioner of the Andaman and Nicobar Islands.

15. Snake-charming ? No. Enjoying a feel of the python on his nacked backneck. Prof. Vidyarthi with the "informants" and villagers while working with the Maler tribe in the Rajmahals in 1958.

Vidyarthi describes the political structure of the whole India. For example, in the Himalayan region, in Assam and Meghalaya the traditional village Darbars look after the business. At the same time statutory village Panchayats have also been constituted. In some cases the Darbars have been recognized as such. In Manipur and Arunachal Pradesh the tribal councils have been recognized and any innovation in their traditional set-up, such as election, has been resisted. Nagaland has recognised the traditional set-up of the Village Council, Range Council and Tribal Council which had wide powers to deal with administrative and development matters along with cases involving breaches of customary law. In Himachal Pradesh, the most distinctive institution in Lahaul and Spiti is the monastery which is a joint product of the Lama system and of the social and economic organization of the tribes. Its hold, however, is not as strong as it used to be. Another traditional institution in Spiti is the Novo whose office is hereditary and has always been vested with certain criminal and civil powers.

Regarding middle India, he says, "In Bihar, where the Munda Manki system has been in vogue for a long time, the Mundas exercise considerable influence over the tribal community in religious and social affairs and even now are entrusted with the work of collection of revenue. In the Santhal Parganas, for every tribal village there is a village council which is presided over by a Manjhi and gives its decision on all important matters and disputes and levies penal ties against defaulters. In West Bengal, among such tribes as the Santhal and Munda the traditional councils exist even now but in many areas they are not effective. These councils settle disputes relating to connubial and commensal restrictions, rights and obligations of the family, inheritance and so on. They also help in the organization of village festivals.

"In Orissa the tribal communities have distinct social institutions and in some areas the traditional councils function as judicial, developmental and socialization bodies. Their internal affairs are governed by their laws derived, modified and administered in a purely democratic way by a penal of village elders and a headman. In Madhya Pradesh, every tribal community has its own organization which is comparatively strong in the more inaccessible tracts but is weakening in areas where the world influence has been increasing."

Regarding western India, Vidyarthi says, "in Gujarat, groups of small villages have tribal councils which wield considerable influence. They usually deal with social matters. In Maharashtra, the conditions of existing tribal institutions vary from region to region. The general pattern is that there is a council of elders which has a supreme voice in the socio-religious matters. In Rajasthan, except in social and religious matters, the traditional tribal councils do not perform any other function. It is felt that they have enough vitality to look into the village business. In South India, the institution is Muppan (headman) and Muppathy (headman's wife). The village headman is respected and his decisions are accepted."

Structure in the traditional political field

According to Vidyarthi, the traditional political field of the tribals is confined to the institutions like the Council of Village Elders, Village Headman, Village Panchayat and so on. All these institutions consisting of a single person or a group of persons have interrelated, cross-cutting fields where one surpasses the other depending on the situation. He says that these institutions are mainly of five kinds :

1. The Council of Elders, a temporary body of selected villagers, generally coincides with clan elders to look into cases brought before them.
2. The Village Headman, a hereditary post and/or subject to villagers' opinion if and when required.
3. The Village Panchayat, a body of the panchs headed by the village Headman. The panchs are elected by the villagers directly.
4. The Union of Villages, a regional panchayat headed by the regional head.
5. The tribal chief, a hereditary post of supreme judicial authority at the tribal level.

The Council of Elders

Regarding the Council of Elders, he says that it is a temporary council of selected village elders who take up particular problems at a particular time and solve disputes like quarrels between two villagers, and tackle sex offences, intrusion by outsiders in village affair, etc. He thinks that it is not a formally constituted Village Council, but the elders of the village customarily gather every morning at daybreak in the village centre, youth dormitory or a particular place in the village. Here the men sit around, smoke biris and discuss village business. Very often there is no real "business", so that the gathering can be regarded as primarily social. In any case, there is no sharp division between the business and social aspects of any meeting. This type of Council of Elders exists in most of the tribes of India. He substantiates it with the other tribes of India like the Lushais, tribes of the North Cachar hills, the Ao clan, the Apa Tanis of Arunachal Pradesh, the Khasis of Tripura, the Eastern Rengma Nagas, the Tharus of the Central Himalayas, the Kamars of middle India, the Saoras of Orissa, the Koli Mahadevas of western India (Maharashtra), the Kathodis and Koli Malhar, the Dubla, etc. He also describes it among the south Indian tribes, among the Konda Reddis, the Kadras, the Chenchus and so on.

The village headman

Vidyarthi considers the headman as the spokesman for all the villagers in dealing with outside authorities. He finds that the headman himself has no formal authority beyond that which his own personality and powers of persuasion permit him to exert. In everyday dealings with his fellow villagers he is not unlike them although his position as mediator between the village and the external administration provides him with a source of prestige which he can manipulate to advantage if he so desires. The position is hereditary and usually belongs to the largest clan group of a village. He finds that the village headman is a man who commands majority of the villagers, whom the followers consider a guide and keeper of traditional values, and who has the betterment of his followers at heart. Such a headman is an informal leader of the village, but he wields a great deal of power and influence over all village decisions and actions. He finds, "Even the gods go to the headman for help". He goes on to describe the position of the headman in the north-eastern Himalayan region, central Himalayas, middle India, south India and so on.

Assistants to the village headman

In some of the Indian tribes Vidyarthi finds the village headman is given extra hands by the villagers to run the village administration. He is helped in the discharge of his duties by certain minor officials. Among the Purums of Manipur there is a band of seven village officers who help and work for the Khullakpa. The eighth man, i.e., Changlai, is the orderly of the headman whereas the second man of the village, the Luplakpa, functions as the assistant headman of the village. Likewise, he has described the position of the whole of India like middle India, western India and south India.

Traditional village panchayat

Vidyarthi finds that the Village Panchayat has universal membership. Villagers sit together to discuss village affairs of diverse nature. There is never any formal voting. Each man states his opinions and the dominant attitude is immediately apparent. Rarely is an issue sufficiently controversial to evoke a heated argument. During many ceremonies the village acts as a corporate body. The village Panchayat is different in its character. The common man of the village starts taking part in the activities of the Panchayat when he reaches the age of about 20 or so. Usually the Panchayat meetings are attended by at least one member from each house. In their traditional village Panchayat, they have their village headman known by different names in different tribes as Munda, Mahto, Pradhan, Mukhiya, Mukhi, Patel, etc. They govern the village with the help of one or two assistants. The common will of the village community is expressed through the medium of the Panchayat which practically includes the entire population of the village.

Vidyarthi describes the Panchayats of Ao Nagas, the tribes of central Himalayas, middle India, western India, south India and so on.

The union of villages : Pargana panchayat

Among some tribes, Vidyarthi says, villages are grouped in loose unions, the strength of each such union going up to 200 villages or even more. Such a union is known among different tribes as Pargana, or Parha, etc. Its legal authority is vested in the Pargana Panchayat. This institution constitutes a court of appeal from decisions of the village Panchayat ; moreover it is the only authority competent to try certain types of offences. Though the Panchayat is, in some cases, empowered to pass a sentence of ex-communication, re-admission to the tribal fold can be effected only through the agency of the wider representative body. Vidyarthi goes on to describe the union of village in the north-eastern Himalayan region, middle India and southern India.

Tribal chief or chieftainship

The Chieftainship was a common feature of the tribals like the Nagas, Khasis, Garos, Lushais, etc., living in the north-eastern Himalayan region. The post of the chief was hereditary and he was not only to look after the region or tribe but was also the supreme judicial authority at the tribe level. Regarding the Himalayan region, the most remarkable feature about the tribals in the hills of Assam, Meghalaya, Nagaland, Tripura, etc., is the fundamentally democratic basis of their social and administrative organizations. With exceptions the land belonged to the community and not to any individual. Although in the Garo Hills the Nokma, in the Khasi and Jaintia Hills the Siem or the Doloi or the Raja, and in the Lushai Hills, till recently, the chief was the nominal proprietor of all lands within his jurisdiction, every villager could cultivate a plot of land everywhere as a matter of right. In society, there is no distinction between the high and the low. Wealth and income do not confer social privileges. The one powerful Lushai chief and the Khasi Siem were commoners as the humblest of the humble. Vidyarthi finds that rich is always ready to help those of their co-villagers who are in need and the strong is similarly inclined to help the weak. In fact the Lushai chief, who wielded enormous authority over his subjects, was the de jure father of the villagers over whom he ruled. In times of scarcity, if the villagers committed robbery of grain from the chief granary they committed no offence.

Vidyarthi describes this democratic spirit in the indigenous tribal administrative organizations. He describes it among the Khasis and others. In the autocratic Konyak village the Chieftainship called Ang or Wang still exists but the chief is gradually losing his status to the new elected and educated leaders. The Wanchu chiefs of Arunachal Pradesh have retained their traditional position and the halls of their enormous houses are still teeming with retainers and wives. Except for the fact that they could no longer have offenders put to death, the chiefs retain their judicial powers which they exercise in conjunction with the Village Council. Likewise he describes it among the Tangkhul Nagas and Tripuries.

The above-mentioned facts amply describes the political structure of almost all tribes of India.

Vidyarthi's contribution towards tribal development, tribal administration and tribal welfare are invaluable. He states that the approaches to tribal development/administration can be divided into two periods, viz., pre-Independence and post-Independence. On the pre-Independence period he says that in the ancient India the people considered the tribals living in the remote forest and hilly areas, part and parcel of Indian population. It was in the immediate past in the British period of Indian history that these people were approached in quite a different way. The national leaders never regarded them as a separate section of the Indian population. However, he has criticized the Indian Government of following the stereotyped policy of the British Government administration in a modified way.[20] He nevertheless says :

> Experience of a decade or so of the administration of free India, constant thinking of social references, political leaders of the nation and the Indian anthropologists as experts on the tribal ways of life found out a most desirable course for the integration of the tribal people in their respective regional and national setting.

Historically, he says, there have been three main approaches to tribal welfare/administration :

(1) Policy of Segregation :

(i) In pre-Independence period.
(ii) In post-Independence period.

(2) Assimilation : A result of constant contact of the tribes with the rest of Indian population and the efforts of social reformers.
(3) Integration of the tribes in regional and national setting.

These approaches may be viewed in some detail.

Policy of segregation : In pre-Independence period

Vidyarthi opines that the foremost policies which were adopted by the British rulers were to isolate these people from the general mass and separate the tribal areas from the purview of the normal administration. This administrative segregative adjustment was not at all realized by the rest of their countrymen as they were either too subdued or too ignorant to understand what was happening. This isolation, he says, led to much exploitation by non-tribal moneylenders, contractors, zamindars and middlemen. In the segregated areas, however, only a few such people could enter through the administration. But they were not welcomed by the tribes. Also their contact with non-tribals added to their strain of fighting a lone battle against nature in the hilly and forest areas.

The policy of isolation by the British Government was largely effected by their deliberate efforts not to develop communication in the tribal areas which, as a result, remained cut off from the rest of the population. He cites the example of the north-eastern Himalayan tribes. They had no communication with the rest of India and consequently a sense of separatism has developed in them.

In isolated tribal areas, he says, "a very small number of people were allowed, i.e., some contractors, Government officials and a few businessmen. They grouped together and started business on their own terms. They were there to interpret the rule, and their terms of business swept in purchase and sale of the goods and thus exploitation of an extreme degree pervaded." In some areas, he adds, "the British rulers also created 'excluded' and 'partially excluded' areas and gave them separate political representation." He supports the feeling of the national field that it was a wicked conspiracy to create a new separatist minority . . . And ultimately this precipitated the creation of Nagaland, a separate State, in 1960 with the population of a few lakhs.

He goes on to describe the "Scheduled Tracts" of the Government of India Act of 1870, "Scheduled District Act" of 1874, Acts of 1919 and 1935.

Segregation in post-Independence period

In the early period of Independence, Vidyarthi finds that the Government of India too adopted the policy of isolation though in a slightly modified form. He blames these policies for the separatist move, for instance the demand for an independent Naga State and an autonomous Jharkhand. The enlisting of the Scheduled Tribes, he says, also created the wrong impression of the tribals being under a special law. The constitutional safeguards, he adds, created constitutional gaps between general population and tribal population.

The assimilation

The assimilation of the tribal people with the rest of the population, says Vidyarthi, is another approach and is a continuous process and the culture contact with the neighbouring population is held responsible for it. In India, he finds, the tribal people have come in contact with different Hindu and other communities and situations have different degrees of culture contact leading to assimilation in different parts. Some tribals have gradually accepted the Hindu way of life and others have converted to Christianity. This culture contact has given rise to so many types of tribals and has created a set of different types of tribes on acculturation level. He finds that the process of assimilation has been a part and parcel of the Indian tribal culture. Citing examples of various tribes, like the Bhumijs, the Bhutias, the Gonds, the Mundas, the Oraons, the tribes of the north-west and central Himalayan regions, including Kols-Bhils, and the south Indian tribes, he says that the tribal people of different regions have assimilated themselves in the neighbouring folk people and have been in fully intimate contact with them.

Integration of the tribes in regional and national setting

Vidyarthi says "the base of India, i.e., 'unity in diversity' once again got its due importance. The social reformers, politicians, anthropologists as experts on the tribal ways of life and the administration combined their skills and adopted an integrated approach towards the tribals." Appreciating the Panchsheel, he says, "for the first time the late Jawaharlal Nehru gave a 'Panchsheel', i.e., five fundamental principles for the tribal upliftment, as an integrational approach which was later confirmed by the researches of anthropologists." He says the latest approaches for integration of the tribes are the following : (i) single-line administration, (ii) comparatively small districts due to communicational difficulties, and (iii) area development approach, etc.

Approaches to tribal welfare

Vidyarthi opines that there are mainly five approaches which have been employed so far for the welfare of the tribals in India. These are : (i) Political Approach, (ii) Administrative Approach, (iii) Religious Approach with special reference to Missionary Approach, (iv) Voluntary Approach, and (v) Anthropological Approach.

(i) *Political Approach* : The Political Approach, according to Prof. Vidyarthi, may be understood in the context of the pre- and post-Independence periods. We have already discussed his views on pre-Independence days. Coming to post-Independence period he describes the provisions of the Indian Constitution. Having described the constitutional provisions Vidyarthi opines that "the tribal people are politically democratic in nature. Their leaders respect each of their fellowmen. They have also received a share of about seven per cent in the Indian Republic through the Lok Sabha and Vidhan Sabha reserved seats. Only a tribal can stand for election to these seats. With the emergence of such new tribal leaders, no doubt, the tribal issues are getting politicized but he hopes that with the enlightened tribal leadership the solution of the problems of poverty will be accelerated in a peaceful democratic way. Lauding the work of various conferences he says,

> Various all-India tribal conferences organized by the Government or actively supported by it are indirectly creating a new solidarity in tribal India. In the context of present-day separatist trends specially numerous all-India and regional parties, the possible implications of such a development will have to be closely watched and analyzed.[21]

The division of whole of north-eastern India, he adds, into different full-fledged States like Nagaland, Meghalaya, Manipur and Tripura and Union Territories like Mizoram and Arunachal Pradesh has to be viewed not only from the point of view of tribal interests but also against the wider canvas of regional and national life.

(ii) *Administrative Approach* : The present structure of the administrative set-up for tribal welfare, opines Vidyarthi, has evolved through interactions among the national leaders, social workers, tribal elders and applied anthropologists. He explains the powers of the President of India to safeguard the interests of these communities. He also explains the works of the State Ministers in this regard. Likewise he goes on to explain the control of Parliament on the welfare activities and works of the different commissions and committees.

(iii) *Religious Approach with Special Reference to Missionary Approach* : Religious Approach has been attempted by different religious agencies like the Christian missionaries, the Ramakrishna Mission, the Arya Samaj and other local religious institutions. These agencies are also engaged in the welfare work for the tribals. At the same time conversion of tribes to a new faith, viz., Christianity, has also taken place. Vidyarthi finds that this conversion activity has formed in-groups among the tribals. The missionaries of various denominations have been active in different parts of tribal India specially in tribal Bihar, eastern Madhya Pradesh, north Orissa, in middle India and Meghalaya, Nagaland, and Mizoram in north-eastern Himalayas. Though they have been primarily interested in evangelization, the welfare work—educational, economic, hygienic and social called "work of mercy"—has invariably followed. He, however, has disapproved the separatist feeling created by the Christian missions. He opines :

"Although the advantages flowing from the social welfare measures introduced by the Missionaries have been of tremendous help to the tribals they would be greatly discounted when viewed in the context of the feeling created by Christian Tribals and Non-Christian Tribals in middle India and the separatist move . . . in north-eastern Himalayas.[22]

In view of the above, he concludes that if the conversion of tribes to a new faith adds to their social solidarity, without alienating them from the majority of neighbouring communities, and equips them better for participation in modern life, it cannot reasonably be opposed. But if it de-tribalizes and disintegrates these communities without offering them any alternative satisfaction, the approach can hardly be said to be offering any meaningful solution to the tribal problem.

(iv) *Voluntary Agencies Approach* : Under the Voluntary Agencies Approach, Vidyarthi opines, social workers, social welfare agencies, social movement agencies, social reformers, etc., are working to uplift the weaker sections of our society in their own ways.[23] He considers the Bhartiya Adimjati Sewak Sangh as the foremost. Describing the various voluntary agencies he opines :

> Voluntary social service organizations have done considerable humanitarian work in the tribal area, but often their idealism and spirit of service have not been matched by their understanding of tribal organization, values and problems. They sometimes went into the tribal areas with an omnibus solution to the tribal problems as they understood them, while in reality the problems for different tribal groups, and even for sections of one tribe, were often different. Their motives were probably laudable in their own cultural frame of reference, but not so against the tribal scheme of values. They failed to realize that their well-intentioned 'reforms' may be injurious to the tribes in terms of their socio-cultural life.[24]

(v) *Anthropological Approach* : Vidyarthi says that there is not one anthropological approach, there are anthropological approaches ; instead of offering an omnibus solution to tribal problems, the anthropologists have been thinking of possible solutions. He has a high opinion of Anthropological knowledge. He opines, "anthropological knowledge in the changed situation of the country as a Welfare State is again of great importance. By and large anthropologists believe in the ultimate integration of the tribes into the mainstream of Indian life. Some controversies took place in the thirties, forties and early fifties of the present century about contributions of anthropology to the tribals." Nevertheless, he concludes, "if the welfare projects are implemented with understanding and caution the first effective steps against primitiveness will have been taken. There is tribal life that can be preserved without reducing the tribals to the position of museum pieces and without bearing their logical development, and there is no doubt that this could be with imaginative planning and a carefully designed strategy of implementation.

Vidyarthi has thoroughly examined the administrative policies of the Scheduled Tribes since Independence.[25] Here we summarize his ideas on tribal development administration since Independence.

Reasons for poor impact of Tribal Development Programmes

The principal deficiencies (of tribal development) of the earlier plans, according to Vidyarthi, are in brief :

(1) Lack of special attention to tribal and scheduled areas in spite of constitutional provisions ;
(2) Very inadequate allotment of funds in both general and special sectors to cover all aspects of development of the tribal areas. As, for example, in the Third Plan the per capita expenditure on the tribals comes to Rs. 13.08, when both State and Central sectors are added together ;
(3) The major programmes of Tribal Development Blocks with a coverage of 25,000 tribal population per block was not significant enough for carrying to the tribal areas all the services essential for their full development ;
(4) Inadequate administrative machinery to integrate all the sectoral programmes. Coupled with it is the lack of coordination and integration at inter- and intra-departmental levels of the State and the Centre ;
(5) Lack of effective personnel policy of the Government which is reflected in the frequent transfer of key personnel in the administration, inadequate incentives to work in and for tribal areas, lack of specialized training in tribal culture as well as non-inculcation of the spirit of social service in them ;
(6) Failure on the part of the Government to adopt scientific planning and to ensure implementation based on research materials and findings ; and
(7) Excessive politicization of the tribal issues and failure on the part of tribal societies to throw up dedicated, articulate and enlightened local leaders.[26]

Separate Tribal Development Programme

It is high time, he believes, that the Scheduled Tribes and Scheduled Areas are classified in terms of ecosystems and levels of development. He opines, "believing that there is a similar pattern of poverty and exploitation, two ethnic groups of Scheduled Tribes/Castes have been lumped together for the purposes of diagnosing their maladies and improving their socio-economic conditions". He believes that it is an inappropriate approach, as it blurs the correct understanding of their problems, and steps taken for their amelioration become inadequate and faulty. He gives the following reasons for a separate tribal development programme :

> Ecologically, while the tribals are isolated, the scheduled castes are exposed. Demographically, the former are concentrated in certain continuous geographical areas, while the latter are scattered in the villages of high castes. Economically, while the former are tied up with land and forest, the latter are mostly dependent on the high caste villagers ; culturally the former enjoy a distinct style of life characterized by a distinct language and heritage, love for freedom and respect for self-identity while the latter occupy the lowest rung in the caste hierarchy and suffer from social disabilities and loss of self-respect. To a social doctor they will appear as two groups suffering from two distinct types of maladies deserving different therapies.[27]

Area Development Approach

Vidyarthi believes that the constitutional configuration of "Scheduled Areas" needs rethinking as it includes certain tribal areas which could have been declared as "Scheduled" in view of its tribal concentration and ecosystem. The divisions of tribal areas under Tribal Development Blocks, delineated on national criteria earlier, have been realized, of late, by the Government of India as too small for planning integrated economic development of the area. In the new area development approach, these Tribal Development Blocks may constitute for the purposes of planning and implementation "micro-areas". Such a meso-area may fall within or coincide with the district boundary. A still larger area of tribal concentration (e.g. 50 per cent of the total population) may be termed as "Macro-Development Region". Within this macro-development region a categorization of extremely backward and backward areas may be envisaged. He felt that the criteria for the classification of "regions" and "backwardness" required more careful study.[28] He suggested the following diagnostic features :

(a) Proportion of tribal population engaged in the primary sector of economy (hunting, food-gathering, shifting cultivation, agriculture, craft, etc.) ;

(b) Percentage of literacy to be determined with reference to average literacy in the State as well as average literacy of tribals at the all-India level ;

(c) Eco-social system, topography, soil, climate, drainage, density of population, nature of labour supply, etc. ;
(d) Health and sanitary conditions ;
(e) Nature and extent of drinking water supply ;
(f) State of irrigation and power ;
(g) State of industry ;
(h) Condition of roads and state of transport ;
(i) Percentage of urban population and employment in urbanized industries.

In the light of adequate materials, the areas of tribal concentration are to be grouped into Development Regions considering the coverage of area, population, ethnic composition and other factors of natural resources, level of development, and other related factors. They are to be further classified in terms of meso- and micro-regions for the purposes of planning and implementation of schemes through administrative machinery. In the case of Bihar, for example, the existing region of Chotanagpur and Santhal Pargana may be carved out as one such Development Region.

Welfare Development

Vidyarthi believes that the concept of "welfare" needs to be partly replaced by that of "development". The existing approach of giving doles to tribals, he thinks, has not yielded the desired results. He feels that this emphasis on development of tribals and tribal areas will necessitate changes in the Government policy, reorganization of their departments and intensive training programmes for officers who will work in tribal areas. The whole training programme in the tribal areas needs to be reviewed and reinforced, along with the question of personnel policies to ensure the implementation of the accepted policies. For example, it is conceded by everyone that better officers should be posted in tribal areas and that such areas should not be treated as places for punishment postings.

Single Line Administration Approach

In view of the simplicity of the tribals, a unified single-line administration for tribals was suggested by Vidyarthi. He advised that the head of the regional authority should be made responsible for the implementation of tribal policies and programmes. At such a level, an expert in tribal culture should function as his adviser, who should also share his responsibility in the implementation of the programmes. In the light of the new strategy for tribal development, these and other related issues should be carefully studied with the help of experts on tribal culture, tribal economy, personnel management and tribal administration.

Special Scheme for Primitive Pockets and Isolated Tribes

The tribes living in isolated hilly and forest areas of certain districts in the country, according to Vidyarthi, have remained the least beneficiaries of all. These are numerically minor tribes and have not been able to attract the attention of policy-makers and the administrative machinery so far owing to their isolation and lack of preparedness to face the challenge of backwardness. The problems of these less developed tribal communities of India, according to Vidyarthi, need to be taken up on an urgent and priority basis. In view of their unique economic, educational as well as other specific problems, a community-based scheme should be prepared on the basis of their felt needs. It is heartening to note that the Ministry of Home Affairs has started implementing these proposals of the Planning Commission from 1975. The new strategies also ensure the use of research materials and involvement of specialists in a big way.

Thus, it is to the credit of Vidyarthi whose efforts have brought together the worlds of the academician and the administrator. The two worlds were completely apart and its denizens lived in water-tight compartments, unaware of what was going on beyond the walls created by themselves. The result was that theory and practice remained poles apart. Now both sides can derive benefits from the experiences of each other.

Administration is said to be culture bound. The relationship between culture and administration has been fully established by Vidyarthi. He opines :

"In their zeal to "better the lives", of others, planners and administrators overlook the cultural background of the community and make desperate efforts to alter the way of life by introducing modern technology and methods even in tradition-bound societies. Such desperate efforts to interfere with the life-style of the people sometimes by a team or by sponsors of cross-cultural missions is bound to meet with "resistance".

"Our researches among the various dimensions of Indian society go to establish that people resist such changes that go to interfere with their respective core culture or their basic cultural adjustments. They also resist the proposed changes they either do not understand or interpret differently in their respective cultural backgrounds. In some cases, the resistance is of an emotional nature too, as a plan or project is imposed on them without taking them into confidence."[29]

He classified the tribes of Bihar in terms of their cultural, ecological and economic adaptations into five categories : (1) Forest hunting type, (2) Hill cultivation type, (3) Settled agricultural type, (4) Simple artisan type, and (5) Industrial and non-industrial labour type.

Vidyarthi believes that development means "growth" plus "change". It involves both the materials and the human factors.[30] He suggests that administrators and planners should not ignore cultural factors and the traditional background of the tribes while developing them. Instead of making all tribes agriculturists, make hunters better hunters, shifting cultivators better shifting cultivators, agriculturists better agriculturists introducing modern methods, artisans better artisans, labourers better labourers by giving them simple and sophisticated training and so on.

Having explained the above-mentioned views of Vidyarthi on History, Politics and Administration the author is fully convinced that he has not been able to do full justice to Vidyarthi. In fact his writings are so vast that it is not possible to condense all his views in one short paper. However a sincere effort was surely made.

References

1. L.P. Vidyarthi and B.K. Rai, *The Tribal Culture of India*, Concept Publishing Company 1977, pp. 26-29.
2. Ibid., p. 26.
3. W.W. Hunter, *Comparative Dictionary of the non-Aryan Languages of India and High Asia*, with a dissertation, London, 1868, pp. 1-32.
4. L.P. Vidyarthi and B.K. Rai, *The Tribal Culture of India*, op. cit., p. 29.
5. Ibid., pp. 30-31 and L.P. Vidyarthi and K.N. Sahay, *Dynamics of Tribal Leadership in Bihar*, Kitab Mahal, 1976, pp. 30-31.
6. Ibid., p. 33.
7. L.P. Vidyarthi and K.N. Sahay, *Dynamics of Tribal Leadership in Bihar*, pp. 36-37.
8. L.P. Vidyarthi and B.K. Rai, op. cit., p. 36.
9. Ibid., p. 36.
10. L P. Vidyarthi and K.N. Sahay, *Dynamics of Tribal Leadership*, op. cit., pp. 41-80.
11. L.P. Vidyarthi and B.K. Rai, *The Tribal Culture of India*, op. cit., p. 231.
12. L.P. Vidyarthi, "Some Preliminary Observations on Emerging Patterns of Leadership in Tribal India". Emerging Patterns of Rural Leadership in Southern Asia, Govt. of India, National Institute of Community Development, Hyderabad (1965), 180.
13. Ibid., p. 188.
14. *Tribal Culture of India*, op. cit., p. 231.
15. "Some Preliminary Observations on Emerging Patterns of Leadership in Tribal India", op. cit., pp. 179-184. *Tribal Culture of India*, op. cit., pp. 231-235.
16. *Rise of Anthropology in India*, Concept, Delhi, 1978, Vol. I, p. 16 ; Vol. II, pp. 222-226.
17. *Dynamics of Tribal Leadership*, op. cit., p. 262.
18. Ibid., pp. 359-367.
19. *The Tribal Culture of India*, op. cit., pp. 195-235.
20. Ibid.
21. *The Tribal Culture of India*, op. cit., p. 412.
22. Ibid.
23. Ibid., p. 428.
24. Vide Peasant Organization in India, Council of Social Science and Cultural Research, Bihar, Ranchi, 1977.

25. *The Tribal Culture in India*, Concept, *Tribal Development and its Administration*, Concept, New Delhi, 1981, *Tribal Development in India* (ed.), Buddhadeb Chaudhuri, "The Profiles of the Marginal and Pre-farming Tribes of Central Eastern India", Report of the Task Force submitted to the Planning Commission in 1973, etc.
26. L.P. Vidyarthi, "Problems and Prospects of Tribal Development in India", *Tribal Development in India* (ed.), Buddhadeb Chaudhuri, Inter-India Publications, New Delhi, pp. 376-377.
27. Ibid., pp. 376-377.
28. For details see report of the Task Force submitted to the Planning Commission in 1973.
39. L.P. Vidyarthi, The Cultural Factors in Development Process : Case Studies from Tribal Bihar, *Tribal Development and Its Administration*, Concept, 1981, pp. 3-4.

REVIEW ARTICLES

REVIEW ARTICLES

The Sacred Complex in Hindu Gaya, *by L.P. Vidyarthi,* Concept Publishing Company, (New Delhi, 1978 Second Edition), Bombay, Asia Publishing House, 1962 (First Edition).

—*Reviewed by* D.N. MAJUMDAR

Dr. Vidyarthi has done me a great honour by asking me to write a foreword to his book. *The Sacred Complex in Hindu Gaya*—a study of the Gayawal of Bihar. Good wine does not need any brush and neither does Dr. Vidyarthi want me to give him a testimonial. As a distinguished pupil, and a loyal one, he has roped me in to show his courtesy, and I am indeed happy to be associated with his useful work, on a levitical sect which has had a spectacular past but today faces an anxious future. I had some acquaintance with an earlier manuscript of his, on his field assignment, for his M.A. degree at Lucknow where Dr. Vidyarthi recorded the Culture of the dying Gayawal Community. In the present volume Dr. Vidyarthi has given an analytical study of the sacred complex that had motivated the survival of the Community in the past. The changing values and attitudes in popular Hinduism have made significant dents into the Cultural life of the Gayawal, their ritual status has declined and the structural facades are showing signs of fissures which are widening into schisms likely to destroy the structure itself. In the present volume, Dr. Vidyarthi comes to grips with theoretical problems and has selected the part of Gaya, which incidentally shapes into the study of a traditional city, and of a traditional city, and of a traditional community and brings out the importance of Gaya as a pilgrim city with its sacred specialists, the Gayawal. The methodological orientation is the unique feature of Dr. Vidyarthi's contribution. The theoretical stand and the rich material on which he elaborates provide an excellent analytical study of a levitical sect that faces evil days.

In the context of the growing tourist traffic, the question of a professional order, alive to the needs of the tourist public with adequate education and training associated with our larger temples and sacred cities, has assumed significance. One feels unhappy, if not bitter, when one meets the temple priests and guides who sell our religion and mythology to the inquisitive tourists and pilgrims, for they are indeed a miserable lot, both physically and mentally. These render a dubious service to the visitors and pilgrims, and they are more pitied than liked, for most of them have been reduced to penury and social incompetence, and parade the temples and their precincts with the beggar's bowl. The proposed institution of a cadre of temple guides, for more informed service to the public and international tourists is so far so good and will certainly raise the effectiveness of our foreign exchange approach, but it would be pertinent to ask how far our temple and religious lore will be safe in the hands of the new initiates, and how far the values of our society will remain intact when secularization is pushed to its logical end. The rehabilitation of the levitical communities, particularly of those that cater to our religious education in the centres of sacred contacts, requires a planned approach, and it would be a halfway measure to replace for traditional caterers of religion by a new order whose interests and orientation may be entirely secular.

Our temples and centres of religious pilgrimage are our heritage and give the configuration of India's personality. The folk beliefs, rituals and learning that are associated with them are difficult to separate, or even identify. The story is not merely in the scriptures and temple art and architecture, but in the folkways and the mores which are inextricably woven into the "sacred complex" of the cities and temples. The levitical community which still survives, possesses this knowledge, and even the illiterate among it have a deep interest and knowledge of the oral literature that provides the benchmark data on the religious life of our people. It is necessary to recover this knowledge ; to rediscover them from the memory of these people and from the palimpsest manuscripts that some families do still preserve. What is needed is not a sudden divorce from traditional practice, but a *modus vivendi*, which will secure the sacred lore and ritual practices on the one hand, and provide an orientation for the levitical community on the other, both of which will help in the rehabilitation of the latter, particularly those that already manifest signs of exhaustion and maladaptation. The Gayawal, or for that matter any priestly community who live on temple traffic and the benefits of pilgrimage (and there are many such communities in India) need to develop initiative, which they had and have lost, and the Government of the country owes it to them to find out solutions for their miseries and maladaptation.

To millions of Hindus in India, Gaya is holy and very important. Volumes have been written by the sacred character of the place, its architecture, its traditional history and its place in orthodox Hindu society. Gaya is the passport for the future life of the pious Hindu and his happiness beyond. Prof. Kane has discussed the "sacred complex" of Gaya in his inimitable erudite style, and has opened up the hidden recesses that have stored up the knowledge, and wisdom of our saints and prophets, of bygone days, (*History of Dharmashastra*), Vol. IV, Poona,

1953). Prof. Kane writes of Gaya as follows, "Gaya appears to have passed through several vicissitudes. Some centuries before the Christian era it was in existence and was a flourishing town. By A.D. 400 it had been reduced to desolation." But in the seventh century the Chinese traveller Hiouen Th Sang notes that Hindu Gaya was a town with a thousand Brahmin families. Later on when Buddhism waned and vanished, Gaya came to comprehend even Buddhist remnants since the *Vayu-Purana* speaks of Gaya as extending from Pretasila to the Mahabodhi Tree (a distance of about 13 miles, according to R.L. Mitra).

It is no use entering into an academic discussion about the antiquity of Gaya. Our problem is that of the Gayawal. Prof. Kane writes, "The Gayawals are notorious and ignorant and they are a dying race." According to O'Malley, "the families of Gayawals were 1,484." In Buchaman Hamilton's time they numbered about 1,000. In 1893, Gayawal families in the Census of 1901, there existed 168 males (as pure Gayawal) and 153 families (*Ibid.*, p. 644).

Writing about the literature on Gaya, Prof. Kane says "the most important work on Gaya relied upon such works as the *Tristhali* Setu and in modern times is the *Gaya-Mahatmya* that occurs at the end of the *Vayu-Purana* (Chapter 105-112 of the Amandasrma Edition)." Scholars differ about the antiquity of the chapters. Rajendra Lal Mitra assigned the *Gaya-Mahatmya* to the third or fourth centuries A.D. O'Malley was inclined to hold that the legend of Gayasura was invented in the fourteenth or fifteenth centuries, principally on the ground that the Gayawal profess the Vaishnava faith established by Madhavacharya and acknowledge as their spiritual head the Mahant of Hari Nara Singhapura (Vide *J.A.S.B.*, Vol. LXXII, 1903, No. 4, p. 644, *History of Dharamshastra*, Vol. IV, Poona, 1953). Dr. Vidyarthi has given an account of the legned of Gayasura.

The Gayawal claim to have been especially created by Lord Brahma. They minister to the needs of ceremonial service to the Hindus, at the time of the *Shraddha*, and they are supposed to be the sole ministers at the latter ceremonies. Dr. Vidyarthi has collected a lot of first-hand data on the Gayawal community and the analytical study he has presented will be of immense value in the field of "current" anthropology, which reduces, and eliminates in some cases, the distance between urban and rural, tribal and caste societies. The methodology that Dr. Vidyarthi has projected into this analytical study probably would be open to challenge for the concepts like "great" and "little" traditions, cultural specialists, cultural performances and cultural media have not been standardized and we do not always speak with the same voice. Dr. Vidyarthi knows the strength and weakness of the concepts, like "great" and "little" traditions, which now have come into fashion. Again the concept of continuity of folk and urban traditions has its zealous champions in our country, but Dr. Vidyarthi has a critical and yet appreciative mind. He has, for example, shown the process of conflict and compromise between Hindu and Buddhist ways of life and thought, and, incidentally, similar conflict between urban and rural living. This is in keeping with the background of our culture-history. Our sacred literature depicts the succession of cultural traditions. Imposition of one culture on another, and the mixture and assimilation of culture by culture. Neither is there ample nor convincing proof of the cultural continuity in India as Prof. Milton Singer has figured out. There has not been any systematic study of urban and rural life in India, there has not been much meticulous analysis of Indian Culture, as such, and our concepts of Indian Culture, particularly those that are now being imported, are based on meagre and often superficial acquaintance with Indian life and institutions. Indian Culture, if it admits of reconstruction, is characterized by diversity rather than unity, and a superficial acquaintance with it has underlined similarity and strangeness.

In a paper on Japanese folk-beliefs Prof. Ichiro Hori (*Am. Anth.*, Vol. 61, No. 3, pp. 405, 436 ; 1959) has referred to the Japanese folk-belief the essence of which he writes "lies in the interaction of two beliefs systems, a little tradition which is based on blood or close community ties, and a great tradition, introduced from without which is adopted by individual or group choice." By "little" tradition Prof. Hori means the native or folk religions including the advanced Shinto which came out of the ancient Japanese geographic and cultural circumstances ; by the "great" tradition, he means Confucianism, Taoism and Buddhism—highly developed religious and philosophical importations. Apparently Prof. Hori could not give more specific "configuration to "little" and "great" tradition, and he coined another phrase "the more advanced little traditions". This is inevitable, when one delves into the belief systems in countries which have a continuity of civilization for thousands of years, and had to receive and accept beliefs, practices and values, imparted from outside, producing a complex web of life and culture. There are little traditions, big traditions and great traditions, even greater, and it is hardly possible to isolate them, to be of use as diagnostic recipes.

Dr. Vidyarthi has formulated and used terms like sacred centres, sacred segments, sacred cluster, sacred zone, sacred ground, sacred geography, to describe the social organization of the temples. He describes the sacred complex of a place of pilgrimage, and thinks that such a concept is applicable even to tribal religions in India, with their sacred groves, sacred performances, and sacred rituals. Dr. Vidyarthi, however, does not use "sacred" in the same way in which E. Durkheim had used it, i.e., "sacred" as distinguished from profane. He has used "sacred" as distinct from "secular" and has shown the possibility of a reorganization of the sacred complex, which might show the way to rehabilitate the sacred community of the Gayawal.

Dr. L.P. Vidyarthi has done a good piece of original work, he has not followed the traditional path that anthropologists in India have so long preferred to follow ; which has been uptil now the "great tradition" of Indian Anthropology, viz., the study of tribal cultures or rural life. He has pointed to the new foci of anthropological interest, the study of cities and centres of culture, and I am sure others will follow in the study of problems of urban complexes and the process of "secondary urbanization", as he prefers to categorize it.

I am happy that I could add a few words to highlight the rich fare the book has provided, both for the professional anthropologists and for the anthropologically oriented laymen.

The Sacred Complex in Hindu Gaya, *by L.P. Vidyarthi,* Asia Publishing House, 1961. New York. *American Anthropologist,* Vol. 64, No. 2, 1962.

—*Reviewed by* MORRIS E. OPLER

The north Indian city of Gaya and its environs in the State of Bihar have long been a centre of ritual activity. A few miles south in the city proper is the site of the Bodhi tree under which the Buddha is said to have received enlightenment. This shrine draws Buddhist pilgrims from many parts of the world, and Hindus, too, worship there, for the Buddha has been absorbed into the Hindu pantheon as one of the Avatars of Vishnu. At Gaya there are temples and shrines to every important god or goddess of Hinduism. Consequently, as calendrical rites in honour of this deity or that occur, there is a constant round of ceremonies. But despite the variety of religious functions that take place at Gaya, a devout Hindu from any part of India can explain that Gaya is especially noted as the place to which one goes to carry on the shraddha ceremony (memorial sacrifices) in honour of deceased relatives of the paternal line. In this book, Dr. Vidyarthi gives us an overview of the many strands of ritual that meet at Gaya, but his main emphasis is upon the Gayawal, the priests who have primary responsibility for the shraddha ceremony, and upon the details of the ceremony through which they lead the pilgrims.

The Gayawal are a group of 120 Brahman families which claim the hereditary right to conduct the shraddha ceremonies at Gaya. Their claim goes back to a sacred legend which tells how a demon, Gaya, Asur, became so powerful through his performance of austerities that he threatened to rival the gods themselves. He was slain by the deities and rites were performed on his body. According to the legend, the ancestral Gayawal were created by Brahma to aid in the sacrifice. The outstretched remains of the demon became the portion of the city of Gaya given over to religious activities, the Gayawal and their descendants were made responsible for the rites to be carried on at this spot for the benefit of the dead.

The Gayawal, as Dr. Vidyarthi describes them, are a compact group. They are endogamous but are divided into 14 exogamous patri-clans or gotra. Consciousness of lineage is strong, and ritual privileges of considerable economic value ordinarily are inherited in the male line. The Gayawal have a strong preference for the joint family. All the Gayawal live in the same quarter of Gaya and are further unified and set aside from others by peculiarities of food habits, dress, and speech.

Other features of the contemporary Gayawal are their orthodoxy and conservatism. They have been cool to newer forms of education and consider every liberal trend in social or political life a threat to religion. Consequently, they are being increasingly isolated and alienated from events in modern India.

The relationship of the Gayawal with their customers and with other Brahmans and ritualists is complex and fascinating. Members of each Gayawal lineage have the right to conduct ceremonies for pilgrims from some specific section of India. In order to stimulate interest among potential customers in coming to Gaya, priests or their representatives pay visits to the areas from which their allotted pilgrims come, and they give lectures on the glories of Gaya. At Gaya the shrine priests keep elaborate accounts of the visits of pilgrims which record the names, villages, and other details about the sacrificers. Pilgrims are gratified to see proof of the visits of their ancestors in years past to the same shrine city.

The Gayawal have the central place in the conduct of the shraddha ceremony, but they interact with other ritualists and participants who have become involved in the procedures. A group of Brahmans, called Acharya, carries on some of the rites under the direction of the Gayawal. Non-Brahman ritualists, called Dhami, lead the pilgrims to certain sacred centres by arrangement with the Gayawal, barbers, florists, grain sellers, and others are present to offer commodities and services when needed.

Dr. Vidyarthi tries to give as much time depth as possible to his discussion of Gaya and the Gayawal. He produces evidence to show how various shrines and centres of Gaya have become more prominent or have lost favour with pilgrims over the centuries. He suggests that symbols and images which once were associated with Buddhism or with local folk belief have gradually been absorbed into the shraddha complex.

The author believes that "the style of life" of the Gayawal has changed markedly through the years, too. He thinks that before 1800 the Gayawal were mainly concerned with the proper discharge of their priestly duties. After 1800 better communications and the suppression of banditry made travel easier for wealthy and highly placed pilgrims, and the Gayawal flourished. Many of them succumbed to luxurious living and shallow thinking. Now, because of the abolition of landlordism, secularization, partition, and other causes, patronage has decreased sharply and the Gayawal are in economic distress.

Perhaps the least satisfying aspect of the study is the attempt to force the data into the Redfield-Singer "great tradition—little tradition" mould. The pilgrims come to Gaya in part to carry out filial obligations to ancestors and in part out of fear of the ghosts of the departed. There are rituals in Gaya to take care of both of these concerns. Yet we are given to understand, for no convincing reason I can see, that the practices to allay the fear of ghosts are part of the "little", "rural", or "local" tradition and those having to do with other kinds of sacrifices to the spirits of the dead are "great tradition", "Sanskritic", "universal", and "urban". But the fear of ghosts is hardly local in principle. It is found all over India. It is as "Sanskritic" as anything else in Hinduism. References to it are found in the Vedas, Sutras, and the Puranas. It is as characteristic of a city like Gaya as it is of the villages from which the pilgrims come. I am suspicious of the attempts to read sequence or "greatness" and "littleness" into these matters. What is called the "great tradition often appears to be the more abstract and philosophic component of Hinduism, and what is called the "little tradition" seems to be the more earthy and emotionally laden segment.

But whether or not we accept all of Dr. Vidyarthi's terminology and theory, we are sure to be impressed by the amount of information and illumination he has provided in this pioneering effort. We have been sadly in need of some analysis of the internal organization of the religious centres which dot India, and Dr. Vidyarthi has so well demonstrated how rewarding studies of this kind can be that others are sure to follow. Another happy feature of the book is the personal life histories of Gayawal informants which are included in an appendix. They reveal more about Brahmanical family life than anything else I have seen in print.

The Sacred Complex in Hindu Gaya, *by L.P. Vidyarthi,* Asia Publishing House, Calcutta, Bombay, New York, London, 1961. *Sociology.*

—*Reviewed by* S.C. SINHA

Dr. L.P. Vidyarthi is to be congratulated for traversing off the beaten tract of conventional ethnography in this volume on the Sacred City of Gaya. Rather than collecting data on yet another "Tribal Group" or "Village Community" he has attempted to reach the core of Indian civilization by studying clusters of Sacred Institutions or "Sacred Complexes" that have grown around the ancient and yet modern city of Gaya. With admirable skill he presents his complex data, representing cultural accretions over 2,000 years, through a number of descriptive devices of his own. Even in his essentially synchronic presentation of the data, one never fails to grasp the dynamics of the transformation scene.

The book consists of six chapters with a thought-provoking Introduction to the theoretical formulation by the author and a very appreciative foreword by late Professor D.N. Mazumdar. The first chapter outlining the "Sacred geography" of the city of Gaya brings out the varying spatial and temporal significance of the numerous sacred centres in Gaya. In the second chapter, the different types of sacred performances including the shraddha observed at Gaya have been discussed with a view to bringing out the processes of Continuity, Compromise and Combination of the great and little traditions in Indian civilization. The following three chapters are mainly devoted to the study of the Gayawal as an example of "sacred specialists". In these chapters, the style of priestly life, the network of structural relationship of the Gayawal with the rest of Hindu universe, and then the dynamics of their social and religious organisation have been analysed in order to understand the roles that the Gayawal as high priests and other such sacred specialists have played in transforming the folk traditions of the Indian villages to higher Brahmanical traditions. Thus, analysing the "Sacred Complex" of a traditional city of India Dr. Vidyarthi not only brings to our light concrete data on Gaya and the Gayawal but opens up a large area for scientific research on Priestly groups, on Indian towns and cities, and on evolution and change within Hinduism as such. I have been pleased with the skill of the author's presentation of a wealth of data compressed into a reasonable size, in the very able combination of concrete data and abstraction in a way that the result is neither an ineffective jabbering of formula nor an unweildy mass of irrelevant data.

To my mind, it is one of the most significant contributions to social anthropology of India by an Indian author.

With very attractive get-up, nice-printing, suitable illustrations and numerous appendices and tables, the book is very reasonably priced and is sure to attract the attention of both professionals and laymen of all over the world.

The Sacred Complex in Hindu Gaya, *by L.P. Vidyarthi*, 1961, Asia Publishing House, Calcutta, *Man in India*, Vol. 42, No. 1

—*Reviewed by* N.K. BOSE

Dr. L.P. Vidyarthi has tried to strike a new note in Indian social anthropology. He has picked up one of the sacred institutions of the Hindus which is not only clothed with ritual significance but is also intimately related to the Hindu's association with the departed. Gaya is a famous pilgrimage in Bihar to which people resort from all parts of India in order to perform prescribed funerary ceremonies. A geographically well-marked area is held sacred, while there are attached areas of subsidiary importance. A class of priests has sprung up here to serve the needs of visiting pilgrims.

Dr. Vidyarthi has taken a detailed census of the priests, and tried to describe how their functions have varied in course of history. Priestcraft incorporates here not only elements of high Hindu religion but also those derived from more restricted "folk-cults'. The priests of Gaya subscribe to certain values ; but history tells us that they have not always remained steady in their adherence. Wealth has exercised its temptations, and conspicuous ostentation has been followed by a decline in morals.

Certain historical facts have been utilized by the author in course of his analysis. But his main reliance has been on the questionnaire method supplemented by copious observation. As a result, there emerges a satisfactory picture of Hindu ritualism and it functions at the levels of social operation and religious beliefs.

In one of the appendices, there is presented a series of seven autobiographies of Gayawals, as these have emerged in the course of Dr. Vidyarthi's prolonged interviews. The biographies have not been woven into the texture of his main picture, but form a supplement helpful in explaining how life has undergone changes in recent times. As such, they form an independent material of great interest.

While closely reading the book, one is likely to gather the impression that the work was done in parts, and then woven into a whole. Consequently, there is a faint lack of cohesion. Facts stand out a little more obstreperously than the inward relation which binds them together. As the facts are meaningful, and as they are of an original nature in Indian anthropology, we are hopeful that the author's present work will open up further ways of understanding Hindu civilization for which an anthropologist is perhaps better fitted than a historian.

The Maler : A Study in Nature-Man-Spirit Complex of a Hill Tribe in Bihar, *by L.P. Vidyarthi*, Bookland Private Ltd., Calcutta, 1963.

—*Reviewed by* JULIAN H. STEWARD

Professor Vidyarthi presents a vivid, penetrating and sympathetic analysis of the Maler, a primitive hill tribe of India. The Maler, or Paharia, constitute an enclave within the great civilization of India and are even linked tenuously with the larger society in several ways, but they fail to share the basic institutions of that society. The "little tradition" of the Maler, to use Redfield's term, does not reflect the "great tradition" of India. It has no castes, occupational specialists, urban concentrations, or States. Its supernaturalism has been influenced little if at all by Buddhism, Islam, or Christianity. Particulars show considerable borrowing from their neighbours on the plains, the Santhal, but much less from Hinduism.

Like several other hill peoples of India, the Maler live in an infertile and rather inaccessible habitat which has insulated them from fundamental impacts of the larger society. Moreover, their local traditions, which are very old ones, are unable to assimilate alien patterns. They represent social and spiritual adjustments to omnipresent threats of starvation, sickness and death. The Malers' anxieties are deep, constant and rarely below the surface of consciousness.

Despite the extreme difficulties of fieldwork, Professor Vidyarthi and his students from Bihar University (now Ranchi University) made extended visits to the Maler over the course of several years. They were able to win the confidence of the people, analyse their economic, social and religious life and record other special kinds of data. This volume is a basic ethnographic monograph, which covers virtually all aspects of culture, but the emphasis is upon the subsistence activities, social arrangements, and supernaturalism involved in the struggle to survive. Professor Vidyarthi has wisely relegated other materials to a series of appendices.

The central theme is that the Maler are motivated by two basic drives, hunger for food and need for sex, which the Maler also conceive as a hunger. The unrelenting anxieties that surround subsistence, health and sex are expressed in a religious system, which includes a considerable complex of supernatural beings, religious personnel and ceremonialism. Professor Vidyarthi's analysis makes the religious complex extremely interesting, not because its ingredients are unique, but by demonstrating how the Maler have related the beliefs and practices functionally to the needs and fears of the people and to different levels within the social structure: the individual, the family, the lineage, the village, and the region. Professor Vidyarthi shows how the structuring of society within each of these levels in turn represents organizations of the people for the purposes of subsistence, sexual satisfaction, procreation, socialization of children, and patterns of interaction and co-operation appropriate to these goals. An important orienting concept is that of cultural ecology or the adaptation of social arrangements to the requirements of surviving in this harsh environment by means of a certain technological inventory.

The relationships of the family, lineage and community to one another and to productive processes are especially provocative in view of their significance for comparative studies. Despite a fairly rich inventory of crops, including maize and rice, domesticated animals, including cattle, goats, hogs and chickens, and forest products, the rocky hilly and forested lands make subsistance very precarious. Slash-and-burn cultivation requires a new clearing each year, for land is usually cultivated a second time only after the lapse of at least five years. Frequently, the crop is partly or entirely lost owing to wild animals, insects and other adversities.

Social structure consists of interpersonal arrangements adapted to the exploitation of resources, satisfaction of sex, child rearing and manipulation of supernatural beings. The basis of society is the nuclear family, which, in six villages, averages only 3.8 persons. The family, which is sometimes polygynous, occupies its own hut, own forest lands for slash-and-burn farming, and is the ultimate unit of consumption. But the isolated family is unable to cope with many crucial tasks. In clearing and preparing the forests for planting, in constructing houses, and in other chores, it needs assistance. The first call for co-operative help is always to other members of the patrilineage.

Professor Vidyarthi's detailed analysis of the Maler lineage raises some interesting questions. The lineage is reckoned through only three generations, and it consists of an average of four nuclear families. Each family has an average of 3.8 persons—a total of 15.2 lineage. Marriage is forbidden within three generations of each line of descent. The Maler have a term to distinguish the lineage from other social units, but it seems structurally to be little more than an extended family which is patrilineal in inheritance of farm lands. These lineages are very small as compared with lineage segments or primary lineages elsewhere. They are minimal in size, perhaps subminimal. Families average only 1.8 children, and the population of Professor Vidyarthi's principal village has shrunk to one quarter of its size of 50 years ago. The patrilineal hunting bands among the Australians, Bushmen, Fuegians, and others consist of lineages of 40 or more persons. Some of the single-house lineages of the Northwest Amazon are still larger. Lineages in Africa and Asia discussed by Leach, Bohannan, Fortes, Evans Pritchard and others are so large as to have segmented into many primary corporate units.

A population which barely perpetuates is numbers must average two offspring per family who in turn produce two offspring and so on. If relationship is traced through the male line for only three generations, the minimum cannot be less than three families—grandfather, father and son with additional kin and children of the son. The total lineage membership might range between 10 and 20 persons. A large lineage means either that the population is expanding or that descent is reckoned beyond three generations.

In the light of Professor Vidyarthi's data, two ways of enlarging the sphere of co-operation of the lineage or extended family suggests themselves. First, the family or minimal lineage may be enlarged by reckoning relationship back to five or six generations. Thus, four generations would double the average of 15 persons of the three generational lineage to 30 persons. Five generations would make it 60 persons, and so on. Knowledge of ancestry to five or six generations among a people without a sense of history or genealogy would be lost only if there were taboos which erased knowledge of deceased ancestors. Extension of lineage beyond five or six generations ordinarily occurs only where there is a fairly sophisticated society. large population, and sense—or myth—of genealogy. Second, instead of lineage expansion, other lineages within the same community may participate in co-operative enterprises. The Maler village consists of three to seven lineages, which are related through intermarriage and cooperate in many village-level functions. Without detailed cross-cultural comparisons, one cannot be sure in any instance whether co-operation within an enlarged lineage of four to six generations or between smaller lineages within the village is a function of the nature of land use, residence patterns, and other factors. It seems clear that patrilineal hunting bands reckon relationship which five or six generations because lineage land tenure and co-operative hunting within territories of optimum size would be badly disjoined if lineages were to split after three generations. Maler land tenure is on a family basis, and there appears to be no reason why regulation of sex, ceremonialism and other activities within the village cannot be carried on by inter-lineage co-operation.

Among other provocative features of Professor Vidyarthi's monograph is the relationship of various types of social interaction, especially of co-operation, to levels and territories of integration. The village achieves cohesion through marriages between its lineages, through common shrines, ceremonies and sacrifices, through a hereditary priest (*majhiye*) who is also the secular leader, through a youth dormitory, and through association of village members in daily activities which creates bonds that cross-cut kinship ties.

The nuclear family, extended family or lineage and village are the basic, and probably the oldest, patterns. Social interaction fades beyond the village, but it is not absent. Members of a Maler village may intermarry, offer co-operative assistance, attend ceremonies and visit weekly markets at other Maler villages. The Maler area or region of social interaction includes about 80 villages within a radius of 8 to 10 miles. That of the lowland Santhal includes 500 villages within a 40-mile radius. "The Maler have a regional headman, *sardar*, whose office dates from pre-British times, but whose duties are ill-defined. Today, he collects taxes and maintains law and order. Interaction with the lowland people, especially the Santhal, is largely economic. The Maler sell local forest products, borrow money, and sometimes hire labour. Borrowing of money and hiring labour, however, seem to be functions of a marginal, transitional situation. Plough cultivation with its greater cash requirements is moving up from the lowland, but it has not penetrated the culture of the true hill Maler. These inter-regional cash transactions have introduced money to the Maler to the extent that fines for breaches of taboos or customary behaviour are paid in rupees, but this has not affected the older subsistence patterns nor the structure and functions of the family, lineage and community.

Professor Vidyarthi has also related the beliefs and practices concerning the supernatural very clearly to the basic drives and anxieties of the people and to the levels of socio-cultural integration and co-operation. The religious complex is surprisingly rich for so simple a society, owing partly to fairly extensive borrowing from the lowland Santhal and slightly to infiltration of Hindu ingredients. There are nature spirits, both beneficent and evil, and deceased ancestors which need to be placated. There are innumerable fetishes, household and village shrines and sacred places. Religious personnel includes shamans, curers, oracles, ceremonial leaders, and witches. Sacrifices, offerings, magic and counter-magic are all prominent.

Among malicious forces, there is witchcraft, in which everyone believes but to which no one admits. The Maler, like so many societies that consist of tight in-groups which suppress hostilities, ascribe many misfortunes to the malevolence of some neighbour. But there are also many evil nature spirits, which may cause abortions, sickness, death, starvation and other calamities. These must be avoided, propitiated and guarded against.

The more benign spirits are called upon to prevent sickness and other misfortunes and to further food production, but ceremonial lapses and violations of taboos may turn them against the people. The religious functionaries include shamans and curers who deal with individual troubles and illness, the family heads who conduct household rites, and oracles and ceremonial leaders who operate on behalf of the village.

It is apparently a function of the extremely small size of the primary lineage and of the fairly tightly integrated village that while the lineage operates ceremonially mainly in life-cycle functions, the village as a whole carries out the principal ceremonials. The village and the nuclear family, however, are usually counterparts of the same religious activities, which relate principally to the two basic "hungers", food and sex. That is, village ceremonies are accompanied by household rites.

The principal annual village ceremony follows the harvest. It includes offerings to the spirits for the harvest (but smaller offerings if the harvest is not good—a kind of chastisement of the spirits), feasting and merry-making, and sexual licence. Since blood sacrifice is efficacious in proportion to the size of the animal, buffalos, which can be purchased only through contributions from the whole community, are sacrificed at the major ceremonies. The sex play at the harvest ceremony relates to the marriage system and to the nature of controls of pre- and extra-marital sexual relations. The sexual hunger of unmarried Maler youths leads to many affairs, but, since these are prohibited, they are carried out clandestinely in the forests. Affairs between youths or between married persons are matters of village concern. One who denies them is put under oath and subjected to the ordeal of licking salt or a hot axe head. While maintenance of pre-marital chastity or marital faithfulness is not usually treated so rigorously in primitive societies, the Maler regard these as offences against the village as well as the family or lineage. The sexual licence permitted at the annual harvest festival is essentially an occasion for the selection of marriage partners, and it therefore has village approval. Thus, oaths, ordeals and ceremonies serve to enforce customary law in the absence of formal law and law-enforcement agencies.

In these vital areas of Maler life it appears that the lineage is frequently bypassed. The nuclear family operates in some measure as the basic productive, consumption, sexual and ceremonial unit. The several other families within the lineage, or extended family, co-operate in production and some ceremonialism. But, because the lineage is small and the multi-lineage village has deep interest in such matters as maintenance of the family against promiscuity, insurance of subsistence productivity, protection against disease, disaster, predatory animals and other threats of concern to all village members, the multi-lineage village, instead of an expanded lineage of five or six generations has become the integrated unit that deals with the problems arising from the hunger for food and sex and with the ever-present threats to existence.

Professor Vidyarthi's generous request that I write this Foreword has led me to speculate about a number of interesting matters. A monograph less rich in a sense of problem and less incisive in relevant detail would not stimulate such thought. The highest compliment I can pay Professor Vidyarthi is that his analysis is so provocative event hough its substantive reporting is not vitiated by excessive theorizing or imposition of preconceived notions upon the data.

The Maler : A Study in Nature-Man-Spirit Complex of a Hill Tribe in Bihar, *by L.P. Vidyarthi,* Foreword by Julian Steward, Bookland Private Ltd., Calcutta, 1963, ***Boekbesprekingen.***

—*Reviewed by* M.K. GAUTAM*

Professor Vidyarthi with an absorbing experience among the people of Chôtānāgpur plateau presents in this book a vivid, penetrating and sympathetic analysis of the Maler tribe. The present study of the Maler or the Paharia hill tribe is noteworthy not only for its competence, as a descriptive ethnographic monograph, but also for the theoretical and practical questions that have been raised by Professor Vidyarthi.

The value of the study lies in clarifying many interesting points which were never studied by any trained anthropologist. Recently Chôtānāgpur has become a cynosure not only to anthropologists but to the national planners as this region is enormously rich in mineral resources. The region

* Institute Kern, Leiden University, Leiden, The Netherlands.

on the whole needs various studies which may provide a better understanding of tribal behaviour for the rapid industrialisation in the country. Professor Vidyarthi despite extremely difficult conditions has conducted his researches together with a team of students of Ranchi University over the course of several years. His approach to the material lies in terms of three phenomena "Nature-Man-Spirit" complex. He shows an interrelation among the Malers which he calls "cultural ecology and functionalism". The phenomenon of Nature, being the ecological, links up with the material culture and economic activities of the Maler which is further interwoven in social interaction.

The first three chapters describe the economy of the Malers, who are a simple, little known backward people. They are primitive cultivators. Their tribal economy apart from culling, fishing and hunting is limited to the so-called "slash-and-burn cultivation" (shifting cultivation) or "Khallu cultivation". This is not purely a shifting cultivation in the neolithic sense. The ownership right of each family on the forest is well defined and confines its agricultural operations to its fields. This cultivation is widely practised in a rotational way covering a period of seven to ten years. Changes from shifting cultivation to plough terrace cultivation are also noticed. In what way this change has occurred is not clarified, although a masterly description of the actual agricultural operations is given.

The further three chapters explain the social organization of the Maler which is surprisingly simple. The actual basis of the Maler community is the nuclear family, averaging 3.8 persons ; and having interpersonal arrangements to maintain the exploitation of resources, sex satisfaction, child-bearing and supernatural magico-religious manipulations. Co-operation between the members on village and family level goes hand in hand with all sorts of socio-religious and economic pursuits. One of the interesting phenomena is that the Malers unlike neighbouring tribes neither have totemic clans nor village exogamy. The lineage or "byare" is reckoned through only three generations, prohibiting the marriage contact with three generations of each descent line. Thus the Malers form the smallest lineages, comparable to those of the Fuegeans, the Bushmans and Australians. Professor Vidyarthi doesn't explain the reasons for this limitation. However, he explains in detail the various types of social interaction such as co-operation which promotes village unity and cohesion through marriage between its lineages or extended family ; through common shrines, religious offerings and sacrifices ; through various ceremonies and youth dormitories and through various leaders of the village. Like many other tribes of North-eastern Central India the Maler have youth dormitories known as "Kodadda". The sex relations are rather loose ; pre-marital sex relations are common, though they are not tolerated. The popular terms for sex among Maler is "bhookh" (hunger). "To a Maler sex is as inevitable, natural and common as hunger". Perhaps the absence of totemic clans and the prevailing of village endogamy have enhanced this free intercourse. Certain festivals such as "Thadi" or "Pillai" or "Bhadon" also provide ample opportunity for this purpose.

The political structure of the Maler is well organised and elaborate. The village community, like that of the Santhals, is headed by a "Manjhi", whereas a further congregation of various villages is headed by a "Sardar". Governmental organizations also play a part. In the last two chapters, in his religious analysis of Maler society, Prof. Vidyarthi demonstrates how the Maler have related the beliefs and practices functionally to the needs and fears of the people, and to different levels within the structural framework of the individual, the family, the lineage, the village and the region. Almost all sorts of economic and social activities on village as well as on family level are directly related to the worship and offerings to the various spirits, deities and places, without which their social life would come to a standstill. The "sacred complex" of such a simple society is described by three concepts : sacred geography, sacred performers and sacred specialists. The influence of Hinduism is not very great, but a combination or synthesis of Hinduism and tribal spiritism is emerging. The book does not go further in theorizing and analysing the causes of socio-cultural changes which are easily traced among the Maler. However, the intention of Professor Vidyarthi has been more concentrated towards the "Nature-Man-Spirit Complex" relations, that is, the interrelations between the ecology, social organization and the religion of the tribe. The whole set-up of the book shows that the Maler in spite of their own cultural setting are going through an enormous cultural change. Many of the words of the Maler language are factual indications of borrowings from Hindus or non-tribals, perhaps through Santhals. To mention some :

Maler	*Hindi*	*Eng.*	*Source*
'Jungli"	Jungli	wild	(p. 19)
"Khajoor"	Khajoor	date	(p. 13)
'Bans"	Bāns	bamboo	(p. 13)
"Lathi"	Lāthī	stick	(p. 27)
"Magh", "Falgun"	Māgh, Phālgun	month of Hindu	
"Kartik", 'Bhadar"	Kārtik, Bhādra	calendar	(p. 44)
"Rama", "Rupa",			
"Surja"	Hindu names	names	(p. 34)
"Bhai"	Bhāi	brother	(p. 63)
"Bazar"	Bazar	bazar	(p. 71)
"Bhookh"	Bhookh	hunger	(p. 90)
"Bhut"	Bhoot	ghost, spirit	(p. 141)
"Guru"	Guru	specialist, teacher	(p. 143)
"Jarana"	Jharanā	stream	(p. 151)
"Mahadeo"	Mahādeva	Lord Shiva	(p. 155)
"Sima"	Seema	boundary	(p. 155)
"Deva"	Deva	God	(p. 160)

All these similarities, between the spoken language of the Maler and Hindi, demonstrate some linguistic acculturation which must have commenced long ago.

Cultural Configuration of Ranchi, Calcutta Bookland, 1968.

—*Reviewed by* S.N. SEN

Professor Vidyarthi presents a systematic, comprehensive and factual description of the emerging industrial city of Ranchi, located in the heart of the tribal belt of middle India. The growth of this city, till recently, remained stunted because of its geographical isolation, ethnological characterization and technological backwardness. A critical reading of the preliminary chapters of the book on the historical, geographical and demographic settings of the city reflects very vividly the factors which led to the growth of Ranchi from a cluster of tribal villages to a regional centre for administrative, commercial, transportational, cathedral, military and educational activities. When this study was undertaken in the year 1960, Ranchi had just entered the phase of industrial urbanization with the establishment of the heavy industries and other associated ancillary factories around it.

It was rather of great methodological significance to plan the study of this tribal town of Ranchi at a time when it was at the threshold of industrial urbanization. Such a timely field inquiry rightly gave Professor Vidyarthi and his team a unique opportunity to observe, describe and analyse very vividly the "tribal past" and the "industrial future" of the changing city of Ranchi.

The city of Ranchi, described so systematically from different angles, is obviously different in many respects from other cities of other regions in India. At the ethnological level, the city is the headquarters of a district which has 60 per cent and of a division which has 30 per cent of their total population as tribals. This ethnic element, though considerably reduced in the city, still accounts for 30 per cent of its total population and in the tribal *bustees* located in the heart of the city, the density of tribal population is still higher. In terms of material status, 43.2 per cent of the total families continue to live in *kachcha* houses, while only 19.3 per cent of them are living in *pucca* houses, 63.3 per cent of the families have no electricity, 78.8 per cent of them have no water taps, and 35 per cent of them have no latrines in their houses. A drainage system is yet unknown, and in spite of new colonization and growing insanitary conditions, the dependency on natural drainage flowing from upland to lowland continues to be the chief feature. In terms of occupation as well, which has found special treatment in the book, agriculture figures quite prominently, 7.7% of the earners are engaged in agriculture as their primary occupation but it provides a subsidiary occupation for 51.8% of the total earners. This, obviously, is due to the presence of a tribal element in the urban population, and also because of the legal provision of the Chotanagpur Tenancy Act which prohibits the transfer of land from the tribal to the non-tribal families.

In the light of such materials from a sample survey, the comparative description of the tribal localities in the city as well as the description of the culture of the migrants, the rural characteristics of the Ranchi community become quite evident. In the case of Ranchi, as the picture emerges, the dichotomy between "rural" and "urban" is more of a theoretical concept than a division based upon the facts of community life. It seems that any definition of an Indian city, unless it is purely arbitrary, must include within the scope the characteristics of rural as well as urban communities.

Along with the meticulous analysis of the historical, ecological, demographic and economic character of the city, the author has wisely included the investigation of the sociological dimensions of (i) leisure and recreation, (ii) religion and festivals, (iii) class and caste, (iv) urban leadership, and (v) social life of the urban tribals and the urban impact on the tribals of the neighbouring villages. In all these chapters one is intrigued to find the combination of two styles of life of the tribal and non-tribal systems, which obviously is smoothening the process of integration, though the rate of such social integration seems to be considerably slow in comparison to the rate of growth of urbanization.

In terms of class structure, the sample survey has clearly thrown in relief the overwhelming number and cultural characteristics of lower class people living in the city. These lower class people (41.6% of the total number) belong mostly to the Muslim and non-converted tribal communities. In view of social anthropological interests of the author, the functions of castes as well as the style of life of the urban tribals have received due attention. In this treatment one will not be surprised to learn that the migrants belonging to different castes and communities have settled in the respective localities, and have given rise to what is termed as clear-cut "social geography". Along with the caste-geography in Ranchi one finds *mohallas* which are organized on the basis of linguistic, religious and even denominational considerations around the respective types of churches. Again, with certain modifications and exceptions, the barbers, potters, bhangi, chamar and washermen are seen to have continued their traditional occupations.

Urbanization has brought about manifold changes in the life of the tribal people. The primary changes are noticed in the occupational sphere, but these changes are followed by changes in the field of social relations, customs, values and beliefs. It has also been established that while the younger, educated and Christian tribals have ordinarily accepted the challenge of urbanization, the older, uneducated *Sarna* or non-Christian tribals have maintained a link between tribal and urban style of life. It is an interesting study to see thousands of tribal males and females in the city in a phase of transition. From the data on the dynamics of their social and family life, it becomes evident that there is a great strain on them as they are passing through a phase of transformation from tribal-peasant life to an urban-industrial society.

In describing the urban pattern of Ranchi, very unconventionally, of course, Professor Vidyarthi goes to describe the political role of Ranchi in providing leadership to the fast developing region of Chotanagpur. He refers to the facts, how Ranchi has become the regional centre of caste Panchayat of the Nai and Chamar, and how the caste leaders from the city visit the villages to solve serious disputes that arise from time to time among the caste members or between the caste specialists and their clients. Considering the ethnic characteristics of the region, he wisely devotes a separate chapter to the origin and development of tribal leadership and brings out the roles that Ranchi has played to provide a congregation of political intellectuals who, in turn, provide leadership not only to the city but to its entire hinterland. His authentic and well-documented analysis brings out the fact that under the impact of urbanization and democratization, rural-bred, charismatic and tradition-oriented leadership in Chotanagpur is in fact being replaced by a new model of "secularized" leadership. The historical analysis of the political activities and the biographical survey of the tribal elite makes it abundantly clear that Ranchi as the regional centre has been also the exclusive seat of tribal politics for the whole of Chotanagpur.

Methodologically, again, Professor Vidyarthi does not stop by describing the city in isolation. In his framework, the impact of the city has been viewed from the other end of the village as well. The influence of the city on every aspect of the life of the people who live beyond its border has been very distinct. Distance is an important consideration and it is found that, other things being equal, these villages lying adjacent to Ranchi are under greater urban influence. In the study of these two sets of exposed and isolated villages it has been noted that the exposed villages near Ranchi have become somewhat heterogeneous in terms of economic, occupational, ethnic, religious and linguistic composition, material culture and social relationships while the isolated ones, however, continue to maintain certain type of traditional homogeneity in their style of life.

In the light of the rich wealth of data, Professor Vidyarthi, in conclusion, has summarized several social and civic problems of the fast expanding city. The fact of the unsatisfactory function of the Ranchi Municipality, the Ranchi Improvement Trust drainage, public health service, transport and public safety, etc., to the expanding population has been well brought out. The author has given a timely note of caution to the civic authorities for utmost vigilance at the time of initial expansion. Highlighting the vast potentialities for its future expansion, the problems of planning the expanding city have been well emphasized, a failure in which will obviously lead this "rural town" of Ranchi into an "industrial slum". In the true spirit of a social anthropologist, he has made a plea to look [at the civic problem from the angles of ethnic composition and class stratification. Along with many recommendations, which I am sure the civic authorities will find useful, Professor Vidyarthi rightly advocates the need for regional planning, as a city in many respects is moulded by the social system of which it is a part.

At the methodological level, I very much appreciate the efforts of Professor Vidyarthi to supplement the sample survey techniques with anthropological methods of microcosmic investigations. This research project goes to establish that the microcosmic study of certain sections of the urban community and its institutions combined with a sample survey brings out a clearer and more intimate picture of an urban pattern as well as its cultural roles in the various spheres of a society. The intensive study of various administrative, missionary, religious and political functions of the city viewed in historical perspective have definitely proved to be useful in understanding the various processes and factors of urbanization.

At the level of generality, Professor Vidyarthi's work can also be viewed as an intimate appraisal of the process of transformation from primitivism to industrialization. Considering it as a caste study, it reads like a story of the evolution of folk and peasant culture to pre-industrial urbanization, and then to rapid industrial urbanization. Owing to his multi-disciplinary orientation, Professor Vidyarthi has ably succeeded in portraying the multiple facets of the career of Ranchi, and the personality of the city that his study reflects is both rich in substantive reporting and theoretical findings.

Professor Vidyarthi's generous request that I write this Foreword has led me to highlight a number of interesting matters which are of general interest as well in the study of modern urbanization in India. I am sure this book will be considered as a valuable contribution to the urban studies in general and to urban anthropology in particular. Professor Vidyarthi has indeed done a pioneering piece of research and I wish him fruitful future as an urban-industrial anthropologist.

WHAT MEDIA SAYS

WHAT MEDIA SAYS

Durant's Press cuttings : 29-39, Mount Pleasant, London, W.C.1, 16 August, 1961.

SACRED CENTRE OF HINDU PILGRIMAGE

—SONYA RICHMOND

In the State of Bihar, in the Eastern part of India, lies the sacred city of Gaya, a place of Hindu pilgrimage. It is remarkable in that it is divided into two distinct zones, the secular and the sacred.

The sacred zone, called by the residents "Andar Gaya" or the Inner Gaya, is inhabited by the Gayawals, the "people of Gaya", which is the special caste of Brahmans controlling the Gaya shraddah. This shraddah is the common name for the ritual performed in honour of the departed spirits of dead ancestors, a custom which exists among other primitive races of the world.

DYING RACE

The Gayawals claim to have been especially created by Lord Brahma, and to millions of Hindus in India the city of Gaya is a holy place ; but in actual fact the Gayawals are notorious, ignorant, beggarly, and a dying race who live on temple traffic and the benefits of pilgrimage, while the sacred zone of the city itself is becoming more and more desolate and disorganized. In contrast, the secular zone is expanding in population, area and activities.

The fascinating study of the Gayawal community, set into the framework of India and Indian culture, is related in a doctoral thesis by Shri L.P. Vidyarthi entitled *The Sacred Complex of Hindu Gaya*, published by the Asia Publishing House at 30s.

The city of Gaya is described in terms of three analytic concepts : a sacred geography, a set of sacred performances, and a corps of sacred specialists. These three concepts, considered collectively, are termed a sacred complex. It represents the higher form of Hinduism as reflected in the all-prevailing influence of the Brahmanical priesthood and sacred intelligentsia.

The incisive mind of Dr. Vidyarthi, head of the Department of Anthropology at Ranchi University, has concentrated on new foci of anthropological interest—the study of cities and centres of culture – rather than on the traditional ones, namely, those of tribal cultures and rural life.

The author is a man of great distinction in the field of Anthropology. Editor of the *Journal of Social Research*, he was selected for the Bihar Government State Scholarship for advanced training in anthropology, and is the winner of a gold medal for the best dissertation in his chosen subject in the year 1953.

NEW FACTS

Besides his teaching work at Ranchi University he carried on field researches among the tribes of Bihar. In 1955 he was awarded the Ford Foundation Grant to complete the study of the pilgrim city of Gaya, the result of which is this valuable contribution to the study of Indian civilization.

This comprehensive ethnology is a pioneering work of high quality and provides an abundant source of new facts and concepts not only for the professional anthropologist but also for the interested layman.

The Sunday Standard, August 27, 1961.

PRIESTLY COMMUNITY

The Sacred Complex in Hindu Gaya, *by L.P. Vidyarthi*,
Asia Publishing House, Bombay.

—A. D. PUSALKER

Based on fieldwork in the sacred city of Gaya and among the Gayawal, the caste of sacred specialists, this book constitutes an ethnography of the sacred city of Gaya and represents the first study of any priestly community in India.

The first chapter (The Sacred Centres of Gaya) deals with the geographical aspect, wherein several sacred centres in the holy city have been considered according to their spatial and temporal influence, under the heading of local, regional and universal.

Particulars about the sacred performances at Gaya are given in Chapter II of which the second section is devoted to shraddha, which is almost the sole religious performance for which millions of Hindus start on a pilgrimage to Gaya. The next three chapters give the study of the Gayawal as an example of sacred specialists in all aspects. We get a complete picture of the life of the Gayawal through the ages and their impact on the sacred intelligentsia and the common man. The last chapter presents in a nutshell the author's conclusions.

CHANGING VALUES

In the Introduction, Dr. Vidyarthi has explained the methodology and also the concepts of "great" and "little" traditions, cultural specialists, cultural performance, cultural media, etc., which have not yet come into general use and are employed with different notions.

With all his critical and scientific background and outlook, Dr. Vidyarthi rightly approaches the problem in a sympathetic and appreciative spirit. His extensive fieldwork and analytical study of the Gayawal show how the changing values and attitudes in popular Hinduism have effected corresponding changes in the cultural life of the Gayawal and deteriorated their religious status. Dr. Vidyarthi's investigations show that "while the secular zone of Gaya is expanding in population, area and activities, the sacred zone is becoming more and more desolate, unimportant and disorganized."

Dr. Vidyarthi's analytical study of the sacred specialists is a valuable contribution to current anthropology. It is to be hoped that the book will inspire similar studies of sacred specialists at other centres in India.

The printing and get-up are excellent. We strongly commend the book to all libraries interested in Indian culture.

Sunday, May 21, 1961

GAYA : A PLACE OF HINDU PILGRIMAGE

The Sacred Complex in Hindu Gaya, *by L.P. Vidyarthi*, Published by Asia Publishing House, Bombay.

—MALATHI SRIRAM

The temples and centres of religious pilgrimage are a rich cultural heritage of India. According to the late Pros. D.N. Mazumdar, "The folk beliefs, rituals and learning that are associated with them are difficult to separate or even to identify. The story is not merely in the scriptures and temple art and architecture, but in the folk ways and the mores which are inextricably woven into the "sacred complex" of the cities and temples."

Gaya in Bihar is such a sacred place of Hindu pilgrimage. Dr. L.P. Vidyarthi's attempt to explain the "sacred complex" in Gaya is really praiseworthy. Essentially an anthropological study of the Gayawal community "who live on temple traffic and benefits of pilgrimage", the book will be of particular interest to those with a religious bent of mind.

A sacred place with its sacred rituals undertaken by the sacred priests forms a "sacred complex". Gaya is divided into "sacred" and "secular" Gaya. Sacred Gaya is the actual place of the Shraddha rituals near the sacred river Phalgu and the well-known temple Vishnu Pada. It is again divided into "sacred clusters" and "sacred segments" on the basis of the worship of different gods.

The various types of worship such as Puja, Homa, etc., have been explained in detail. Also there is a notable mention of the birth of Buddhism in Gaya and also of the conflict and compromise between Buddhism and Hinduism.

One of the most important Hindu rituals is Shraddha yagna which is observed on an elaborate scale in honour of the ancestors, the dead fathers and other progenitors for their happiness beyond. The rituals are carried on in the temple, whereas the devotional performances signifying group-singing and story-recitation are carried on in the small places of worship.

The "Gayawal" is a Brahmanical community who had once lived up to the standard of culture as expected of them. Gradually they declined to a most degrading state, which is the result of the state of affluence they felt when they received huge gifts of lands, houses and large sums of money from the Maharajas and rich landowners who came to Gaya on pilgrimage. Once very orthodox the Gayawal community have now undergone a vast change, which has certainly been conditioned by the changes in the outside world.

The book well-equipped with detailed appendices, notes and glossary provides a glimpse into the religious heritage of Hinduism. It is no doubt a book on a new line of venture.

The Times Literary Supplement, Friday, June 9, 1961

CASTE AND CEREMONY

The Sacred Complex in Hindu Gaya, *by L.P. Vidyarthi*, Asia Publishing House, Bombay.

Since the war there has been a considerable development in the detailed study of Indian villages by social anthropologists. The initial assumption that the village might be a microcosm of Indian civilization, the catch-phrase that "India is to be found in her villages", have slowly given way as each investigator is driven by the facts to take in a wider and wider field of study and knowledge. India is a self-conscious civilization and neither its present problems nor its traditional form is to be understood if it is treated only as a mass of isolates joined quite unconsciously by a common culture. One of the most striking features of this civilization is the country-wide fame and attraction of certain religious centres such as Banaras, Ujjain, Madura and Gaya, which is the subject of this book.

Dr. Vidyarthi limits his discussion to Hindu Gaya and mentions only briefly Buddhist Gaya, which is perhaps better known in the West as the site of Buddha's enlightenment. He describes the clusters of temples in Gaya, lists the type of worship most commonly found in each, and considers the rise and fall in the fame of certain of these clusters and the wealthy patronage which they have enjoyed from all parts of India.

Hindu Gaya is a specialized centre in that it is particularly associated with the shraddha ceremony for departed ancestors and relatives. The performance of this ceremony here is a monopoly of a particular caste of Brahmans, the Gayawal. Dr. Vidyarthi describes the internal organization of this caste and the relationships which it has established with other castes that are either necessary to the performance of the ritual or assist in the business organization and accommodation of pilgrims. Traditionally each Gayawal family has its own clients and the link was maintained through generations. One can get a good idea of the influence of this religious centre from the details which emerge in some of the seven life-histories published in an appendix. Gayawal Brahmans were accustomed to making year-long pilgrimages themselves, in the course of which they visited their clients in places as far apart as Madras and Afghanistan.

Of the ritual specialist with whom the Gayawal have ties in Gaya the most significant are the Dhami who call themselves Pretiya Brahman, or Brahmans having to do with ghosts. The Gayawal do not admit this claim to Brahmanic status but grant the Dhami priestly power and rights. The Dhami certainly appear to violate most of the customs which are the mark of orthodox Brahmanism. The shrines which they serve are, however, of equal importance to the pilgrims with those of the Gayawal and as the author observes 'they are an inseparable part of the same ritual complex".

Dr. Vidyarthi avoids the mistake of earlier writers who assumed that the Dhami were survivors of some pre-Brahman period, but one could have wished for a greater elaboration of his argument on this point. The Dhami seems to correspond to the Mahabrahman elsewhere in India who are the Brahmans of death ceremonies and hence low or even untouchable because contact with death pollutes. More and more, research tends to show that Hinduism as a lived religion (as opposed to a religion of edifying texts) includes cults and priests dealing with the inevitable impurity as well as the better-known cults of purity reserved to Brahmans.

The penultimate chapter describes the present condition of the Gayawal and the changes brought about in their life in modern society. Deprived of consistent and wealthy patronage, their economic condition has deteriorated. At the same time indolence has allowed many of their functions to fall into the hands of their former servants. Touting for pilgrims has become more common and the spiritual standards of many have declined. Pilgrimage in India, as in Europe, must always have had an element of tourist enjoyment, sight-seeing and holiday-making, but from this account one has the impression that in Gaya as elsewhere this is coming to predominate. At the same time Dr. Vidyarthi describes the various reform movements that have been and are being attempted, and suggests reasons for their failure.

Among the appendices are to be found some extracts from the Vayu Purana which contains the myth describing the sacred origin of Gaya. Brief as it is, it brings out well enough the opposition between purity and impurity which the traditional specialization of this city presents in an extreme form. Dr. Vidyarthi has produced a notable work and if it has shortcomings these are felt as a result of an appetite that he has stimulated. A more detailed map of Gaya giving the location of temples would be an improvement and we should like to know more details of the rituals performed, the business organization of the temples, the effects upon the Gayawal of local religious variations among their clients, and equally the effect of Gaya upon the localities when the pilgrims return home. The book is short ; only a half is text and the remainder appendices, bibliography and glossary. One must hope that Dr. Vidyarthi will publish in greater detail the mass of facts he must have at his disposal before the changes he describes have their inevitable effect.

Hindustan Srandard, November 26, 1961

The Sacred Complex in Hindu Gaya *by L.P. Vidyarthi*, Asia Publishing House, Bombay.

—S.C.C.

The present study constitutes an ethnography of the sacred city of Gaya, a place of Hindu pilgrimage. The city is described in terms of three analytic concepts : "a sacred geography", a set of "sacred performances", and a corps of "sacred specialists". These three concepts, conceived collectively, are termed "a sacred complex". This, from Chapter VI, in a way summarizes the author's doctoral thesis on Gaya. Dr. Vidyarthi is the Head of the Department of Anthropology at Ranchi University, Ranchi, and Editor of *The Journal of Social Research*. We hope this brilliant pioneering work will be competently followed by studies of other cities by other researchers, contributing to the construction of an overall picture of India's present religio-social situation. The present book is a study not only of the sacred city, but also of the levitical communities, "notorious" for their pilgrimage trafficking. The author has shown how their life-style is undergoing an alteration by the impact of general secularization. The book has been exhaustively indexed and the plates and a glossary given will be greatly helpful to the readers. The headings of the five appendices, viz., (1) Gaya Mythology, (2) Sacred Centres of Gaya Through the Ages, (3) Professional Lineage Titles of the Gayawal, (4) Gayawal Gotra and Their Corresponding Divisions, and (5) Seven Life Histories of the Gayawal will be enough to give an indication of the author's method of approach.

THE INDO-ASIAN CULTURE

The Sacred Complex in Hindu Gaya, *by L.P. Vidyarthi*, 1961, Asia Publishing House, Bombay.

—SUMATI BHATTACHARYA

This is a study along anthropological lines of the history, geography and mythology of the famous Hindu shrine, performance of sacrificial rites at which place in honour of the departed is considered most efficacious in securing their spiritual welfare in the life after death as well as conferring merit on their decendants. An additional special feature of the book is the study of the history of the hereditary class of priests, known as the Gayawal—"the community who live on temple traffic and benefits of pilgrimage"—who officiate at and guide the religious rites performed by the sacrificer around the shrine. The work embodies the results of field-work, in addition to studies of literary or archaeological material. As would be expected in an anthropological study, the author gives an account of the processes of conflict among different historical, cultural, geographical and mythological trends, and the compromises effected, of course chiefly in the interest of the continuity of the sacred trade. We see in Dr. Vidyarthi's analysis how traditions of cultural import have succeeded one another, how a stronger cultural force has imposed itself on other weaker forces, and how cultural trends have mixed with and assimilated each other in the life of the priests, their functions and their scope, in and around this important shrine. Historians would welcome similar studies on the life and history of the other great ancient religious centres of Hinduism.

PACIFIC AFFAIRS

The Sacred Complex in Hindu Gaya, *by L.P. Vidyarthi*, Bombay, Asia Publishing House ; New York, Taplinger Publishing Co., 1961.

—R. MORTON SMITH

Anthropology seems to begin and end in description. This book by the head of the Department of Anthropology in Ranchi does so in presenting a full account of the sociology of the priesthood at Hindu Gaya in Bihar. To the outside world Gaya is Buddhist, but in the changing pattern of India its fame is due to the rather artificial revival of Buddhism there and that site is six miles away from the city. The antiquity of Hindu Gaya is attested by the shrines (detailed in the Vayu Purana, Chapters 105-12) ; I am not aware of any critical examination of these chapters for dating purposes, but the work as a whole was probably finished by 400 A.D. It is, however, interesting to note that the Purana account of Gaya as first ruled by Gaya, son of Sudyumna, is ignored in the myth of Gaya Asura in Vayu 105-6.

Many interesting facts are elicited in the book, illuminating processes of change in the officially changeless society of India in the past, and the rapid corrosion of national change today. This has led to degeneration of internal and external relationships and chief priesthood caste (the Gayawal) who find those they used to employ as servants now have the status rather of partners, when the diminished revenues of pilgrimage must be divided between many more ; pilgrims estimated at 300,000 in 1906 are now only about 80,000 and those poorer. Historical change at the site can be seen from the number of shrines (nearly 400) that can be traced as being or having been sacred. It is also interesting to note the enormous increase in pilgrimage under the British raj, owing to the improved safety of the roads. The all-India character of Gaya is also well brought out.

The investigation of the Gayawal class has been thorough. One or two biographies of their assistant sacrificial castes would have been interesting. Blemishes are minor. Misprints seem to occur mostly at the beginning. The author has provided useful tables, appendices, glossary and bibliography. He has successfully followed his teachers, Redfield and Singer, and no political or contemporary bias is visible in his work, which can be fully recommended.

National Herald, Sunday, March 18, 1962

THE GAYAWAL COMMUNITY

The Sacred Complex in Hindu Gaya, *by L.P. Vidyarthi*, Published by Asia Publishing House, Bombay.

—V.S.N.

Until recently anthropological research in India was almost entirely confined to the study of primitive communities. Consequently, there are very few works devoted to contemporary complex societies in India. L.P. Vidyarthi's study of the Gayawal community will, therefore, be welcomed as an important contribution to modern anthropological scholarship. We have here a careful analysis of the extremely fascinating but also highly complicated process by which cultural traditions are superimposed and get telescoped into each other.

The author begins with an outline of the sacred geography of Hindu Gaya. He goes on to discuss the significance of certain forms of ritual prevalent here and compares these forms with their counterparts in other sacred centres in India. This is followed by the main body of the work in which all the aspects of the Gayawal's life are treated in detail with reference to the various types of relationships that have been evolved in the course of centuries.

The study is adequately supported by tables and by records of personal interviews with a number of Gayawals representing a cross section of the community.

British Book News, October, 1961

The Sacred Complex in Hindu Gaya, *by L.P. Vidyarthi*, Asia Publishing House.

This stimulating and well-written anthropological study, based on field-work and literary sources, is important for two reasons : it shows the interaction of the higher, unifying Brahmanical (Sanskrit) socio-religious tradition and the many variegated local and regional peasant and folk cults and it describes the impact of modern Western civilization which is bringing about a transformation and decline of the "sacred complex". Dr. Vidyarthi gives an illuminating analysis of this continuous process of conflict and compromise, of the imposition of one culture on another. The "sacred complex" consists of the combination of the "sacred centres", i.e., the places where ritual and devotional activities are carried on ; the "sacred performances", i.e., offerings, rituals, prayers, etc. ; the "sacred specialists" who depend for their livelihood on their services, i.e., the priests and monks and their serving acolytes (astrologers, sacred singers, etc.). The author describes in particular the "Gayawal", the priests who are at the apex of the caste hierarchy and who supervise the shraddha ritual. The book sheds considerable light on the tribal, rural and urban (sacred and secular) situation as well as on caste developments.

A CULTURAL STUDY OF THE GAYAWALS

The Sacred Complex in Hindu Gaya, *by L.P. Vidyarthi*, Asia Publishing House, Bombay.

This book is devoted to a study of the cultural characteristics of the Gayawals of Bihar. Gaya is a place sacred to the Hindus and Buddhists alike. The special significance of Gaya to the Hindus is that the pious Hindu belonging to any part of India goes there to perform a Shraddha for the ancestors and he considers it a fulfilment of a holy debt that he owes to them. Gayawals are a set of people who constitute a distinct group with traditions and ways of life that have persisted through the centuries. With the acquisition of a proprietary interest in the sacred spots of Gaya, to them belong the perquisites of officiating at the ceremonies performed there by the Hindu for the satisfaction of the manes of his forefathers. Endogamic in character, they have preserved their distinct individuality and form an interesting subject of study for the anthropologist.

In this book Dr. L.P. Vidyarthi has delved into the history and given an exhaustive description of this notorious, ignorant, and dying race" of people who claim to have descended from Brahma himself. Distinguishing Gaya from other "secular" places of India, the author details at length what he calls "the sacred complex" associated with it in its topographical and human aspects. He has endeavoured with remarkable success to describe the cultural consciousness of the Gayawals with a measure of sympathetic understanding so necessary to a discerning anthropologist. He has gathered his materials by researches into recorded history, tradition and personal interrogation of the people. This last is revealing of the attitudes and aspirations of the persons questioned and of the changes that are slowly though reluctantly creeping into that community due to "westernization and modernization of the Indian universe".

The first chapter of the book deals with the "Sacred Centres of Gaya", Buddhistic and Hindu, and mentions the conflicts between the two religionists in respect of the Bodhi tree. The author advances the view that the Brahmin priests might have adopted the tree as a suitable object for veneration on the decline of Buddhism and in this way made profitable use of the worship it received from the Buddhists. Writing about the "Sacred Performances at Gaya", the author gives a detailed account of the Gaya Shraddha and the motives of people from different parts of India in performing it. The common motive is in terms of "filial piety" sentiments of love and attachment, and, above all, consciousness of the social and religious duty to one's father and other progenitors. There are quite a few whom the author mentions who do it for conformity and not from conviction. The next three chapters deal intensively with the "Sacred Specialists", namely, the Gayawals, their orthodoxy, the guru-sishya tradition among them, their different types and their antecedent history, how from an exclusive conservative body they got transformed into a proletarian type infected with lapses and vices to which they became a prey changing "from orthodoxy to de-sanskritization". One cause of this disintegration and fall seems to be that "the Gayawal pandas are slaves in the hands of goondas whose number is increasing every day". The goondas are rozgariyas who inflict themselves between the pious Yajamana and the priestly panda to the chagrin of the former and the undoing of the latter.

The author concludes his book with a doleful observation : "The Gayawal style of life, which is essentially the Sanskritic way of pious life, has become so degenerate that both the Gayawals themselves and the people in general are greatly concerned. The Gayawals who were once famous for their holiness and sacredness are now being labelled as a degenerate group of pandas and their names are remembered with a certain amount of contempt and ridicule." It would appear that between the instinct to live within a social in-group of his own and the impact of the external world on it, Gayawals are in the danger of "accepting secular jobs instead of their traditional profession". It is a moot point whether the sacred complex of Gaya will lose by this phenomenon or gain by it. But it will be a sad day when this community which has functioned through the centuries in the scheme of Hindu orthodoxy disintegrates by the compulsion of circumstances.

Enriched by a number of illustrations and explanatory tabular statements, the book is a solid contribution to the understanding of an interesting levitical group that still survive and maintain individuality in one of the famous spots of India.

The Weekly Mail, December 9, 1961

THE GAYAWAL

The Sacred Complex in Hindu Gaya, *by L.P. Vidyarthi*, Asia Publishing House, Bombay.

Dr. Vidyarthi has blazed a new path in Indian anthropology by undertaking a study of the sacred complex of a place of pilgrimage. He makes an analytical study of the Gayawal community who cluster round the Hindu pilgrim city of Gaya, the bathing ghats of which have had, through the centuries, a strange allure for India's humanity. Three chapters are devoted to the study of the Gayawal who claims to have been created by Lord Brahma, and who ministers to the needs of the Hindus at the time of the Shraddha. The ways of life of this priestly community are described at length, and the author relates them to the different roles within the caste group and with the other local sacred specialists.

Dr. Vidyarthi has assessed the direction of some of the social and economic changes in the sacred complex of Gaya. It is pointed out that while the secular zone of the city is expanding in population, areas, etc., the sacred zone is becoming more and more "unimportant", "desolate", and "disorganised". The importance of the priest is rapidly decreasing, and his monopolistic right in dealing with the pilgrims is rapidly disappearing. Pointed attention is drawn to the fact that the priests are a miserable lot, both physically and mentally, that most of them have now been reduced to poverty, and that "they parade the temples and their precincts with the beggar's bowl."

The author has dealt with the Gayawal under the theoretical and methodological influence of the functional school. He has tested some of the concepts and hypotheses put forward by Robert Redfield and Milton Singer, and used them under certain specifications. He has shown that the sacred complex of Gaya is "predominantly tradition-oriented".

COMMENTS FROM IMPORTANT JOURNALS, NEWSPAPERS, INDIVIDUALS

The Sacred Complex in Hindu Gaya, Asia Publishing House, Bombay, New York, London, 1961.

1. . . . Whether or not we accept all of Dr. Vidyarthi's terminology and theory, we are sure to be impressed by the amount of information and illumination he has provided in this *pioneering effort.* We have been sadly in need of some analysis of the internal organization of the religious centres which dot India, and Dr. Vidyarthi has so well demonstrated how rewarding studies of this kind can be that others are sure to follow. Another happy feature of the book is the personal life histories of Gayawal informants which are included in an appendix. They reveal more about Brahminal family life than anything else I have seen in print.—Morris Opler in *American Anthropologist*, Vol. 64, No. 2.

2. . . . It indicates a new trend of thought among anthropologists in India who have till now devoted perhaps over much attention to tribal monographs and studies of rural communities. . . . We warmly congratulate Dr. Vidyarthi upon this absorbingly interesting study. We hope that it will inspire further work along these lines.—F.R. Allchin in the *Bulletin of the School of Oriental and African Studies,* University of London, Vol. 25, Pt. 2, 1960.

3. . . . Dr. Vidyarthi has produced a notable work.—*The Times Literary Supplement*, London, June 9, 1961.

4. . . . This is a valuable contribution to the study of Indian civilization. . . . This comprehensive ethnology is a pioneering work of high quality and provides an abundant source of new facts and concepts, not only for professional anthropologist but for the interested layman.—Sonya Richmond in *Psychic News*, London, August 19, 1961.

5. . . . Dr. L.P. Vidyarthi has tried to strike a new note in Indian social anthropology. He has picked up one of the sacred institutions of the Hindus which is not only clothed with ritual significance but is also intimately related to the Hindu's association with the departed. . . . As the facts are meaningful, and as they are of an original nature in Indian anthropology, we are hopeful that the author's present work will open up further ways of understanding Hindu civilization for which an anthropologist is perhaps better fitted than mere historians.—N.K. Bose in *Man in India*, Vol. 42, No. 1.

6. . . . Glimpses can be had of his scientific insight and initiative and brilliance ; and of useful pilot enquiries. . . . Dr. Vidyarthi should, therefore, be congratulated for his pioneer attempt in a direction of sociological research not usually undertaken in India.—Prof. R.K. Mukherjee in *The Eastern Anthropologist.*

7. . . . Dr. Vidyarthi's analytical study of the sacred specialists is a valuable contribution to current anthropology. It is to be hoped that the book will inspire similar studies of sacred specialists at other centres in India.—A.D. Pusalker in *The Sunday Standard*, August 27, 1961.

8. . . . It is a nice job ; the analysis of the sacred geography and of the priest's relationship is very good and adds some new concepts.—Milton Singer, Chicago.

9. . . . It is extremely well written, and breaks new grounds. How I wish that we have more studies of this type.—S.C. Dube, Director of Research, National Institute of Community Development, Mussoorie.

10. . . . Dr. Vidyarthi's book, "The Sacred Complex in Hindu Gaya" is a pioneering work of high quality, comparable to Dr. Irawati Karve's "Kinship Organisation in India" or to Prof. D.N. Mazumdar's The Affairs of a Tribe.—McKim Marriott, Chicago.

11. . . . Dr. L.P. Vidyarthi is to be congratulated for traversing off the beaten tract of conventional ethnography in his volume on the sacred city of Gaya. Rather than collecting data on yet another "Tribal Group" or "Village Community", he has attempted to reach the core of Indian civilization by studying clusters of sacred institutions or "sacred complexes" that have grown around the ancient, and yet modern city of Gaya. With admirable skill, he presents his complex data, representing cultural accretions over 2,000 years, through a number of descriptive devices of his own. Even in his essentially synchronic presentation of the data, one never fails to grasp the dynamics of the transformation scene. . . . To my mind, it is one of the most significant contributions to social anthropology of India by an Indian author.—Dr. Surajit Sinha in *Indian Nation* and *Journal of Social Research*, visiting Professor at University of Chicago and Duke University.

12. . . . Dr. Vidyarthi's study of the Gayawal community will be welcomed as an important contribution to modern anthropological scholarship. We have here a careful analysis of the extremely fascinating but also highly complicated process by which cultural traditions are superimposed and get telescoped into each other.—*National Herald*, March 18, 1962.

13. . . . We hope this brilliant pioneering work will be competently followed by studies of other cities by other researchers, contributing to the construction of an overall picture of India's present religio-social situation.—*Hindustan Standard*, November 26, 1961.

14. . . . Dr. Vidyarthi has blazed a new path in Indian anthropology by undertaking a study of the sacred complex of a place of pilgrimage. He makes an analytical study of the Gayawal community who cluster round the Hindu pilgrim city of Gaya, the bathing ghats of which have had, through the centuries, a strange allure for India's humanity. . . . The author has dealt with the Gayawal under the theoretical and methodological influence of the functional school. He has tested some of the concepts and hypotheses put forward by Robert Redfield and Milton Singer, and used them under certain specification. He has shown that the sacred complex of Gaya is "predominantly tradition-oriented".—*The Weekly Mail*, December 9, 1961.

15. . . . In this book, Dr. L.P. Vidyarthi has delved into the history and given an exhaustive description of this "notorious, ignorant, and dying race" of people who claim to have descended from Brahma himself. Distinguishing Gaya from other . . . and of the changes that are slowly though reluctantly creeping into that community due to ' Westernization and modernization of the Indian universe". Enriched by a number of illustrations and explanatory tabular statements, the book is a solid contribution to the understanding of an interesting levitical group that still survive and maintain individuality in one of the famous spots of India. —*The Hindu*, March 4, 1962.

The Hindu, MADRAS

Neglected aspect of sociology

Many may not be aware that more than the technological sciences it is the social sciences whose study in India is more patterned on foreign models. This has been riling the diminutive and rotund Dr. Lalita Prasad Vidyarthi, 51, who looks the archetype of a Government bureaucrat but is actually the doyen among Indian anthropologists.

Says this social scientist, now Professor and Chairman of the Department of Anthropology, University of Ranchi and Vice-President of the UNESCO sponsored International Social Science Council, "For the past 10 years I have been propagating that there has been blind imitation of the theory and methodology of developed countries. Western models do not provide adequate theoretical background to understand our complex and diverse society. British and American scholars have emphasised consistently the differences in our society, overlooking our cultural unity.

"The social philosophy propounded by our ancient texts—the Vedas, Upanishads, Manusmriti and the like—tend to be ignored by the foreign scholars. For example, we all study Darwin's biological evolution theory but do not pay much attention to the evolution of the mind as propounded in Aurobindo's concept of cosmic evolution."

Dr. Vidyarthi, who got his doctorate in Anthropology from the University of Chicago in 1958, has embarked on a socio-cultural-cum-anthropological study of India's "teerthasthanas" (places of pilgrimage) which he feels are the manifestations of Indian social integration.

Dr. Vidyarthi first studied the "Sacred Complexes in Gaya". His students did research on Varanasi, Tirupati, Rameswaram, Janakpur, Deogarh, etc. Under his guidance, Prof. K.N. Sahay is studying Christian pilgrimage centres in India.

During the sessions of the International Social Science Council, Dr. Vidyarthi stressed that the one-way traffic of researchers from the developed to the developing countries (*They* coming to study *Our* society) needed a form of reversal. Social scientists from developing countries should be encouraged to study the problems arising from over-development (street violence, drug addiction, breakdown of the family etc.).

Dr. Vidyarthi's studies of tribal culture in Bihar are regarded highly. He has also made a special study of the tribals of the Andaman and Nicobar islands. His approach is not to emphasise the esoteric but to present the Nature-Man-Spirit Complex.

Tribals live in certain distinct types of environment which influence their traditions and beliefs and it is this interaction that forms the root of his research. His study of the Maler, a Dravidian speaking tribe in the Santhal Parganas district of Bihar, is a classic. Under the auspices of UGC, he has written a definitive tract called, "Tribal Culture of India".

As Chairman of the Planning Commission's Task Force on Development of Tribal Areas set up during the formulation of the Fifth Plan, he was the first anthropologist to be associated in development plans for tribals.

"We gave in our scheme," says Dr. Vidyarthi, "the concept of integrated tribal development areas instead of the previous blocks which were too small in area. Each area was put under a project officer (the concept of single line administration). All the project officers were put under the Tribal Commissioner. We had also suggested that anthropologists be posted as co-administrators with the project officers and tribal commissioners."

Unfortunately, in actual practice the bureaucrats have tended to treat the scientists as consultants or, worse still, junior employees.

Many tribal sanctuaries have been subjected to the rape of overnight industrialisation. In 1979, the Union Government constituted a committee to assess the impact of industrialisation on the tribal environment. Dr. Vidyarthi, who headed the Research Sub-committee, mentions the following major effects.

Land alienation—tribals become refugees in their own homeland due to displacement ; deterioration of general health level of the tribals and spread of new diseases among them ; spread of unemployment among the tribals ; acceleration of alcoholism ; breakdown of traditional moral order ; generation of industrial nomadism among tribals with their having to shift from place to place as unskilled contract labour ; they are rendered destitute since they waste the compensation they get due to not having the concept of monetary value ; and rise of militant tribal unrest.

A positive influence is that in the fringe areas bordering the industrial townships, the tribals have become agriculturists or livestock farmers and improved their economy.

Asked to spell out the priority research areas for the Social Sciences in India, he listed them as : "Impact of science and technology, rural development, social values and quality of life, unemployment, education and development and ethnicity."

—N.N. SACHITANAND

CONTRIBUTION OF DR. VIDYARTHY TO THE VARIOUS FIELDS OF ANTHROPOLOGY IN *UNDERSTANDING THE MAN IN TOTALITY*

1. In understanding the cultural roles of a traditional city in context with the complexity of Indian Civilization :

The Sacred Complex in Hindu Gaya Asia Publishing House, New York, 1961, 2nd Edition, Concept Publishing Co., New Delhi.

This book carries six long pages of "Foreword" by Dr. D.N. Majumdar. The review of this book appeared in different national and international scholarly journals. While describing about the book these reviews should be highlighted.

Works on Sacred Complex by different scholars

1. '*The Sacred Complex of Janakpur*' (*in Nepal*) by Makhan Jha, United Publishers, Allahabad, 1971.
2. '*Dimension of Indian Civilization*' by Makhan Jha, Classical Publication, New Delhi, 1978.
3. *Mithila and Mahakoshal* by Makhan Jha, Capital Publishing House, Delhi, 1982.
4. *Sacred Complex in Kashi* by L.P. Vidyarthi, B.N. Saraswạti and Makhan Jha, Concept Publishing Company, New Delhi, 1979.
5. *Sacred Complex of Deoghar* by N. Narayan.
6. *The Sacred Specialists of Kashi* by R. Sahu, Ph.D. Thesis (unpublished).

Besides these works on Vidyarthi approach to understand the Indian Civilization a symposium on the Sacred Complex in India was held in Ranchi and the papers have been published in a book.

2. How the primitive man interacts with nature and spirit can best be understood in his book 'The Maler : Nature-Man-Spirit Complex in Hill Tribes of Bihar' Bookland Pvt. Ltd., Calcutta, 1963.

This new approach of Dr. Vidyarthi to study the man in his ecological setting received world recognition and a number of reviews appeared in different journals of India and other countries.

H. Steward has written a long eight-page "foreword" for the book.

Recently a book on *Nature-Man-Spirit Complex* edited by R.S. Mann has been published by Concept Publishing Company, New Delhi (1981). This book consists of papers written by different scholars who have worked on this approach of Dr. Vidyarthi.

A large number of scholars and Dr. Vidyarthi's students worked on this approach for their Ph.D. degree. Here mention may be made of :

1. Dr. A.N. Sandhwar : 'The Korwas of Palamau' (published).
2. Dr. S.G. Morab : 'The Soliga : A Study of Eco-Ecology of a Hill Tribe'.
3. Dr. S. Borbora : 'Cultural Ecology and the Nature in Transformations —Study of the Asur of Natarhat Plateaus'.
4. Dr. V.S. Sahay : 'The Nature-Man-Spirit Complex of Nicobarese'.
5. Dr. A.C. Sahoo : 'The Changing Bondo Highlanders'.
6. Dr. A. Das Gupta : 'The Symbols and Rituals among the Ho of Singhbhum'.
7. A.M. Kurup : 'The Cultural Ecology of the Karkus of Pathalkot in M.P.'.
8. P.K. Singh : 'Maler : A Restudy'.

VILLAGE STUDIES

For the systematic study of Indian villages with a view to testing certain hypothesis and for refining some of the methodological framework developed elsewhere a number of foreign scholars like Morris Opler, Oscar Lewis, David Mandelbaum, McKim Marriott confined themselves to village as a unit of study. Along with these American anthropologists Dube (1955), Srinivas (1955), Majumdar (1950), Vidyarthi (1966) and a few other Indian anthropologists were stimulated to take up analytical study of rural communities in India.

Vidyarthi's book *Ghaghra : A Village in Chotanagpur* has been studied in the light of Robert Redfield's "Little Community". The various social institutions have been studied in depth and a good analysis of the working of these institutions has been presented. Later on Dr. Vidyarthi studied a number of villages of Bihar and focussed the village as a unit of study. Here mention may be made of study of Maler villages (1966). In his book, *Cultural Configuration of Ranchi* (1969) Vidyarthi studied a number of villages in and around the Ranchi town.

In a study, on "Life and Culture in Bihar", several villages of the culture linguistic zones like Bhojpuri, Maghai, Maithil and Chotanagpuri have been studied by Vidyarthi and his research team. Besides village studies, region and civilization studies have also been stressed in this book. The village study on Dr. Vidyarthi's style was followed by different scholars like Purnima Verma who studied "Social Structure of Chotanagpur villages" and N.K. Shukla who studied the Bhagalpur villages. Recently, in December 1982, five villages of Netarhat plateau were covered for the detailed and microscopic study by A.K. Singh and others under the directorship of Dr. Vidyarthi.

WORK ON APPLIED AND ACTION ANTHROPOLOGY

The colonial concept of Applied Anthropology has been partly replaced by the concept of Action Anthropology as developed by Sol Tax and his associates. Professor Vidyarthi terms it as Developmental Anthropology. In the democratic set-up of the nations this realization has marked the beginning about of a new phase in planning and implementation, where administrators and anthropologists have been working together to induce social and economic development and solve other problems of modernization. According to Vidyarthi, "The position of an action anthropologist, from the point of view of both science and action, seems to be the best. As a social doctor, an action anthropologist combines in himself the responsibility for diagnosing the disease, prescribing the medicines, following up the treatment, changing the prescription, if needed and finally bringing obout health and happiness in society. Having this idea in his mind Dr. Vidyarthi published a number of books and articles in Applied and Action Anthropology. Here mention may be made of *Applied Anthropology in India* (1968), *Applied Anthropology and Development in India* (1980), *Tribal Development and its Administration* (1981), *Anthropology and Tribal Welfare in India* (1959), *Indian Anthropology in Action* (1960). Dr. Vidyarthi also wrote a large number of papers on development of the different tribal ethnic groups. Initiated by Dr. Vidyarthi, A.K. Singh, V.S. Upadhyay, A.N. Sandhwar, etc., also conducted their studies on applied research.

Dr. Vidyarthi has achieved such position in the tribal context in India that it is now impossible to think about tribal development or action programme without him. He has been closely associated and has involved with the voluntary organizations of Chotanagpur like Operation Self-help (Lamkana), Kamre, Adimjati Seva Mandal (Kamre) and Vikash Bharati (Bishnupur). He is the President and Chairman of these last two voluntary organizations. He was also the director of the Birhor Action Research Project (1975). Now he has been director of a Social Forestry Project in Netarhat area sponsored by the Swedish International Development Agency and Government of Bihar (Forest Department). Thus he follows the trends—Research and Action—Action and Research.

STUDY ON SCHEDULED CASTE

As Dr. Vidyarthi is interested in the upliftment of the weaker sections and the poorest among the poor, he always tried to understand their problems to bring the national hands for their development. His book *Harizan Today* (1977) earned the national repute. His another edited book *Scheduled Castes in India* (1975) is also of great interest for social workers and social scientists. His article "Thinking about the Problems of the Scheduled Castes" (1976) is also of immense value. Presently he is guiding a large-scale research project on "The Scheduled Castes of Bihar : Problems and Solutions". Now a large number of research scholars of the Department of Anthropology are working for their Ph.D. degree on Scheduled Castes.

WORK ON FOLKLORE RESEARCHES

Folklore has provided man with a method for orally transmitting not only the customs but also the ethical, moral and world views of his particular culture from one generation to the next. Among the anthropolgists Dr. Vidyarthi has done considerable work on "Folklore". In his long paper consisting of 62 pages on "Folklore Research in India" (1978), the trends of development and the various approaches and areas of research in folklore have been analysed in depth. Besides these he has written more than a half dozen articles on folklore in different journals. It is due to his interest that the Department of Anthropology has prescribed folklore as a special paper for M.A. students.

In addition to the review of research publications on folk songs, folk tales, riddles, etc., Professor Vidyarthi, in his writings on folklore, has proposed a methodology for depicting the life-styles on the basis of the analysis of folklore, as such.

WOrK ON URBAN-INDUSTRIAL ANTHROPOLOGY

The urban population in different States has continued to increase and during the last two decades there has been a considerable growth of urban centres in the geographically isolated hilly and forested regions. The growing towns, cities and industries attracted the attention of Dr. Vidyarthi. He took up the large-scale research projects from the various Government sources and published a series of books on urban-industrial population. His books "Bhartiya Nagar" (Indian Cities), (1966), "Cultural Configuration of Ranchi : Survey of an Emerging Industrial City of Tribal India" (1969), "Socio-Cultural Implications of Industrialisation in India : A Case Study of Tribal Bihar" (1970), "Uttar Bharat Ka Ek Sanskritic Nagar : Gaya (A Traditional City of North India : Gaya), (1970), etc., are worth mentioning here. The other traditional towns like Deoghar and Janakpur have been studied by his students.

A large number of scholars from anthropology and other disciplines conducted their studies on Dr. Vidyarthi's approach to study the heterogenetic population of industries and mines. Dr. R. Singh studied Patratu, J.K. Sarkar studied Bokaro, G.R. Sharma studied Jharia, P.K. Roy and G.N. Choudhary studied the H.E.C. Complex, A.K. Haldar studied the mining labourers of Gua and Nuamundi, etc. A large-scale research project on socio-cultural implications, "Industrialization", is under completion by Dr. Vidyarthi himself.

STUDY ON LEADERSHIP

The study of leadership, public acculturation, voluntary organization as an effective machinery of change in the rural and urban communities has also attracted the interest of Dr. Vidyarthi. On the working of a voluntary organization he wrote a book, *The Peasant Organisation in India : A Case Study of a Voluntary Organisation in Tribal **Bihar.*** Another scholar Dr. B.N. Sahay also studied the *Changing Leadership Pattern among the Maler and Santhals.* Dr. Vidyarthi has edited a book, *Leadership in India* (1967).

FIELDWORK TRADITION IN HUMAN WHOLE

Dr. Vidyarthi has covered a wide range of geographical, cultural and ecological area of fieldwork since 1953 till date. He followed the Malinowskian style of fieldwork during his researches among the Maler of Santhal Pargana. He conducted his fieldwork among the most primitive tribe like hunters and food gatherers Andamanese, Jarwas, Sentinalis, Birhors, etc., primitive agriculturists, i.e., hill cultivation type tribals like the Maler. The agriculturist tribes he has covered are the Munda, Oraon and the artisan groups like Asur, Mahli, Chik Baraiks, etc. He has also done fieldwork among the Todas, a pastoral community of South India. Towns, mines and industrial areas have also been covered by him for his fieldwork.

WORK ON ANTHROPOLOGICAL THEORIES

In his Presidential address at the XIIth Annual Vth Special Conference of Indian Anthropological Association, Dr. Vidyarthi made an extensive lecture on "The Current Trends in and Future of World Anthropology". During his speech he dealt with anthropological theories and their internationalization, Cultural Evolutionalism, Diffusion, Culture Area and Innovation, French Structuralism of Levi-Strauss, Ethnoscience, Systems of Symbols, Interaction Theory, Ecological Anthropology, Human Ethnology, Psychological Anthropology and Application of Anthropology (1977).

In his book *Trends in World Anthropology* (1979) Vidyarthi reports not only on the various major international trends and methodologies in Anthropology, like the initial British tradition of studying tribes and castes in their colonies for the purposes of better colonial administration, the American tradition of village studies : Levy-Strauss' Functional, Structural Principle, etc., but also on particular national and regional styles of anthropology and situations peculiar to various countries.

His another book *Rise of World Anthropology as Reflected through the International Congresses 1934-1978* provides a brief survey of the nine international congresses of Anthropology from the first Congress in London in 1934 to the Xth Congress (1978) in India. It reflects upon the major trends in the genesis and development of Anthropology as a science through these congresses, particularly the amalgamation of the two main trends of internationalization and parochialization which has greatly contributed to the tremendous growth of anthropology and made it possible to hold its Xth Congress in a developing country.

In his two-volume book *Rise of Anthropology in India* (1978) Vidyarthi has highlighted extensively the basic factors in the genesis and development of social and cultural researches in India. He has recorded and reviewed the researches that have been conducted by the social scientists on Indian Society.

TEXT BOOKS

He has published a large number of books which are prescribed in different colleges and Universities of the country. These books are not only on anthropology but on other sister disciplines also like sociology, psychology, etc. Some are :

1. *Tribal Culture of India* (1977)
2. *Bihar Ke Adivasi* (1960)
3. *Rise of Anthropology in India* (1978) (2 volumes)
4. *Trends in World Anthropology* (1979)
5. *Theories and Methods in Anthropology* (in Press)
6. *Changing Dietary Patterns and Habits* (1979)
7. *The Sacred Complex in Hindu Gaya* (1961)
8. *The Maler : Nature-Man-Spirit Complex in Hill Tribe of Bihar* (1963)
9. *Manav Shastra Ki Rup Rekha* (Hindi) (1963)
10. *Applied Anthropology in India* (1968)
11. *Conflict and Tension and Social Trend in India* (1968).

In the analytical period Indian anthropology witnessed its expansion through the writings of Vidyarthi. When he entered the teaching profession, he had no alternative but to teach through the text-books written by the American and British scholars mainly based on non-Indian materials.

He organized a series of a half dozen seminars on Applied Anthropology and published the selected papers of Indian scholars under the title, "Applied Anthropology in India". His other volumes on this theme are : "Anthropology in Action", "Anthropology, Administration and Tribal Welfare in India", "Applied Anthropology and Development in India".

In the process of indigenization of anthropology in India, he found very inadequate materials on the life and work of Indian anthropologists. He chose this topic for the Moscow World Congress where he presented the paper on Social Anthropological Research in India in 1964. He wrote another paper in Indian Social Science in UNESCO's journal just after it and finally published his major work *Rise of Anthropology in India* in two volumes. It provides a rich material both for teaching and research on the Indian theme.

He also joined hands with other Cultural Anthropologists (Dr. K.S. Mathur) and a Physical Anthropologist (Dr. I.P. Singh) to prepare a text-book in Hindi on General Anthropology. This book outlines the broader themes of anthropology and is on the pattern of A.L. Kroeber's book, it provides an integrated picture of anthropology for the beginner and the advanced.

DR. VIDYARTHI AS

1. Winner of Awards
2. President
3. Vice-President
4. Chairman
5. Secretary
6. Member of Committee
7. Director-Symposia and Conferences, Xth ICAES
8. Editor
9. Associate Editor
10. Asstt. Editor
11. Director—Different Projects (large-scale).

VIDYARTHI RECEIVES DISTINGUISHED SERVICE AWARD

CHICAGO, NOVEMBER 17, 1983

The Association for Anthropological Diplomacy Politics and Society and the Association of Third World Anthropologists has conferred the Distinguished Service Award on Dr. Lalita Prasad Vidyarthi, University Professor and Head of the Department of Anthropology and Dean, Faculty of Social Sciences, Ranchi University, in a special convocation held here on November 17, 1983, 6-7 : 30 p.m. at Buckingham Hall at Hyatt Regency Hotel, Chicago, in conjunction with the Annual meeting of the American Anthropological Association. This conferment of Honours was also made to Professor Sol Tax of the University of Chicago and Professor Charles Wagley, University of Florida.

The 1983 Distinguished Service Award, the citation mentions, has been conferred on Professor Vidyarthi, "For his significant and distinguished contributions to Anthropology as Professor, Author, Researcher, Editor, Administrator and for his leadership as President of the Xth International Union/Congress of Anthropological and Ethnological Sciences, New Delhi, India, 1978."

Dr. Vidyarthi is the first Scholar from the Third World to be conferred such an award. Dr. Vidyarthi is the 100th Ph.D. in Anthropology from the University of Chicago which he completed in 1958. He is also the recipient of Honorary Fellowship of International Union of Anthropological and Ethnological Sciences.

In the course of his short speech delivered in response to the honour conferred on him, Dr. Vidyarthi observed that his visit to Chicago was taken by him as a pilgrimage as it was there that he had done his doctoral work on Anthropological Approach to Civilization, it was there that he was elected president of the IUAES for five years and to preside over the World Congress of Anthropology held in Delhi in 1978 and it was there that he had been given this Award.

Professor Vidyarthi further observed, that the Science of Man is passing through a crisis. It has to work effectively to give the integrated picture of human culture of the world. The clouds of conflict, tension, war are threatening the world. We live in an age of wonders in invention but blunders in morals. Our Science of man must rise equal to the occasion and ameliorate the condition by its studies.

APPENDIX

CURRICULUM VITAE OF PROF. L.P. VIDYARTHI*

Name :	VIDYARTHI, LALITA PRASAD
Date of Birth :	February 28, 1931
Present Position :	University Professor and Head, Department of Anthropology, Ranchi University, Ranchi-834001, Bihar (India)
Address (Home) :	Lalit Niketan, Adivasi Hostel Road, Nagratoli, Ranchi-834001, Bihar (India), Tel : 23618 (R), 23695 (O)

Education :

1. Ph.D. (Anthropology) :	Chicago University, 1958
2. M.A. (Anthropology) :	Lucknow University (Gold Medallist), 1953
3. Certificate in German :	Lucknow University, 1952
4. M.A. (Part I) (Geography) :	Patna University (First Position), 1951
5. B.A. (Honours) :	Patna College, First Class, 1950
6. I.A. :	Patna College, High Second Division, 1948
7. Matric :	City High School (Rajendra Vidyalaya), First Division, 1946

Position :

1. Dean, Faculty of Social Sciences, April 1983
2. Director, Department of Special Assistance (Under the U.G.C. Scheme of Centre of Advanced Studies), 1978
3. University Professor and Head, Department of Anthropology, Ranchi University, Ranchi, 1968
4. Reader and Head of the Department of Anthropology, Bihar University, 1958-68 (Now Ranchi University)
5. Fellow, University of Chicago, 1957-58
6. Founder Lecturer, Bihar University (Ranchi College), 1953-56

*Published in *Journal of Social Research*, Vol. XXVI, No. 1, 1985, and updated.

Fellowships and Awards

1. Distinguished Service Awards of 1983 : with Dr. Sol Tax and Dr Charles Wagley, Association of Anthropological Diplomacy, Politics and Society and Association of Third World Anthropologists (USA)
2. Rome Civic Reception Bronze Medal (President, IUAES), 1976-79
3. Fellowship of Shastri Indo-Canadian Institute (1974-1977)
4. Indo-USSR Cultural Exchange Fellowship, 1974
5. Indo-GDR Cultural Exchange Fellowship, 1969, 1984
6. Foreign Fellow, American Anthropological Association, 1958
7. University of Chicago Fellowship, 1957
8. Ford Foundation Fellowship, 1957
9. Fulbright and Smithmundt Scholarship, 1956-58
10. Indrajeet Singh University of Lucknow, Gold Medal, 1953
11. Government of Bihar Scholarship in Anthropology, 1950-53

Professional Assignments

President

1. International Symposium on the Development of the Third World Communities, New Delhi, October 1982 (SUNCOM-82)
2. National Conference on Ecology, Economy and Religion, Dehra Dun, October, 1982
3. International Congress of Anthropological and Ethnological Sciences held at Delhi, 1978
4. International Union of Anthropological and Ethnological Sciences, 1973-78
5. Indian Athropological Association, Delhi, 1970
6. Indian Social Science Association, Agra, 1969-74
7. Anthropology and Archaeology Section, Indian Science Congress, Varanasi, 1968
8. Folklore Section, All India Folk Culture, UNESCO, Paris, 1979-82

Chairman

1. Session on (a) Pilgrimage, (b) Anthropology in 2000 A.D., (c) Challenges of Development in XIth ICAES at Vancouver, 1983
2. The UGC Panel on Anthropology, 1978-83
3. IUAES Commissions (i) on Development and (ii) Anthropology of Future, 1978
4. IUAES sponsored Symposium on Rural Development in South Asia during the Inter Congress Amsterdam, 1981
5. National Commission on the Impact of Industrialization on Tribes of Middle India, Home Ministry, Government of India, 1980
6. ICSSD Committee on Anthropological Bibliography, 1979

7. UNESCO sponsored Consultation on Network of Cultural Research Institute in Asia, 1974
8. Committee on the Identification of Primitive Tribes of India, Ministry of Home Affairs, 1974
9. Task Force on the Development of Tribal Areas of Planning Commission, Government of India, 1972--75
10. Standing Committee on Anthropology, Indian Council of Social Science Research, New Delhi, 1968–75
11. Study Team on Tribal Labour, Indian Commission on Labour, 1968
12. All India Social Science Conference, USEFI, New Delhi, 1960

Local Secretary

71st Session of the Indian Science Congress Association, Ranchi, 1983

Important Visits to Foreign Countries

Place	*Year*	*Purpose*
USA (Chicago)	1956 -58	Fulbright and Smithmundt Scholar for Doctoral Research at University of Chicago
USSR (Moscow)	1964	VIIth International Anthropological Congress
Japan, Tokyo	1966	Pacific Science Congress
Japan (Tokyo, Kyota, Hiroshima)	1968	VIIIth International Anthropological Congress
GDR, West Germany, Scandinevian countries	1971–72	Cultural Exchange Programme
USA and Canada	1973	IXth Congress at Chicago, Lecture tours
USSR (Georgia)	1975	Field work—UGC Academic Exchange Programme
U.K. (Cambridge, London, Oxford)	1975	Lectures and Seminar—British Council
Japan, Canada, USA, Europe, several times	1976–80	For UNESCO meetings, Congress work and lectures
Greece (Athens), West Germany,	1982–83	UNESCO Symposium on Race and Racism
Canada	1982–83	IUAES Executive Committee, XIth Anthropological Congress
Japan	1984	Field Expedition among the Ainu
GDR, France, Netherlands	1984	Ethnological Congress at Dresden, lectures and meetings

Member of Committees

1. Honorary (Life) member of IUAES, 1983
2. Forests and Tribals : Social Forestry in Chotanagpur, 1982-83 (Swedish International Development Agency and Government of Bihar)
3. General Assembly of Bureau of International Committee on Social Science Information and Documentation, Paris, 1976-79.
4. Executive Committee of International Social Science Council, 1976–79
5. Committee for the Development of Primitive Tribes of Andaman and Nicobar Islands, Home Ministry, Government of India, 1976
6. General Assembly of International Council for Philosophy and Humanistic Studies, 1974–79
7. Central Tribal Research Institute Advisory Committee, 1973
8. Steering Committee on the Backward Classes, Planning Commission, Government of India, 1972
9. Advisory Committee, Anthropological Survey of India, 1968 -71
10. Founder Member, Indian Council of Social Science Research, New Delhi, 1968 (Government sponsored)
11. Founder Member Advisory Committee of Shastri Indo-Canadian Institute, 1968
12. Panel on Backward Classes, Planning Commission, Government of India, 1964

Director of Symposia and Conferences of International Level

1. International Symposium on the Development of the Underprivileged Communities of the Third World Countries, SUNCOM-82, SUNCOM-83
2. International Symposium on Rural Development in South Asia, Amsterdam, 1981
3. International Congress of Anthropological and Ethnological Science, 1978
4. UNESCO's Regional Consultation on Development of Network of Cultural Research Institute in Asia, 1978 and 1979, Ranchi
5. International Centennial Symposium on S.C. Roy and Hundred Years of Indian Anthropology, 1971
6. XIth International Congress of Anthropological and Ethnological Sciences, Canada, 1983 : Roles and Status

1. Past President, IUAES, 1978–83
2. Member, International Honorary Committee constituted by Canada Congress
3. Chief of the Indian Delegation, Permanent Council of the IUAES
4. Chairman, F. 108-IUAES Commission on Development
5. Chairman, SUNCOM-83

6. Organizer of the Symposia :

(i)	A 412	Anthropological Approach to Development
(ii)	A 414	Task and Challenges of Anthropology before 2000 A.D.
(iii)	E.30	Race and Racism : A New Look at the Old Question
(iv)	E.31	Anthropology of Pilgrimage in Complex Secieties.

Director of Symposia and Conferences of National Level

1. National Workshop Evaluation Methods and Technique, 1983
2. National Seminar on Ecology, Economy and Religion, 1982
3. National Seminar on Himalayan Anthropology, 1981
4. Social Elements in the Ancient Text, 1980
5. Twentyfive Years of Anthropology—Bihar, 1979
6. Post Congress on Tribal World and Its Transformation, Ranchi, 1978
7. Gandhi and Social Sciences (Govt. of India sponsored), 1969
8. Research Methodology in Social Sciences (UGC sponsored), 1968
9. Social Change in Contemporary Indian Society, 1966
10. Conflict and Tension in Indian Society, 1965
11. Cultural Factors in Economic Development and Technological Change, 1964
12. Impact of Modern Forces on the Tribes and Castes in India, 1963
13. Leadership in India, Tribal and Rural, 1962
14. Impact of Urbanization, Industrialization and Social Change in India, 1961
15. Levelling up Tribal and Rural India, 1960
16. Culture Analysis of Contemporary Societies : America, 1959
17. Pattern of Tribal Culture in Bihar, 1954

Editor

Journal of Social Research (Ranchi), 1958—
Indian Anthropologist (Delhi), 1971—
Research Journal of Ranchi University (Ranchi), 1964–1981
International Journal of Asian Studies (UNESCO), 1980

Associate Editor

Case Studies on Human Rights and Fundamental Freedoms : A World Survey in five volumes (1974–76)
The Foundation for the Study of Plural Societies, The Hague

Assistant Editor for India

Review of Ethnology, Institute for Volkerkunde, Vienna, 1980

Field Work : Major and Minor

1. Field Expedition to Andamans (Jarawa), February 1984
2. Visit to Nagaland, March 1984
3. Expedition to the Land of the Ainue of Hokkaido, Japan, July 1984
4. Villages of GDR, November 1984
5. Restudy of Ghaghra : Village in Chotanagpur, 1983
6. Restudy of Ranchi City, 1983
7. Industrialisation in Chotanagpur, 1980
8. Ecology, Economy, Religion in Central Himalayas
9. Bastar : Muria, Maria, Gohotul, Belladilla Mining Complex, 1981
10. Ancient Sacred Complexes of Chotanagpur and other important Sacred Complexes, 1980-81
11. Restudy of the Maler Hill Tribe, 1979-80
12. Andaman and Nicobar Islands, the Four Culture Linguistic Zones of Bihar ; Nutrition Studies in Bihar, Restudy of the Kharia, Action Research Among the Birhor, 1970–78
13. Andaman and Nicobar Islands, Industrial Complexes, Culture in Chotanagpur, Tribal Leadership and Political Systems in Chotanagpur, Scheduled Castes, 1960–65
14. H.E.C. Complex, Tribal Leadership in Ranchi, Munda and Manjhi Villages, and NEFA and Nagaland Tribes
15. Maler, Munda, Ranchi City and H.E.C. Complex, 1958–60
16. Oraon, Maler, Asur, Birhor, 1953–56
17. Sacred City of Gaya, 1955-56
18. Gayawal of Gaya (Priestly Communities), 1952-53
19. Santhals of Santhal Parganas, 1951

Director : Large-Scale Research Projects

1. Problems and Prospect of Social Forestry in Multi-Ethnic Tribals of Netarhat Region of Bihar, Swedish International Development Agency and Government of Bihar, 1982—
2. Socio-cultural Implications of Industrialisation in Middle India, Ministry of Home Affairs, Government of India, 1981—
3. The Scheduled Castes of Bihar : Problem and Solutions, Ministry of Home Affairs, Government of India, 1981—
4. From Cradle to Playground : A Study of the Process of Socialisation of the Tribal Children of Bihar, Ministry of Social Welfare, Government of India, New Delhi, 1980
5. The Cultural Ecology of Netarhat Plateau Region (UGC Research Programmes), 1979
6. UNESCO's Regional Consultation of the Development of Network of Cultural Research Nutritions in Asia, 1978-79 and Follow-up
7. Revival of Indigenous Nutritive Dietary Habits and Recipes in the

Four Cultural-Linguistic Zones of Bihar (Department of Social Welfare, Government of India), 1975–77

8. The Cultural Linguistic Zones of Bihar : A Study in Cross-Cultural Comparisons under Collaborative Programme of Anthropological Survey of India, Calcutta, 1976
9. Restudy of Kharia Tribe, ICSSR, New Delhi, 1975–77
10. Sacred Complex in Kashi, ICSSR, New Delhi, 1972–76
11. Student Unrest in Chotanagpur, UGC Research Progammes, 1969–70
12. Changes in Leadership Pattern in Tribal Society in India, ICSSR Research Programme, 1966–68
13. The Birhor Action Research Project (Government of Bihar and Government of India), 1966 and 1975
14. Monographic Study of a Munda Village—Ghaghra (under the Census Operation, Government of India), 1965
15. Tribal Indebtedness in Two Oraon Villages, Government of Bihar, 1962
16. The Urban Pattern of Ranchi, Research Programmes Committee of Planning Commission, New Delhi, 1960–62
17. From Simple Economy to Industrialization : A Techno-Cultural Implication of Changes in India, Research Programmes Committee of Planning Commission, New Delhi, 1958–66

Books ond Monographs

1. Sacred Complex in Hindu Gaya	Asia Publishing House, Bombay, 1961, 2nd Ed., Concept Publishing Company, New Delhi, 1978.
2. The Maler : Nature-Man-Spirit Complex in Hill Tribe of Bihar	Book Land Pvt. Ltd., Calcutta, 1963
3. Manava Shastra Ki Ruprekha (An Outline of Anthropology (co-author)	Keder Nath Ram Nath, Meerut City, 1963 (2nd Edition 1975)
4. Cultural Contours of Tribal Bihar	Punthi Pustak, 34 Mohan Bagan Lane, Calcutta, 1964
5. Ghaghra : A Village in Chotanagpur	Census of India, 1961, Monograph No. 2, Office of the Registrar-General, India, Ministry of Home Affairs, New Delhi, 1966
6. Bhartiya Nagar (Indian Cities)	Rajkamal Prakashan, New Delhi, 1966
7. Bharatiya Nagar : Indian Cities translated into Gujarati	R.K. Sohni Co., Bombay, 1967

	by A.R. Desai and Neera Desai	
8.	Cultural Configuration of Ranchi : Survey of an Emerging Industrial City of Tribal India	Planning Commission Publications ; Distribution, Council of Social and Cultural Research, Department of Anthropology, Ranchi University, 1969
9.	Socio-Cultural Implications of Industrialization in India : A Case Study of Tribal Bihar	Planning Commission Publications : Distribution, Council of Social and Cultural Research, Department of Anthropology, Ranchi University, 1970
10.	Uttar Bharat Ka Ek Sanskritic Nagar : Gaya (A Traditional City of North India : Gaya)	Bihar Granth Academy, Government of India, Patna, 1970
11.	Dynamics of Tribal Leadership in Bihar	Planning Commission Report (Now transferred, ICSSR), Kitab Mahal, Zero Road, Allahabad, 1970
12.	Student Unrest in Chotanagpur	Punthi Pustak, 34 Mohan Bagan Lane, Calcutta, 1976
13.	South Asian Culture	Orient Publishers, New Delhi, 1976
14.	Bharatiya Adivasi : Unki Samajik Aur Sanskritic Pristhabhumi (Indian Tribes : An Outline of Cultural and Social Life)	Hindi Samiti, U.P. Government ; Lucknow, 1976
15.	First Decade of Social Sciences in Ranchi University	Oriental Publisher, New Delhi, 1976
16.	Tribal Culture of India (co-author)	Concept Publishing Company, New Delhi, 1977 (2nd edition, 1986).
17.	The Peasant Organisation in India : A Case Study of a Voluntary Organisation in Tribal Bihar (ILO and FAO Report)	Council of Social and Cultural Research, Bihar, Ranchi, 1977
18.	Harijan Today (with N. Mishra)	Classical Publishers, New Delhi, 1977
19.	Rise of Anthropology in India in 2 Volumes (Vol. I—The Tribal Dimension,	Concept Publishing Co., New Delhi, 1978.

	Title	Publisher
	Vol. II—Rural, Urban and Other Dimension)	
20.	Trends in World Anthropology	Concept Publishing Co., New Delhi, 1979
21.	The Sacred Complex in Hindu Gaya (2nd Edition)	-do-
22.	Rise of World Anthropoiogy : As Reflected Through the International Congresses (1934-78)	-do-
23.	The Changing Dietary Patterns and Habits (co-author)	-do-
24.	Sacred Complex of Kashi (co-author)	-do-
25.	The Kharia : Then and Now (co-author)	Concept Publishing Co., 1980
26.	Rural Development in South Asia.	Concept Publishing Co., 1982.
27.	Patterns of South Asian Culture (Gen. Editor : Life and Culture in Asian Series)	Books To-day and Tomorrow, New Delhi, 1980
28.	Material Culture in India (Hindi, co-author)	Kedar Nath Ram Nath, 1983
29.	Art and Culture in North-East India	Publications Division, Government of India (in press)
30.	Life and Culture in Bihar (co-author)	(MSS under finalization)
31.	Bio-Cultural Profile of the Netarhat Plateau (co-author)	Punthi Pustak, Calcutta, 1985
32.	Problems and Prospect of Social Forestry in Multi-Ethnic Tribals of Netarhat Pat Regions in Bihar (co-author)	Under publication
33.	Techno-Cultural Implications of Industrialisation of Tribes of Middle India	Under publication
34.	From Cradle to Playground : A Study of Personality Formation in Tribal Children	Under publication
35.	Theories and Methods in Anthropology	UGC Quality Book (under preparation)

Edited Books

	Title	Publisher
1.	Anthropology and Tribal Welfare in India	Council of Social and Cultural Research, Bihar, 1959

2. Indian Anthropology in Action	Council of Social and Cultural Research, Bihar, 1960
3. Bihar Ke Adivasi (Tribes of Bihar)	College Centre, Patna, 1960
4. Aspects of Religion in Indian Society (Majumdar Memorial Volume)	Kedar Nath Ram Nath, Meerut City, 1961
5. American Society and Culture	Council of Social and Cultural Research, Bihar, 1962
6. Aspects of Applied Physical Anthropology (with B.K. Verma)	—do—
7. Leadership in India	Asia Publishing House, Bombay, 1967
8. Applied Anthropology in India	Kitab Mahal, Allahabad, 1968 (2nd Revised Edition)
9. Conflict & Tension and Social Trend in India	Punthi Pustak, Calcutta, 1968
10. Report of Study Group for Tribal Labour (Agriculture and Industrial)	National Commission on Labour, Manager of Publications, New Delhi, 1968
11. Gandhi and Social Science in India (with B.N. Sahay and B.K. Srivastava)	Book Hive, New Delhi, 1970
12. Bihar in Folklore Study : An Anthropology (with G. Choubey)	Indian Publication, Calcutta, 1971
13. Essays in Indian Folklore	Indian Publication, Calcutta, 1973
14. Symposium on Sacred Complex in India (co-author)	Council of Social and Cultural Research, Bihar, Ranchi, 1974
15. Scheduled Castes in India	—do—1975
16. The Tribes of Andaman and Nicobar Islands (Special Number of Journal of Social Research)	—do—1976
17. Research Methodology in Social Sciences in India (co-editor)	Books To-day and Tomorrow, 1985
18. Aspects of Social Anthropology in India (co-editor)	Classical Publishers, New Delhi, 1980
19. Applied Anthropology and Development in India (co-editor)	National Publication, New Delhi, 1980
20. The Profiles of the Marginal and Pre-farming Tribes of Central-Eastern India	Cultural Research Institute, Calcutta, Special Series No. 26, 1981

21. Development of Researches in Anthropology in India under Ranchi Anthropology series	Concept Publishing Co., New Delhi, 1981
22. Tribal Development and Its Administration	Concept Publishing Co., New Delhi, 1981
23. Transactions of the Centre of Himalayan Studies (co-editor)	Council of Social and Cultural Research, Bihar, 1982
24. Ecology, Economy and Religion in the Himalayas (co-editor)	Orient Publication, New Delhi, 1985

General Editor of Xth ICAES Proceedings (Continuing)

1. Xth ICAES The Tribal World and Its Transformation (Ed. Dr. Bhupinder Singh and Dr. J.S. Bhandari), Concept Publishing Co. New Delhi, 1980
2. Xth ICAES Man and His Environment (Ed. Dr. I.P. Singh and Dr. S.C. Tiwari), Concept Publishing Co., New Delhi, 1980
3. Xth ICAES The Communication of Ideas (Ed. Dr. J.S. Yadava and Dr. V.S. Gautam), Concept Publishing Co., New Delhi, 1980
4. Xth ICAES Ideas and Trends in World Anthropology (Ed. Dr. Charles Frantz), Concept Publishing Co., New, Delhi. 1980

General Editor : Ranchi Anthropology Series

(Publisher : Concept Publishing Co., 13, Bali Nagar, New Delhi-110015)

RAS 1 Process, Performance and Pilgrimage, 1979 (By Victor Turner).

RAS 2 Development of Researches in Anthropology in India, 1981 (L.P. Vidyarthi and V.S. Upadhyay).

RAS 3 Nature-Man-Spirit Complex in Tribal India, 1981 (Ed. R.S. Mann and Vijoy S. Sahay).

RAS 4 Microevolution, 1980 (By Dr. B.M. Das)

RAS 5 Tribal Festivals of Bihar, 1982 (By Ajit K. Singh)

RAS 6 The Spectrum of the Sacred : Essays on Religious Tradition of India, 1984 (By B.N. Saraswati).

RAS 7 Folklore : The Pulse of the People, 1985 (By Mazharul Islam)

RAS 8 Social Science and Indian Society, 1985 (By B.N. Varma)

RAS 9 Museums, The Public and Anthropology, 1986 (By Michael M. Ames)

Research Papers

1954

1. Origin and Development of the Gayawal (Priestly Community)	Journal of Bihar Research Society, Vol. XI, Part 2, 1954

1955

2. Education in Tribal Bihar	Man in India, Vol. 35, No. 2, 1955
3. Land and Labour among the Munda of Bihar	Journal of Bihar Research Society, Vol. XIII, Part III, 1955

1956

4. The Nature and Extent of Migration of the Birhor	Paper read before the Vth International Congress of Anthropological and Ethnological Sciences held at Philadelphia in 1956, published in the Proceeding. Also in Men and Cultures by Anthony F.C., Wallau, University in Pennsylvania Press.
5. The Saoria Paharia of Rajmahal Hills	Society in India, edited by L. Balaratnam, Social Science Association, Madras, 1956
6. Synthesis of Tribal Culture in Educational Planning	Bihar Educationist, Vol. 4, 1956
7. Economic Grading of Tribal	Vanya Jati, Vol. 2, 1956

1957

8. The Gayawal : A Case Study of De-sanskritisation	Read before a seminar on Social and Cultural Change in India held at Chicago University, 1957, published in Journal of Social Research
9. Priests, Pilgrimage and Cult of the Dead : A unit of study (mimeo)	Seminar of Redfield on Methods in Anthropology : University of Chicago, 1957 (mimeo), published in Journal of Social Research
10. Cultural Personality of the Gayawal	Seminar of Milton Singer on Culture Personality, University of Chicago, 1957. Revised Paper published in Journal of Social Research

1958

11. Cultural Types in Tribal Bihar : A Methodological Approach	Anthropology Tomorrow, Chicago, Vol. VI, No. 1, January 1958. Revised Paper published in Journal of Social Research, Vol. I, No. 1, 1958
12. The Fiftysixth Annual Meeting of the American Anthropological Association : A Brief Report	Man in India, Ranchi, Vol. 38, No. 2, April-June 1958

13. Adivasi Education (Tribal Education)	Vanyajati, Vol. VI, No. 3, July, Delhi
14. Cultural Types in Tribal Bihar	Journal of Social Research, Ranchi, Vol. I, No. 1, September 1958. Also published in Anthropology Tomorrow, Chicago, 1958
15. Anthropology, Authority & Tribal Welfare in India	The Eastern Anthropologist, Vol. XI, No. 1
16. Culture-Linguistic Zones in India : Bihar—A Case Study	Paper read in the All India Sociological Conference held at Calcutta, December 1958
1959	
17. The Extensions of an Indian Priestly Caste	Man in India, Vol. 39, No. 1, January-March 1959. Read before the Fiftysixth meeting of the Anthropological Association at Chicago, Chicago, 1958
18. Anthropology and Administration in India	Journal of Social Research, Vol. II, No. 1, March 1959
19. The Cultural-Linguistic Regions of India	Indian Folklore, Calcutta, Vol. 2, No. 3, July-September 1959
20. Anthropologists v. Administrators : Case Analysis	Journal of Social Research, Vol. II, No. 1, March-September 1959
21. An Anthropologist Looks at Folklore	Presidential Address to the Folklore Section of the 2nd All India Folk Culture Conference held at Bombay in December 1959 (printed in Folklore and also in Journal of Social Research, Vol. III, No. 1, March 1960)
22. Bharat Ke Adivasi Aur Unki Samasayana Ek Vishleshan (Hindi)	Vanyajati, Vol. VII, No. 1, April 1959
1960	
23. The Birhor : A Study in Ecology, Economy and Wandering	Published in Selected Papers of the Fifth International Congress of Anthropological and Ethnological Science (September 1, 1956) also in Men and Culture edited by Anthony Wallace, Philadelphia, 1960

24.	Thinking about a Sacred City	Paper Read in Convention of Indian Anthropologists held at Lucknow University, January 1960, Published in Eastern Anthropologist, Vol. XIII, No. 4, September 1960, Lucknow
25.	The Kolarian Group in Madhya Pradesh and Uttar Pradesh	Vanyajati, Vol. III, No. 1-2, Delhi, 1960
26.	Cultural Area, Cultural Sub-area and Cultural Types in India : Bihar—A Case Study	Read in the Seminar on Methodology in Social Research at A.N. Sinha Institute of Social Studies, February 1960, Bulletin of A.N.S.I.S.S., 1960, Vol. 1, No. 1
27.	Anthropology and Tribal Policy : A Case Study among the Maler Paharia : Some Preliminary Observations	Read in the Seminar : Levelling up Tribal Bihar, *in* Journal of Social Research, Vol. III, No. 2, September 1960
28.	Bihar Ke Adivasion Ki Sanskritic Prakar	Vanyajati, Vol. VIII, No. 1, January 1960

1961

29.	The Sacred Complex in a Hill-Tribal Village	Journal of Social Research, March-September, 1961, Vol. IV, No. 1-2, also reprinted in Aspects of Religion in Indian Society edited by L.P. Vidyarthi
30.	Red Indian : A Study of American Tribe	Vanyajati, Vol. IX, No. 1, January 1961
31.	The Functioning of Caste in the Tribal City of Ranchi	Bulletin of the Anthropological Survey of India, Vol. X, No. 2, July 1961
32.	The Khallu Cultivation of the Hill Maler : A Study in Slash and Burn Type of Rotational Cultivation	—do—
33.	The Linguistic Affinity of the Oraon and the Saoria : An Application of Lexico-Statistical Dating	Folklore, Calcutta, 1961

1962

34.	A Genetical Study of the Oraon	Journal of American Physical Anthropology, Vol. 20, No. 3, also in Applied Physical Anthro-

	pology in India (ed.), Council of Social and Cultural Research, Bihar
35. Economic Changes in Typical Tribal Villages of Bihar	Leadership in India edited by L.P. Vidyarthi
36. Economic Changes in Typical Tribal Villages of Bihar	Read before the Seminar on Trends of Economic and Political Changes in Villages, Institute of Community Development, Government of India, Mussoorie, published *in* Journal of Ranchi University, Vol. 1, No. 1, 1962
37. Whither Adivasi Dances in Tribal Bihar : Some Preliminary Observations regarding Impact of Christianity and City on the Oraon Dance	Published *in* Folklore, Calcutta, also *in* Cultural Contour of Tribal Bihar
38. The Seminar on Urbanization, Industrialisation and Social Change in India, Introduction	Journal of Social Research, Vol. V, No. 1
39. The Need of Integrated Syllabus on Western Culture : Introducing America in Liberal Education in India	Journal of Social Research, Vol. V, No. 2

1963

40. Appraisal of Conklin's Paper on "The Study of Shifting Cultivation", Vol. 2, No. 1, February 1961	Current Anthropology, Chicago, Vol. IV, December 1963
41. "The Concept of Detribalization and Tribal Bihar"	Read before All India Seminar on Impact of Modern Force on Tribes and Castes in India, published in the Proceedings of the Seminar
42. Tribal Indebtedness in Two Oraon Villages of Ranchi	Journal of Ranchi University, Vol. II
43. Some Aspects of Caste Tensions in India	*In* Anthropology on the March, Social Science Association, Madras, 1963
44. Approaches to Tribal Integration in India	Vanyajati, Vol. XI, No. 2, April 1963

45. Historical Process of Urbanization of Ranchi	Journal of Historical Research, Vol. 1, No. 2
46. The Historic March of Jharkhand Party : A Study of Adivasi Leadership in Tribal Bihar	Indian Sociological Bulletin, Vol. 1, No. 2
1964	
47. The Changing Face of Tribal Bihar	Journal of Social Research, Vol. VIII, No. I-II
1965	
48. Some Preliminary Observations on Emerging Patterns of Leadership in Tribal Bihar	*In* Emerging Patterns of Rural Leadership in Southern Asia edited by S.C. Dube and Prierre Bassaignet, National Institute of Community Development, Hyderabad
49. Nehru's Approach to Tribal Culture	*In* Special Tribal Orientation, Ministry of Community Development and Cooperation and *in* Cultural Contours of Tribal Bihar, also published in Hindi *in* Vanyajati, Delhi
1966	
50. Social Sciences in India : A Social Anthropological Approach	Social Science Information, Vol. V, UNESCO, Paris
51. Social Anthropological Researches in India : A Historical Review	Journal of Social Research, Vol. IX, No. 1
52. Social Change in Tribal India : A Methodological Review	Journal of Ranchi University, Vol. III
1967	
53. Some Preliminary Observations on Inter-group Conflict in India : Tribal, Rural and Industrial	Journal of Social Research, Vol. X, No. 2, September 1967
1968	
54. Cultural Change in the Tribes of Modern India	Presidential Address to the Section of Anthropology and

	Archaeology, 55th Indian Science Congress, Varanasi, also published *in* Journal of Social Research, Vol. XI, No. 1
55. Urgent Anthropology for Tribal Bihar	Presented in a Seminar on Urgent Research in Social Anthropology held in the Indian Institute of Advanced Study, Simla, and also published *in* Journal of Social Research, Vol. XI, No. 2
56. Tribal Village	Cultural Forum, Govt. of India
57. Social Implications of Industrialisation in Tribal Bihar	The Anthropologist, Delhi, Special Number Volume
58. Traditions and Trends in Tribal Studies in India : A Methodological Appraisal	Presented in an All India Seminar on Research Methodology in Social Sciences in India, Department of Anthropology, Ranchi University
59. Urbanisation, Industrialisation and Social Change in India	*In* the Proceeding of the VIIIth International Congress of Anthropological and Ethnological Sciences, Tokyo, Vol. I

1969

60. Cultural, Linguistic Regions in India : Bihar—A Case Study	Language and Society in India : Proceedings of a Seminar, Indian Institute of Advanced Study, Simla
61. Psychological Anthropology : Psycho-Anthropological Researches in India	Journal of Social Research, Vol. XII, No. 2
62. Aspects of Tribal Labour Force	Tribe (a quarterly journal) of the Tribal Research Institute, Udaipur
63. Towards a Unified Discipline of Social Science (as a guest editor)	Editorial, The Social Science Review, Vol. III, No. 2
64. Urgent Anthropology for Tribal Bihar	*In* Urgent Researches in Social Anthropology edited by Behari Lal Abbi and Satish Saberwal, Indian Institute of Advanced Study, Simla, 1969

1970

65. Cultural Personality of the Gayawal	Journal of Social Research, Vol. XIII, No. 2
66. An Academic Visit to European Countries	Journal of Social Research, Vol. XIII, No. 2

1971

67. The Tribal Labour Force in Chotanagpur	*In* Conspectus of Indian Society edited by Rajeshwar Prasad et al., Satish Book Enterprise, Agra
68. Two Hundred Years of Anthropology in India	Annual Conference of Indian Anthropological Association (1970-71) *in* Essay in Social Anthropology, Classical Publishers
69. Notes on Andaman and Nicobar Islands	Tetus Home (Milan), Vol. 3, No. 1
70. Approaches to the Problems of Integration of Tribal in India	*In* Integration in India, edited by M.R. Sinha, Bombay, Asian Studies Press
71. The Dynamics of Tribal Leadership in Bihar	*In* Research Abstract Quarterly of ICSSR, Orient Longman
72. Cultural Diversities in Andaman & Nicobar Islands	Indian Anthropologist, Vol. 1, No. 1
73. The Ranchi Tribals in Andaman & Nicobar Islands	Journal of Social Research, Vol. XIV, No. 2
74. An Experiment in Action Anthropology : The Changing Village Life in Kamre	Journal of Social Research, Vol. XIV, No. 2

1972

75. The Rise of Anthropology and Tribal Ethnography in West Bengal	Presented in the Golden Jubilee of the Department of Anthropology, University of Calcutta, published *in* Bulletin of Cultural Research Institute, Vol. X, No. 1
76. Status of Course in Research Methodology in Anthropology in Indian Universities	Submitted to the ICSSR as Chairman of the Standing Committee on Anthropology and Research Methodology, Abstract published *in* ICSSR Bulletin
77. An Appraisal of Leadership Pattern among the Tribes of Bihar	Tribal Situation in India edited by Kumar S. Singh, Simla, Indian Institute of Advanced Study

78.	University Youths in Chotanagpur : A Study in Campus Life	Journal of Social Research, Vol. XV, No. 2
79.	Needed Urgent Research for the Fifth Five Year Plan for Tribal Bihar	Research Journal of Ranchi University, Vol. VIII
80.	Problems and Prospects of Tribal Development in India	Indian Anthropologist, Vol. 22, No. 2
81.	Causes and Remedies of Students Unrest	Behaviourometric, Vol. 2, No. 2
82.	Social Anthropology in India since Independence	Silver Jubilee issue of Eastern Anthropologist (Man and Society), Lucknow
83.	Tribal Ethnography in India	*In* A Survey of Research in Anthropology, ICSSR, New Delhi, Popular Prakashan, Bombay
84.	Applied Anthropology in India : A Review	Presented *in* the Silver Jubilee celebration of the Anthropological Survey of India
85.	Socio-cultural Implications of Reclamation of Waste Land in the Tribal Belt of Bihar	Bulletin of the Indian National Science Academy, New Delhi, No. 44

1973

86.	The Rise of Social Anthropology in India : An Historical Appraisal	Presented in the IXth ICAES held at Chicago, 1973 (to be published in the volume "Anthropology" Mouton & Co.)
87.	Needed Urgent Research for the Fifth Five Year Plan for the Tribal Bihar	Vanyajati, Vol. XXI
88.	Tribal Researches in the Himalayan Regions	North-Eastern Affairs, Annual, 1973
89.	Report of the Task Force on the Development of Tribal Areas	New Delhi Planning Commission, Government of India
90.	Student Unrest in Chotanagpur, 1969-70	ICSSR Research Abstract quarterly, Vol. II, No. 4, Orient Longman
91.	A Health Survey of Kamre Village, Ranchi	Journal of Social Research, Vol. XVI, No. 1
92.	An Adventure in Social Service	Brief Report published jointly in Journal of Social Research
93.	Problems and Prospects of Tribal Development in India	Samatat Prakashan 18, Supplement (Part I)

1974

94.	Some Basic Postulates in Tribal Administration	Proceedings of the Seminar on the Needed Change in Administrative Structure in Tribal Areas of Bihar, Department of Anthropology, Ranchi University, Ranchi
95.	Sacred Complex as a Dimension of Indian Civilisation	Journal of Social Research, Vol. XVII, No. 1
96.	Research Methodology in Anthropology in Indian Universities	Social Science Information, Vol. 12, No. 4
97.	Pastoral Communities in India	Review of Ethnology (Vienna), Vol. 4, Nos. 10-11
98.	Priorities in Tribal Researches in India	Journal of Social Research, Vol. XVII, No. 2
99.	South Asian Culture	Encyclopaedia Britannica, 15th edition (Helen Hemingway Bentan Publisher, USA)
100.	Inter-Group Conflict in India : Tribal, Rural and Industrial	Presented *in* the Symposium on Conflict and Tension in India at Bidisa, Midnapur (W.B.), December 27-28
101.	Bihar Ke Janjati Ksetron Ke Prashasanik Dhanche Men Abashyak Paribartan	Lok Prashashan (M.P., Hindi Academy, Bhopal), Vol. 1, No. 1-2
102.	Strategy for Tribal Development in India	Inaugural Address to the Lecture Series on India organised by Orissa Government, Bhubaneshwar (published *in* Adivasi)
103.	Bharat Ke Janjatiya Sanskriti Bhang Aur Unka Adhyayan (Tribal Culture of India and Its Studies)	Manav, Vol. 2, No. 2

1975

104.	The Peasant Organization in India : A Case Study of a Voluntary Organization in Tribal Bihar	Research Journal of Ranchi University, 1974-75
105.	The Development, Communication & Application of Social Science Researches in India : An Anthropological Approach	ICSSR News Letter, December Issue and Man and Life, Calcutta, Special Number

106.	Ganatantra Bharat Men Asprishyata Ke Abasthiti (Untouchability in Republic of India)	Lok Prasashan (Bhopal), No. 1
107.	Economic Problems of the Scheduled Castes of Bihar : Some Preliminary Observations	Journal of Social Research, Vol. XVII, No. 2
108.	Problems of Scheduled Castes	Award, Vol. 17, No. 6
109.	The Future of Traditional Primitive Societies : A Case Study of Shifting Cultivation Society	Eastern Anthropologist, Vol. 28, No. 4
110.	The Rise of Social Anthropology in India (1974-77 : A Historical Appraisal)	*In* The New Wind : Changing Identities in South Asia edited by Kenneth David, Mouton Publisher, The Hague, 1977
111.	Trend Report on the Research on Tribal Ethnography : Material Culture Folklore, Applied Anthropology, Religion-Social Anthropology in India during 1969-72	A Survey of Research in Sociology and Social Anthropology, ICSSR, New Delhi, Vol. III
112.	Inter-Group Conflict and Tension in Contemporary Indian Society	*In* Case Studies on Human Rights and Fundamental Freedom : A World Survey, Vol. II, No. 1, Veenahavented, The Hague, Martinus Nyhott (for Foundation for the Study of Plural Societies)

1976

113.	Thinking About the Problems of the Scheduled Castes : Some Preliminary Observations	Indian Anthropologist, Vol. 6, No. 1
114.	Development Plans of the Tribes of Andaman & Nicobar Islands : An Action Oriented Report	Journal of Social Research, Vol. XIX, No. 2
115.	Cultural Diversities in the Andaman & Nicobar Islands : A Preliminary Report	Journal of Social Research, Vol. XIX, No. 2
116.	Applied Anthropology in India	Anthropology in India, Vol. I, Cultural Anthropology edited by

	Surajit C. Sinha, Calcutta, Anthropological Survey of India
117. Foreword to the Book	Under the Shadow of the Cross by K.N. Sahay, Institute of Social Research and Applied Anthropology, Calcutta
1977	
118. The Quarter Century of World Anthropology : Asia	25th Anniversory Round Table, ISSC, UNESCO, 20-21st October
119. Coming of Age of Indian Democracy : An Empirical Perspective	Journal of Social Research, Vol. XX, No. 1
120. Foreword to books on the Korwa and the Parahiya (by Dr. A.N.S. Sandwar and R.N. Prasad)	Institute of Ethnography, Vienna
121. Primitive and Vanishing Tribes of Bihar	Journal of Social Research, Vol. XX, No. 2
122. The Voluntary Organisation in Service of the Tribal Weak : A Case Study of Adimjati Seva Mandal	Dynamics of Development : An International Perspective by S.K. Sharma, Concept Publishing Co., Vol. II, also published *in* Man and Life, Vol. 3, No. 2
123. Current Trends in World Anthropology	Presidential Address to the Annual Meeting of Indian Anthropological Association (December), Ranchi
124. The Rise of Social Anthropology in India (1977—1982) : An Historical Appraisal	In the New Wind-Changing Identities in South Asia edited by K. David, The Hauge, Mouton Publisher
1978	
125. Aspects of Present-day Problems : An Anthropological Focus	Eastern Anthropologist, Vol. 31, No. 1.
126. Folklore Research in India	*In* Varia Folklorica edited by Alan Dundes, The Hague, Mouton
127. Concept of Development : An Anthropological Approach	Presented in the IXth International Sociological Congress held at Upsala, Sweden (to be published in the Proceedings volume)

128. Unity and Diversities in Indian Civilization	Presented in the IXth International Sociological Congress held at Upsala, Sweden (published in a special volume on civilization : One or Many)
129. Presidential Address on Indigenisation v. Internationalisation in India	Xth International Congress of Anthropological & Ethnological Sciences held in New Delhi. Also *in* Trends in World Anthropology edited by Charles Frantz, Concept Publishing Co. New Delhi
1979	
130. The Birhor of Hazaribagh & Giridih Districts : A Study in Cultural Profiles and Action Oriented Development Programme (co-author)	Journal of Social Research, Vol. XV, 1979
1980	
131. Cultural Ecology, Cultural Types and Concept of Tribal Development	Special lecture to the Indian Science Congress, Mysore, Science Congress Proceeding
132. Strategies for the Development of Primitive Tribes : An Anthropological Approach	Guest speech for the Workshop on Strategies for Development of Primitive Tribes organized by the Birhor Tribal Welfare and Research Institute, December 5-6, *in* the Proceeding of the B.T.W.R.I., Ranchi
1981	
133. Development of the Maler : A Case Study in Primitive Hill Cultivation Tribe, Foreword to the Book	*In* the Profiles of the Marginal and the Pre-farming Tribes of Central Eastern India edited by L.P. Vidyarthi, Special Series No. 26 in Cultural Research Institute, Calcutta
134. The Cultural Factors in Development Process : Case Studies from Tribal Bihar	*In* Tribal Development and its Administration, edited by L.P. Vidyarthi, Concept Publishing Co., 1981

135. Trends in World Anthropology	*In* Ideas & Trends in World Anthropology edited by Charles Frantz, Concept Publishing Co., New Delhi
136. The Social Cultural Profiles of the Oraon of Chotanagpur	Plural, Vol. 12, No. 1/2, The Hague Societies. Also published in Collegium Anthropology with revision, Vol. 5, No. 1, Zagreb
137. The Project That Failed : A Study of Birhor in Giridih District	A Note prepared on the invitation of the Governor of Bihar

1982

138. The Emergence of Industrial Anthropology in India	Eastern Anthropology, July-Sept., Vol. 35, No. 3
139. Concensus & Conflict in Contemporary Indian Society	International Journal of Asian Studies, Vol. II, No. 2
140. International Symposium on Problems of Development of Under Privileged Communities of the Third World Countries	Presidential Address on SUNCOM, 1982, New Delhi, under publication in the 3-3 volume Proceedings *in* Rural Development in South Asia (edited by L.P. Vidyarthi, Concept Publishing Co., New Delhi
141. Problems and Prospect of Tribal Development in India	*In* Tribal Development in India edited by Buddhadeb Chaudhuri, Inter-India Publication, New Delhi
142. Race and Racism : A New Look at the Old Question	*In* UNESCO's Race Science and Pseudo Science
143. Report on Socio-cultural Implication of Industrialisation on the Tribes of Middle India	Ministry of Home Affairs, Government of India
144. Religion and Conversion in Tribal India	Valedictory Address to the National (UGC) Seminar on Process of Conversion to Islam, December 1982
145. Effects of Industrialisation on the tribes of Chotanagpur : Case Studies	Ministry of Home Affairs, Government of India : A Brief Report
146. Man and Beasts in the National Park of Betala in Palamau	A Note on living Conditions of the People in the Forest of Betala (mimeo)

147.	Review of the Books : South Asian Civilisation : A Bibliographic Syntheses by L.P. Maureen and Willion J. Alsporngh	International Journal of Asian Studies, 1982, Vol. II, No. 2

1983

148.	Anthropology and Development : Reflection and Experiences	Special lecture, 70th Indian Science Congress. Tirupati, to be published in a Proceeding edited by I.J.S. Bansal, Sectional President, I.S. Congress.
149.	Inaugural Address to Indian Folklore Congress, February 1983	Problems and Prospects of Folklore Research in India
150.	Tribal Culture of India : A General Review	Presidential Address to National Workshop on Tribes of the World, Cultural Research Institute, Hyderabad, 1983
151.	Current Trends of Research in Chhatisgarh of M.P. (including Bastar & Belladilla Mining Complex)	Lecture delivered in the Departments of Anthropology and Sociology at Raipur University in February 1983 (to be published)

1984

152.	Anthropology of the Weaker Section	Presidential Address to the Indian Anthropological Association at Ranchi
153.	The Jarawa Islanders An Expedition	Report to be published *in* The Vanishing Primitive Societies of Andaman and Nicobar Islands edited by L.P. Vidyarthi (under preparation)
154.	The Ainu Tribe of Hokkaido Island of Japan	An Ethnographic Report
155.	Economic Transition among the Chamars in Bihar	Journal of Social Research, Vol. XXVII, No. II
156.	Nutritional Status of Children of Two Primitive Societies in Bihar	*In* A National Seminar on Primitive Tribes of India organised by Tribal Research Institute, Hyderabad, Proceeding
157.	Engels, Evolutionism and Primitive Communism	*In* The Proceedings of an Engels Celebration Congress, Dresden

1985

158. The Strategies for Development of the Underprivileged Communities in India	*In* The Proceeding of the Workshop on Strategy to Communicate with the Underprivileged Communities in India held at Lucknow in February, National Media Centre, New Delhi
159. Needed Studies of Population on Ageing in India	*In* Proceeding of International National Seminar on the Sociology of Ageing Population in India, Trivandrum

Doctoral Research work completed with (Prof. L.P. Vidyarthi)
Degree Awarded

D. Litt

1. Dr. S.P. Sinha	Conflict & Tension of Tribes of Chotanagpur and Santhal Parganas (in press)
2. Dr. Makhan Jha	Mithila & Mahakoshal : An Approach to Study of Civilizational Regions (unpublished)
3. Dr. N.K. Singh	Occupational Goal Values of Indian Teaching Community : A Case Study (published)

Ph.D.

1. K.N. Sahay	Impact of Christianity on the Uraon of the Three Villages in Chotanagpur (published)
2. R. Singh	Impact of Industrialisation on Patratu and Four other Villages
3. S. Prasad	Where the Three Tribes Meet : A Study in Tribal Introduction (published)
4. B.N. Sahay	Changes in the Leadership Pattern among the Maler and Santhals (published)
5. R.K. Prasad	Economic and Social Change among Parahiyas (published)
6. N.K. Shukla	Social Structure of a Village in Bihar (published)
7. Makhan Jha	The Sacred Complex of Janakpur (published)
8. K.K. Verma	Anthropo-Demographic Study of Two Tribes of Bihar (published)
9. J.K. Sarkar	Uprooted Families in Bokaro Industrial Complex
10. G.R. Sharma	Living Conditions of Colliery Workers in Jharia
11. N. Mishra	Cultural Persistence and Change in a Chotanagpur Village (published)

12.	P. Verma	Social Structure of Chotanagpur Villages (published)
13.	R.R. Sinha	Social Structure of Munda and Oraon Villages
14.	S. Narayan	Sacred Complexes of Deoghar and Rajgir (published)
15.	A.N. Sandhwar	The Korwas of Palamau (published)
16.	P.K. Roy	Socio-Economic Impact of Industrialisation on the Indian Family (published)
17.	Kala Rani	Role Conflict in Working Women (published)
18.	Aruna Srivastava	Tribal Women of Central India
19.	G.N. Chowdhury	Impact of Industrialisation in India (published)
20.	A.K. Haldar	Mining Labourers of Chotanagpur
21.	Father V.D. Bogarett	To Stand Together—To Sit Together (published)
22.	Jitendra Singh	Religion & Society among the Tharus
23.	S.G. Morab	The Soliga : A Study in Eco-Ecology Society of a Hill Tribe
24.	V.S. Sahay	The Nature-Man-Spirit Complex of Nicobarese
25.	A.C. Sahoo	The Changing Bondo Highlanders
26.	J.S. Bhandari	Kinship & Family among the Tribes of North-Eastern India
27.	N.G. Nag	A Review of the States of Demographic Research of Scheduled Tribes
28.	A. Das Gupta	The Symbols and Rituals among the Ho of Singhbhum
29.	Mrs. Savitri Sinha	Socio-Economic Implications of Gandhi—An Approach to the Tribes of India
30.	R. Sahu	The Sacred Specialists of Kashi
31.	A.M. Kurup	The Cultural Ecology of the Karkus of Patalkot in M.P.
32.	P.K. Singh	The Maler : A Restudy
33.	Govind Dharma	Interactional Pattern and Its Implications for Scheduled Castes
34.	Uma Sinha	The Changing Personality Structure of the Ho of Singhbhum
35.	Geeta Bhaskar	Ethnic Identity of the Leptchas : A Cross Cultural Analysis of Ethnic Groups in Sikkam with particular reference to the Leptchas

Index